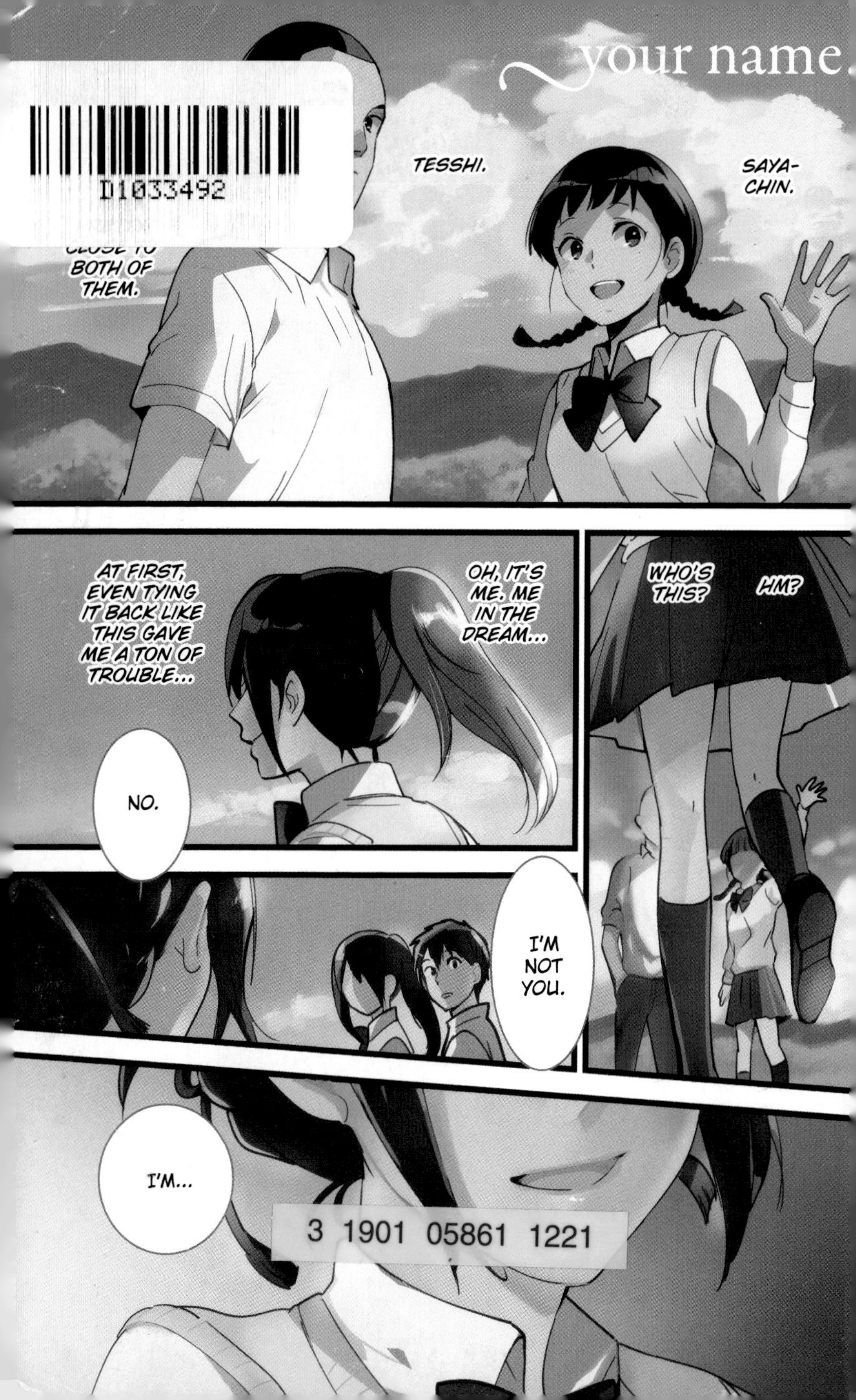

your name.
SAYA-CHIN.
TESSHI.
CLOSE TO BOTH OF THEM.
HM?
WHO'S THIS?
OH, IT'S ME. ME IN THE DREAM...
AT FIRST, EVEN TYING IT BACK LIKE THIS GAVE ME A TON OF TROUBLE...
NO.
I'M NOT YOU.
I'M...

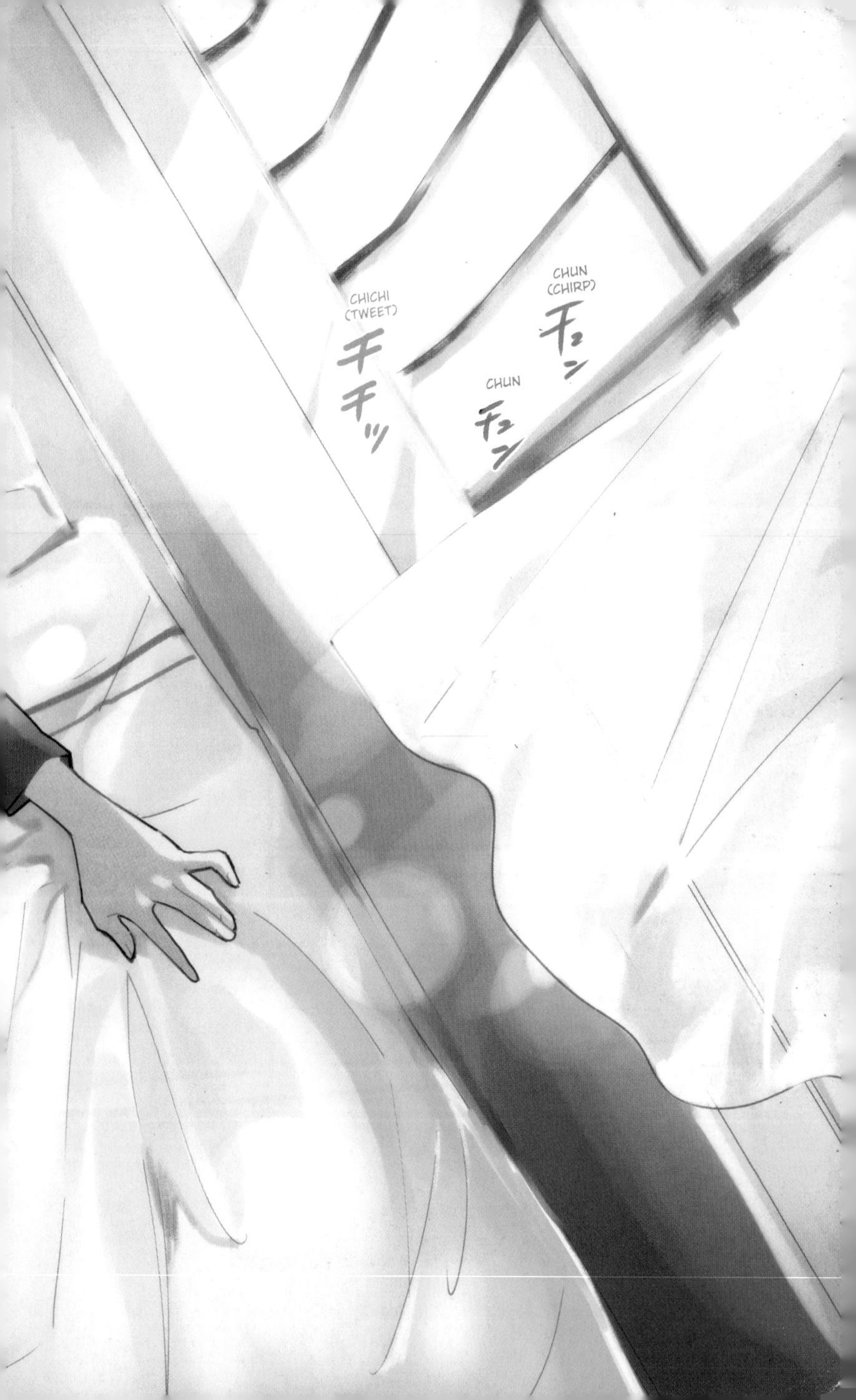
CHUN (CHIRP)
チュン
CHUN
チュン
CHICHI (TWEET)
チチッ

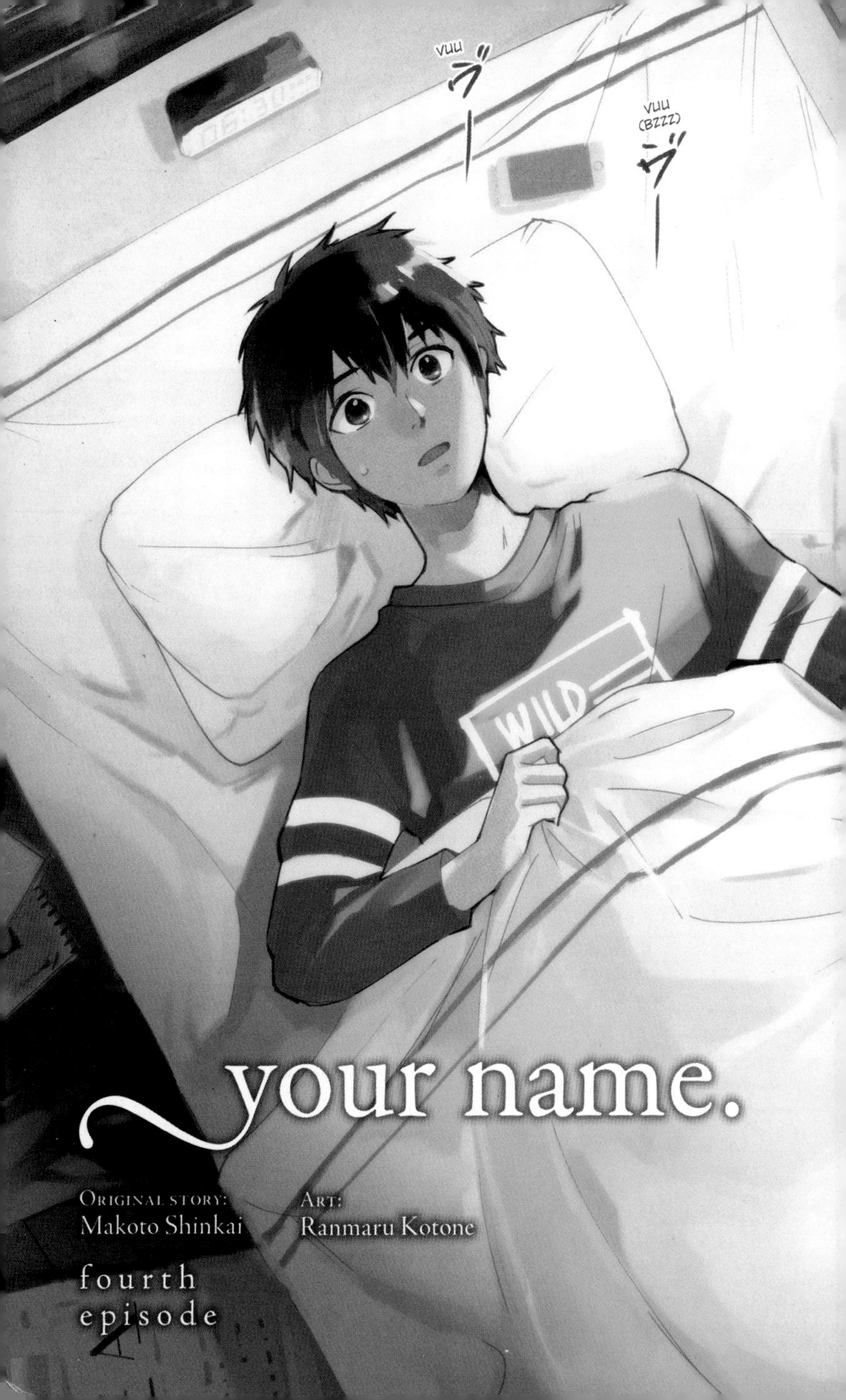
VUU (BZZZ)
ヴー
VUU
ヴー
your name.
ORIGINAL STORY:
Makoto Shinkai
ART:
Ranmaru Kotone
fourth
episode

your name.

Contents

Fourth Episode   001

Fifth Episode   051

Sixth Episode   109

your name.

makoto shinkai

ranmaru kotone

02

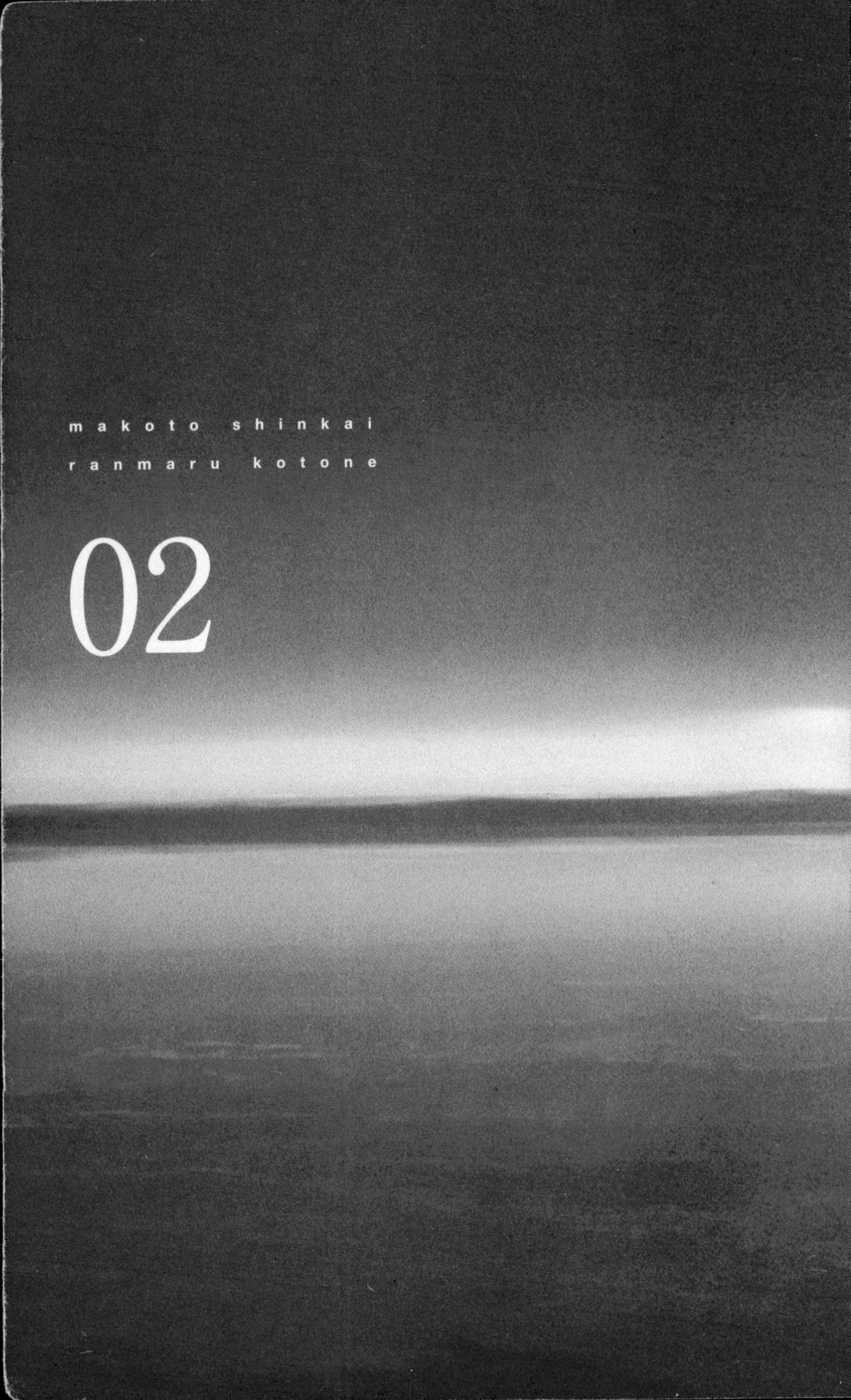

Previously...

Japan. The country eagerly anticipated the arrival of Comet Tiamat, which would be visible for the first time in a thousand years.

Mitsuha, a high school girl living in a rural town deep in the mountains, found herself feeling down most of the time.

The causes: her father's mayoral campaign and the ancient customs of her family's shrine.

Because the town was small and cramped, and because she was old enough to be painfully conscious of the eyes of those around her, her longing for the big city grew and grew.

"Make me a hot guy in Tokyo in my next life, pleeease!!!"

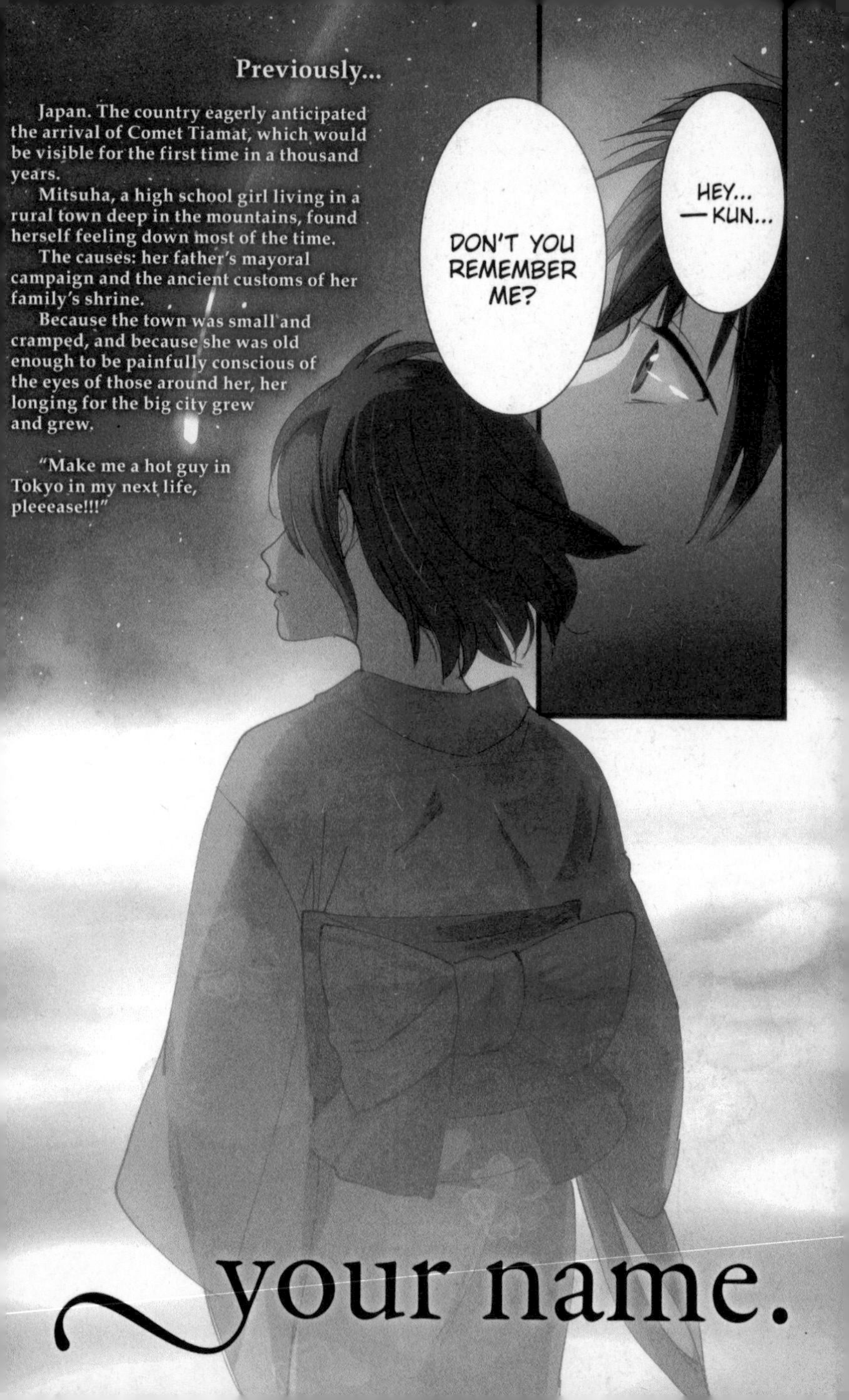
HEY... —KUN...
DON'T YOU REMEMBER ME?
your name.

One day, she dreamed she had become a boy.

An unfamiliar room, friends she didn't know, and the streets of Tokyo opened out before her.

Although Mitsuha was bewildered, she'd wanted a life in the city more than anything in the world, and she enjoyed it to the fullest.

Meanwhile, Taki, a high school boy who lived in Tokyo, was also having strange dreams. He'd become a high school girl in a town he'd never been to before, deep in the mountains.

The mysterious dreams happened again and again. They were also clearly missing memories and time. At last the two of them caught on:

"We're switching!?"

Although Taki and Mitsuha were bewildered that they were repeatedly swapping between each other's bodies and lives, little by little they accepted the reality. They coped with the situation as best they could, sometimes squabbling through notes they left for each other, sometimes enjoying the other's life.

However, just when they'd grown comfortable around each other, the switching abruptly stopped...

A meeting between a girl and boy who'd never meet.

The gears of fate begin to move.

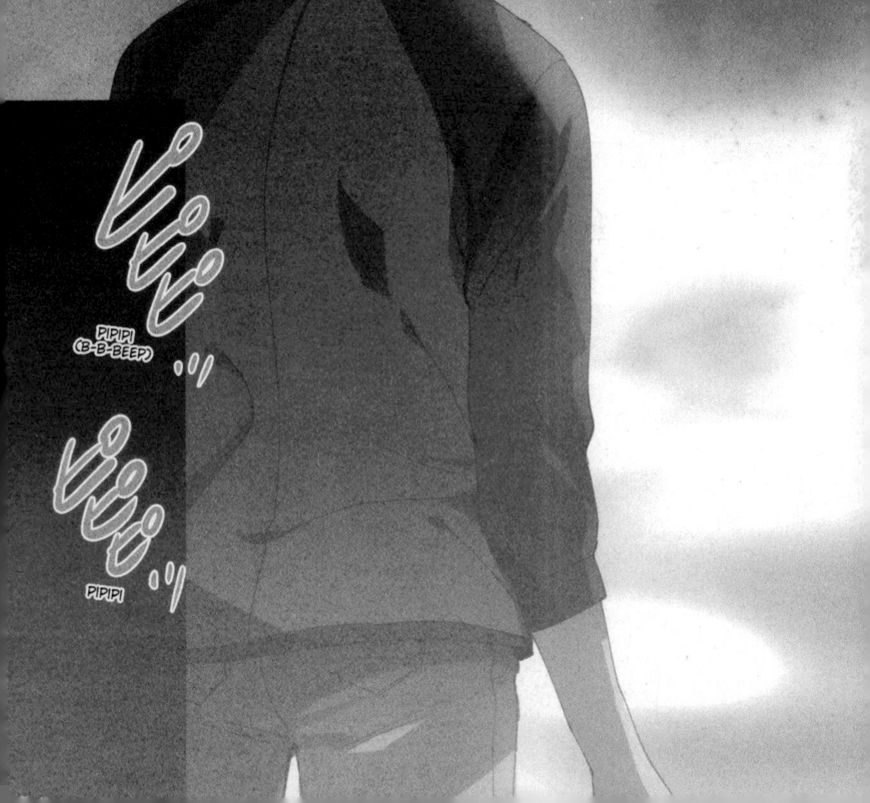
PIPIPI
(B-B-BEEP)
PIPIPI

your name.

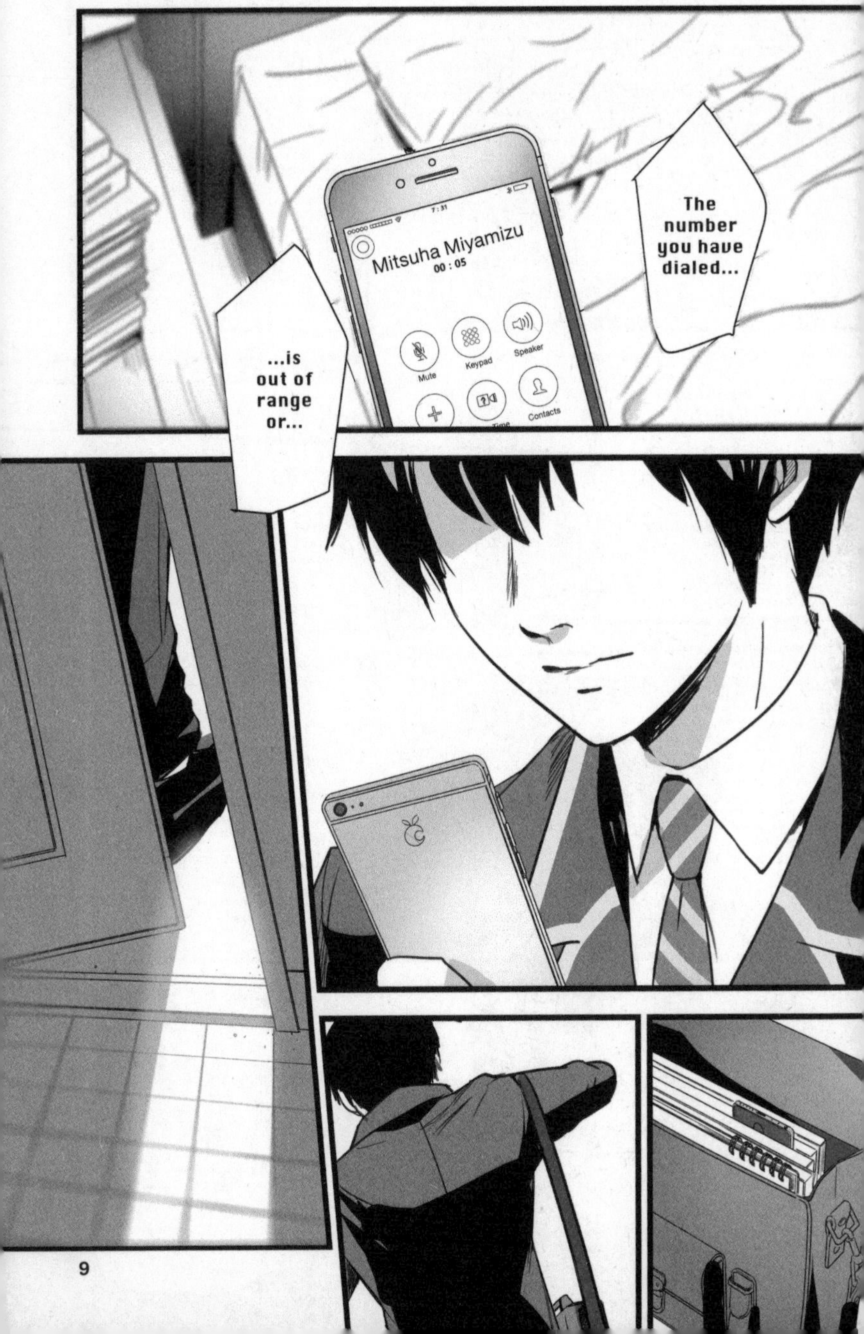
The number you have dialed...
7:31
Mitsuha Miyamizu
00 : 05
Speaker
Keypad
Mute
Contacts
...is out of range or...

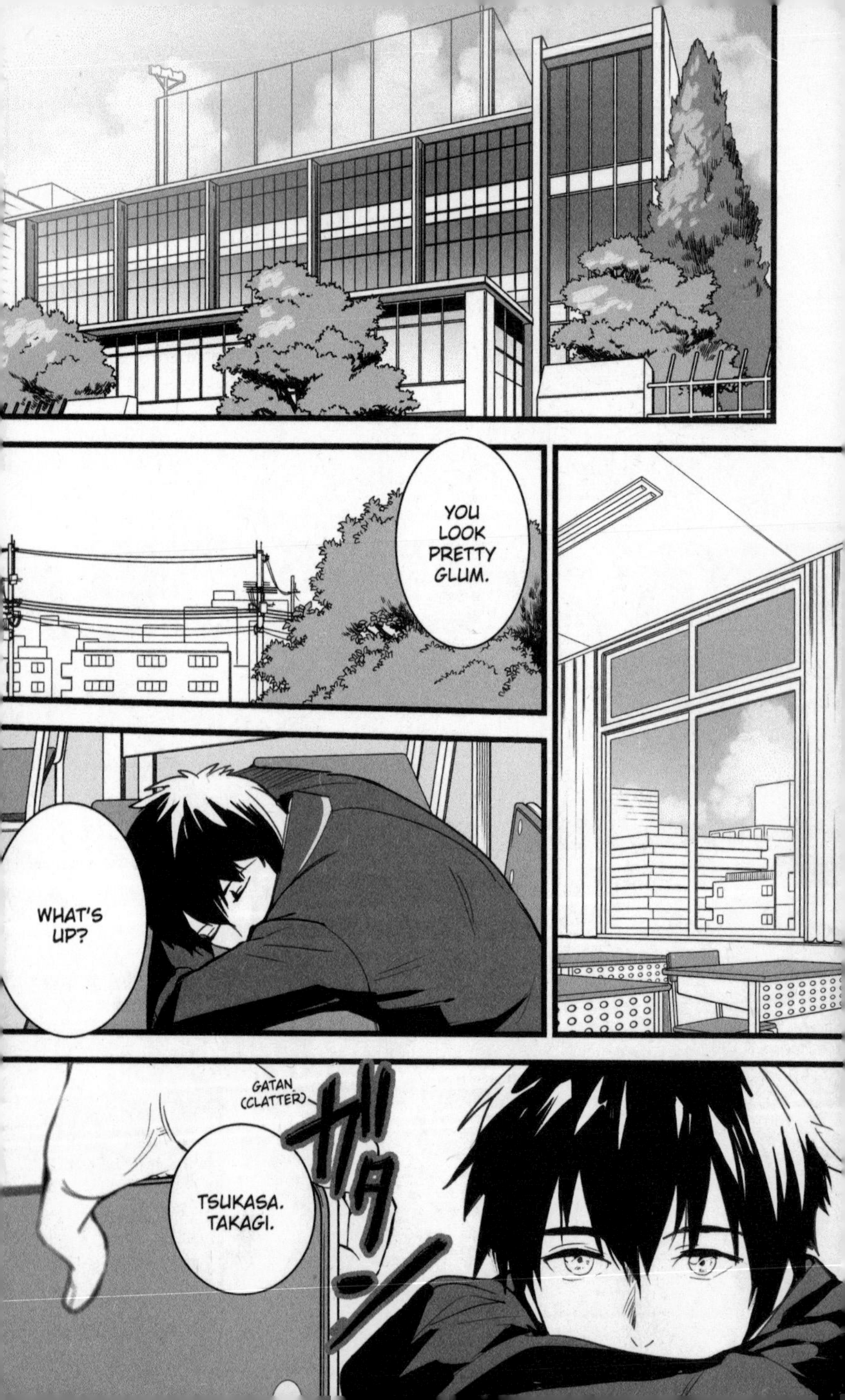
YOU LOOK PRETTY GLUM.
WHAT'S UP?
GATAN (CLATTER)
TSUKASA. TAKAGI.

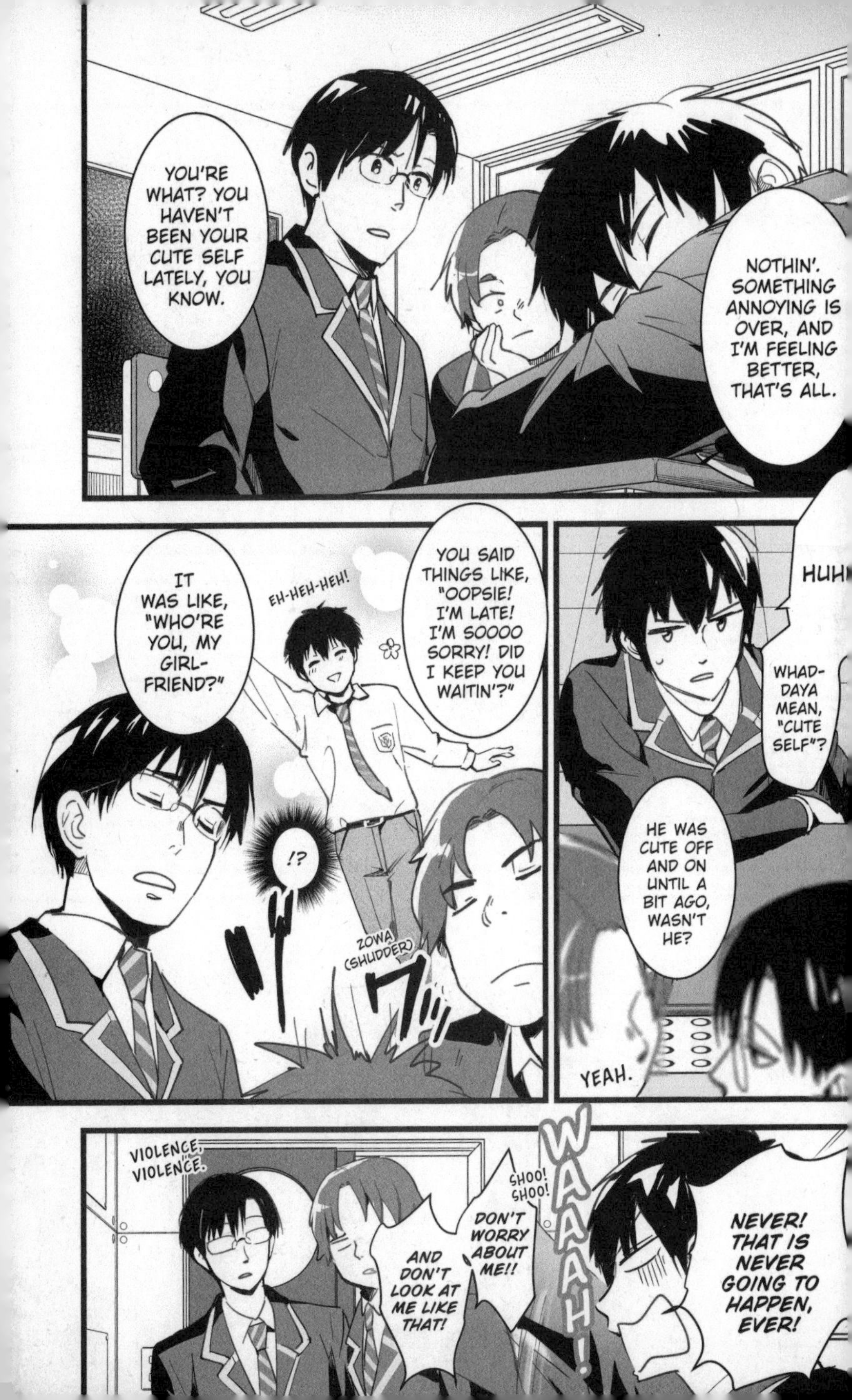
NOTHIN'. SOMETHING ANNOYING IS OVER, AND I'M FEELING BETTER, THAT'S ALL.
YOU'RE WHAT? YOU HAVEN'T BEEN YOUR CUTE SELF LATELY, YOU KNOW.
HUH
WHAD-DAYA MEAN, "CUTE SELF"?
HE WAS CUTE OFF AND ON UNTIL A BIT AGO, WASN'T HE?
YEAH.
YOU SAID THINGS LIKE, "OOPSIE! I'M LATE! I'M SOOOO SORRY! DID I KEEP YOU WAITIN'?"
EH-HEH-HEH!
IT WAS LIKE, "WHO'RE YOU, MY GIRL-FRIEND?"
!?
ZOWA (SHUDDER)
NEVER! THAT IS NEVER GOING TO HAPPEN, EVER!
WAAAAH!
SHOO! SHOO!
DON'T WORRY ABOUT ME!!
AND DON'T LOOK AT ME LIKE THAT!
VIOLENCE, VIOLENCE.

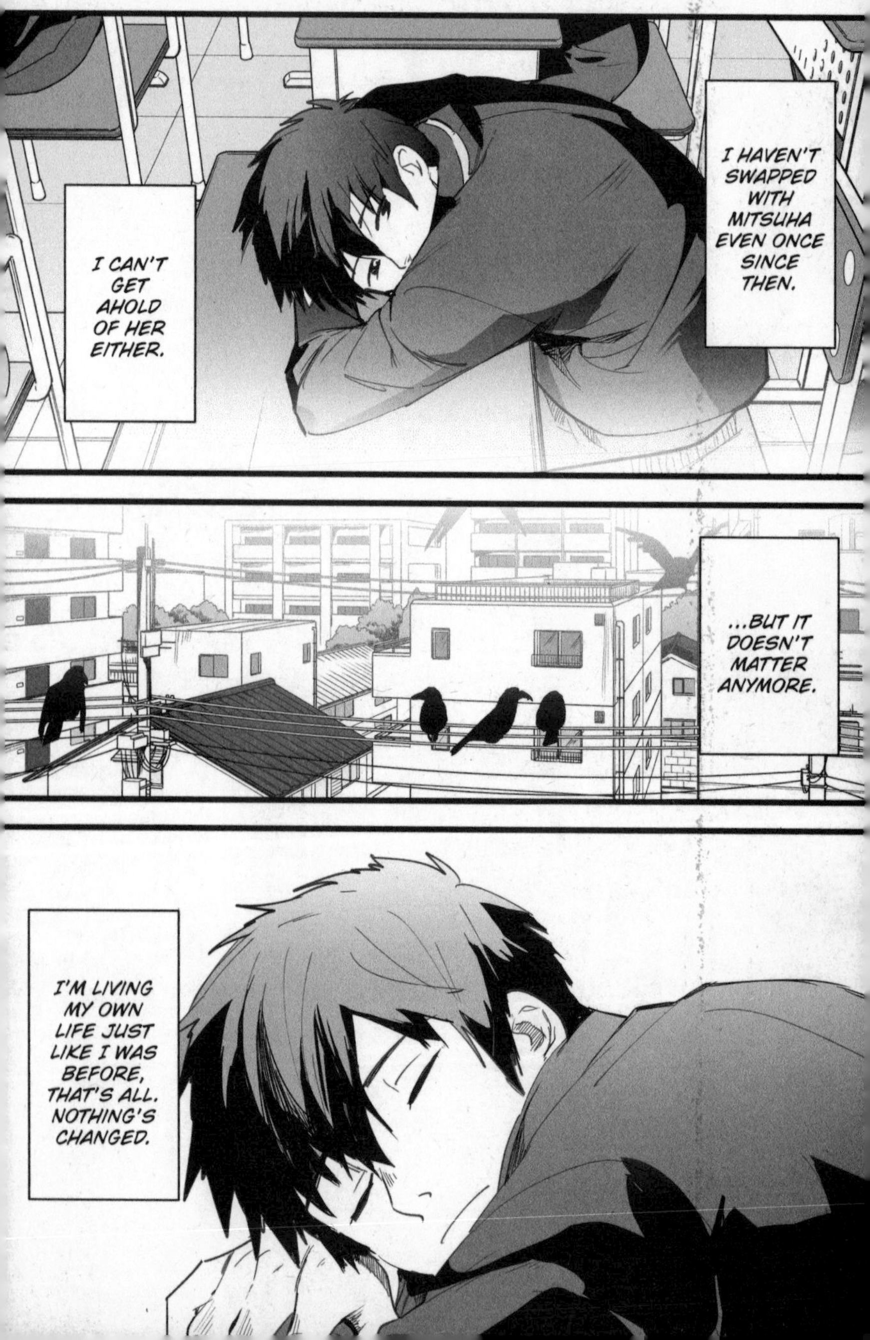
I HAVEN'T SWAPPED WITH MITSUHA EVEN ONCE SINCE THEN.
I CAN'T GET AHOLD OF HER EITHER.
...BUT IT DOESN'T MATTER ANYMORE.
I'M LIVING MY OWN LIFE JUST LIKE I WAS BEFORE, THAT'S ALL. NOTHING'S CHANGED.

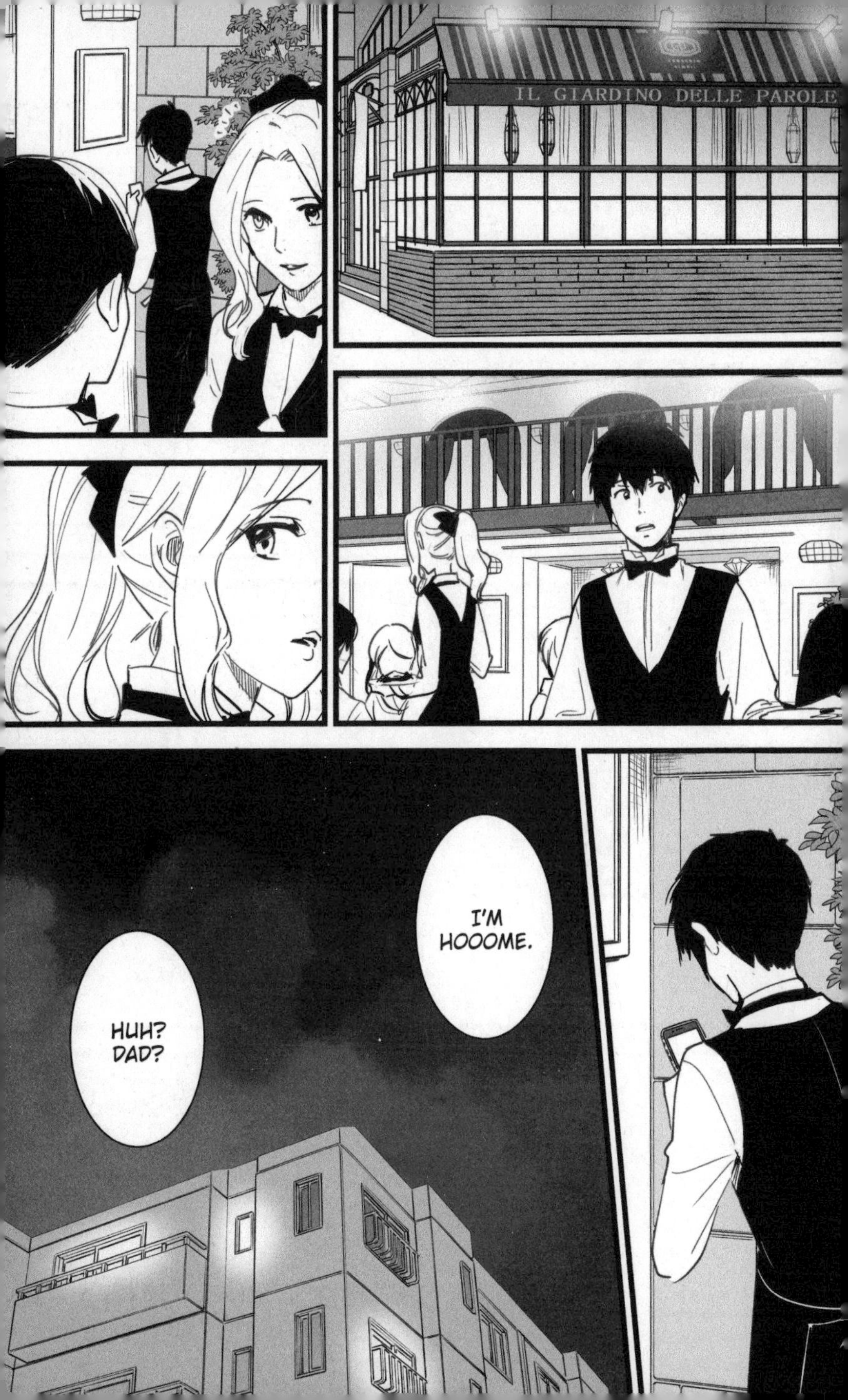
IL GIARDINO DELLE PAROLE
I'M HOOOME.
HUH? DAD?

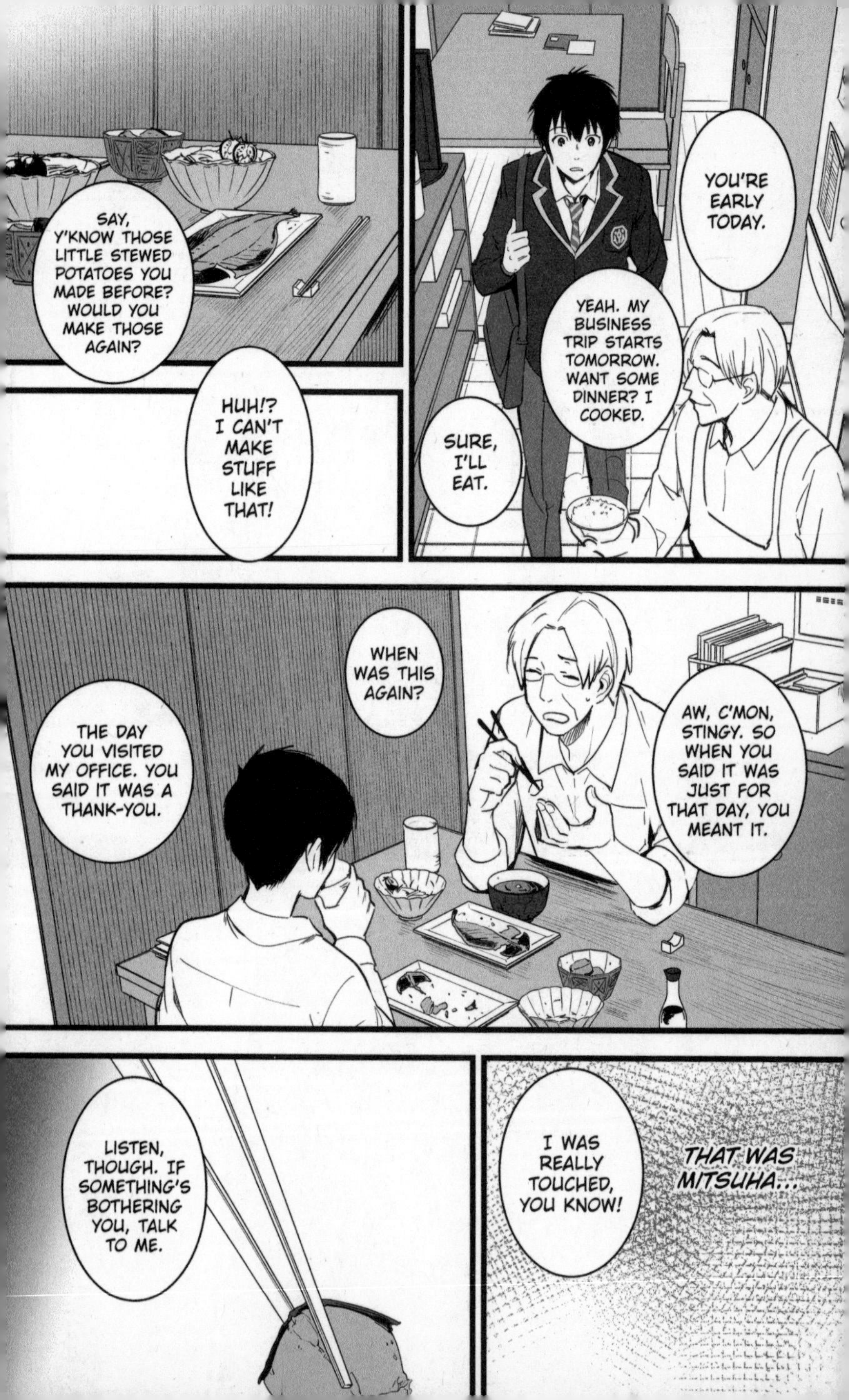
YOU'RE EARLY TODAY.
YEAH. MY BUSINESS TRIP STARTS TOMORROW. WANT SOME DINNER? I COOKED.
SURE, I'LL EAT.
SAY, Y'KNOW THOSE LITTLE STEWED POTATOES YOU MADE BEFORE? WOULD YOU MAKE THOSE AGAIN?
HUH!? I CAN'T MAKE STUFF LIKE THAT!
WHEN WAS THIS AGAIN?
THE DAY YOU VISITED MY OFFICE. YOU SAID IT WAS A THANK-YOU.
AW, C'MON, STINGY. SO WHEN YOU SAID IT WAS JUST FOR THAT DAY, YOU MEANT IT.
I WAS REALLY TOUCHED, YOU KNOW!
THAT WAS MITSUHA...
LISTEN, THOUGH. IF SOMETHING'S BOTHERING YOU, TALK TO ME.

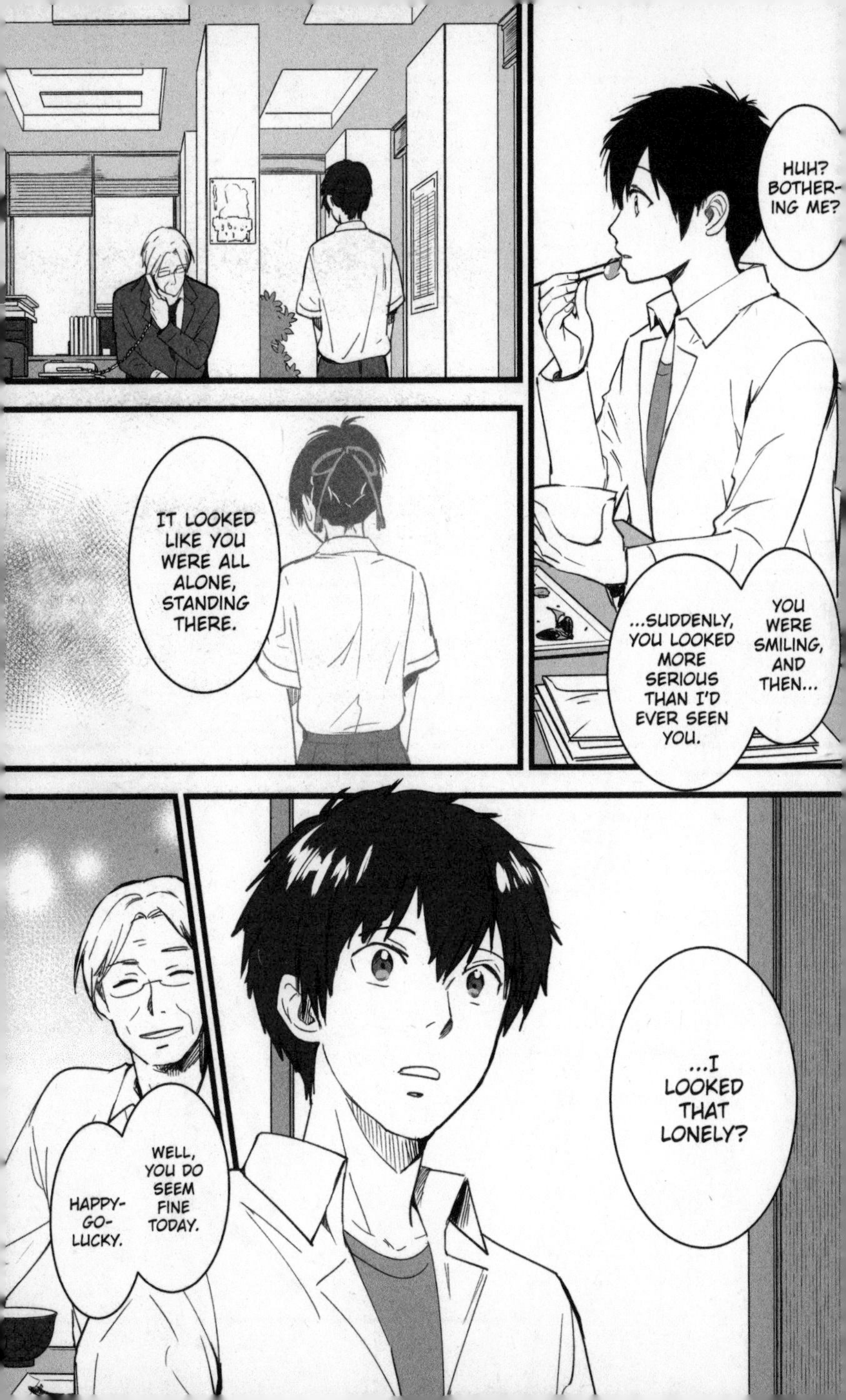
HUH? BOTHERING ME?
YOU WERE SMILING, AND THEN...
...SUDDENLY, YOU LOOKED MORE SERIOUS THAN I'D EVER SEEN YOU.
IT LOOKED LIKE YOU WERE ALL ALONE, STANDING THERE.
...I LOOKED THAT LONELY?
WELL, YOU DO SEEM FINE TODAY.
HAPPY-GO-LUCKY.

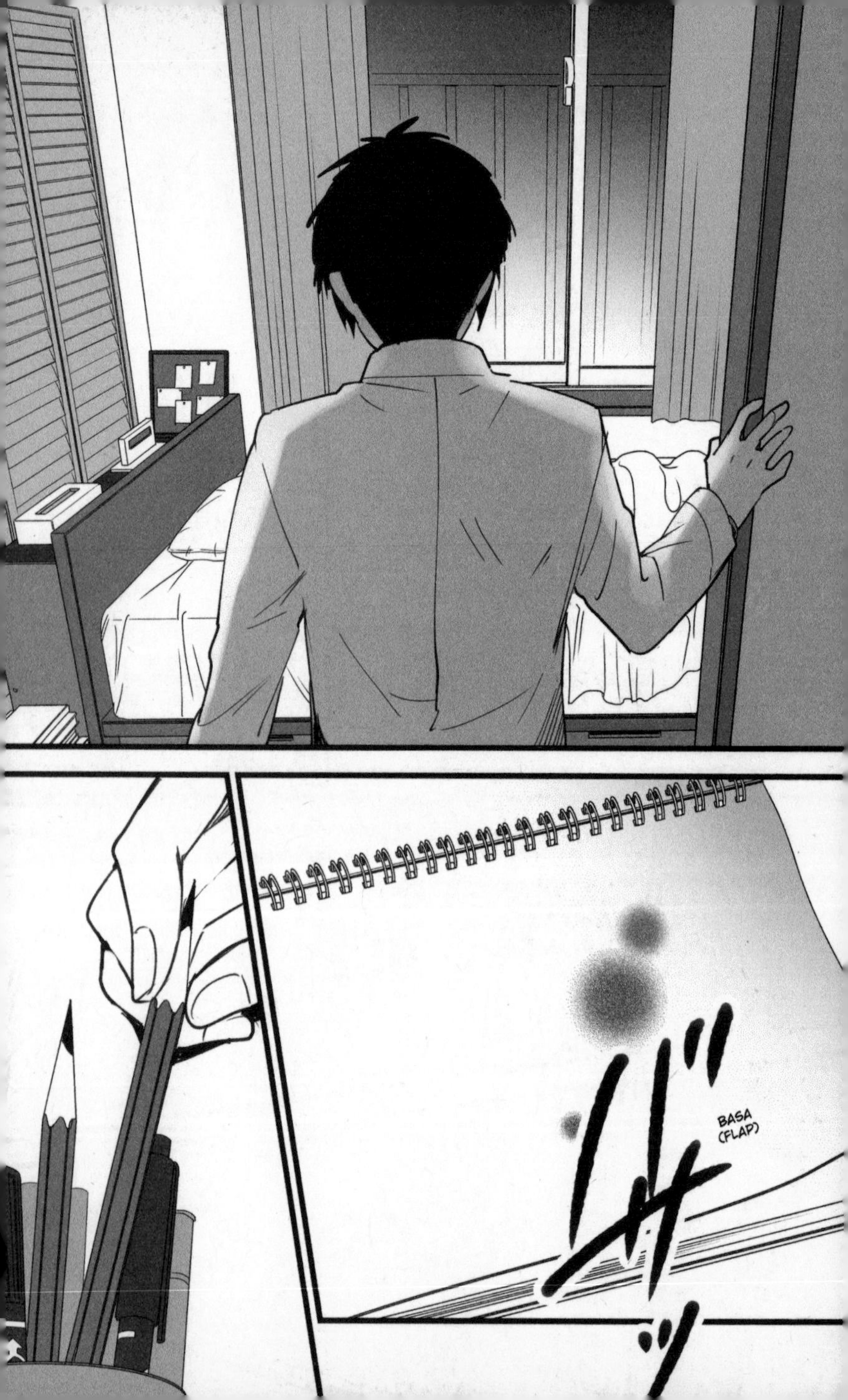
BASA
(FLAP)

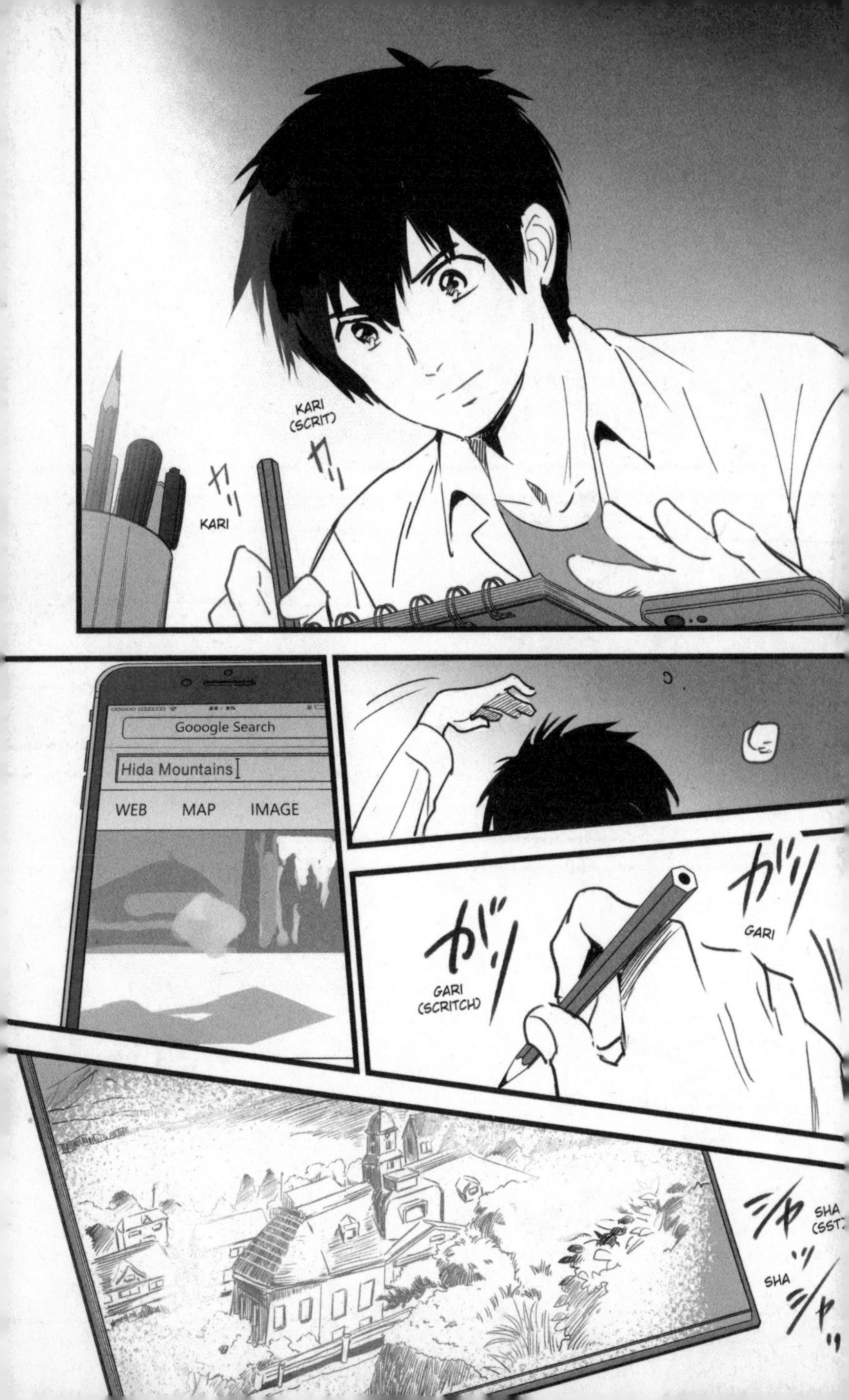
カリ
KARI (SCRIT)
カリ
KARI
ガリ
GARI
ガリ
GARI (SCRITCH)
Gooogle Search
Hida Mountains
WEB
MAP
IMAGE
シャッ
SHA (SST)
シャッ
SHA

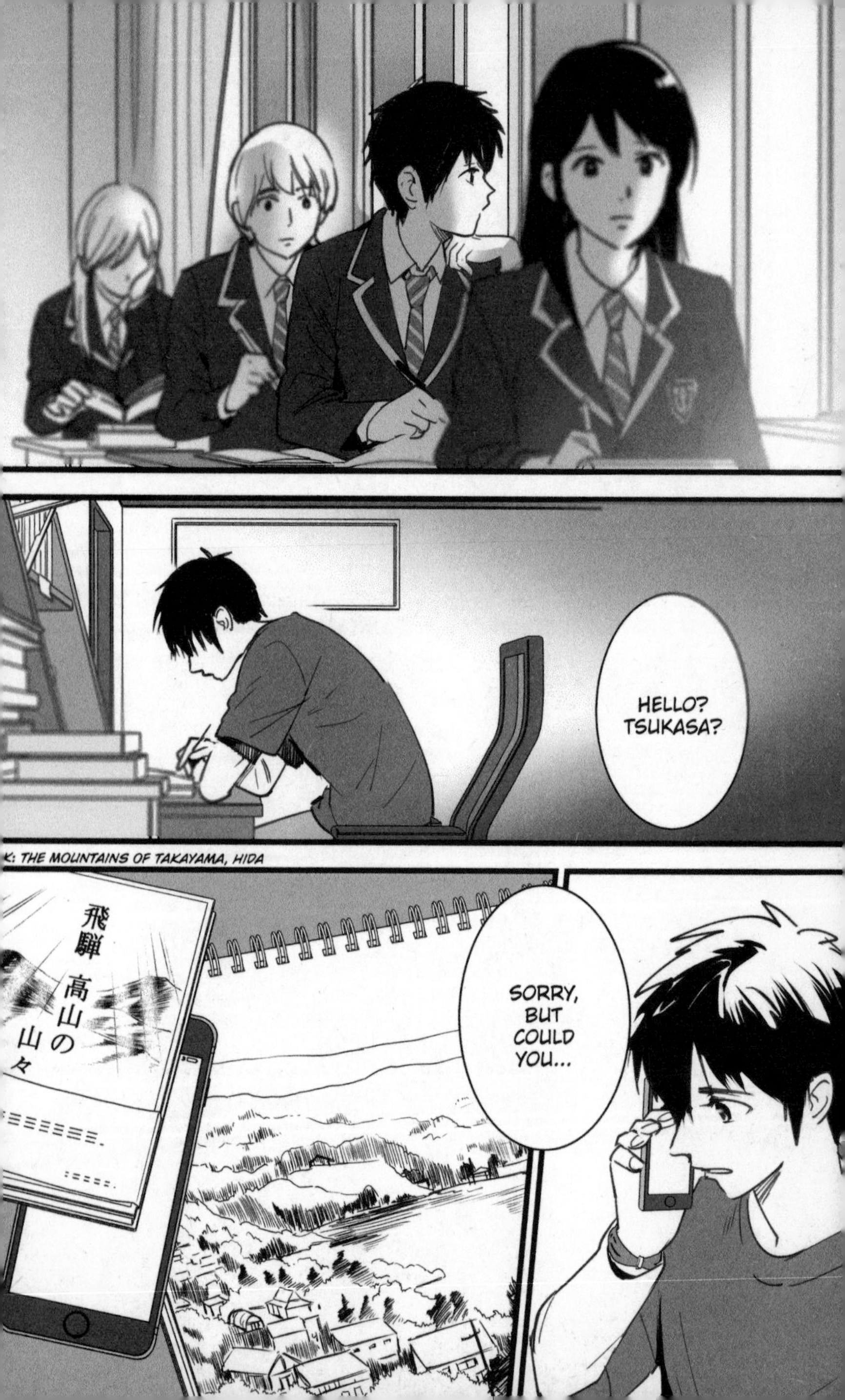
HELLO? TSUKASA?
SORRY, BUT COULD YOU...
飛騨 高山の山々
K: THE MOUNTAINS OF TAKAYAMA, HIDA

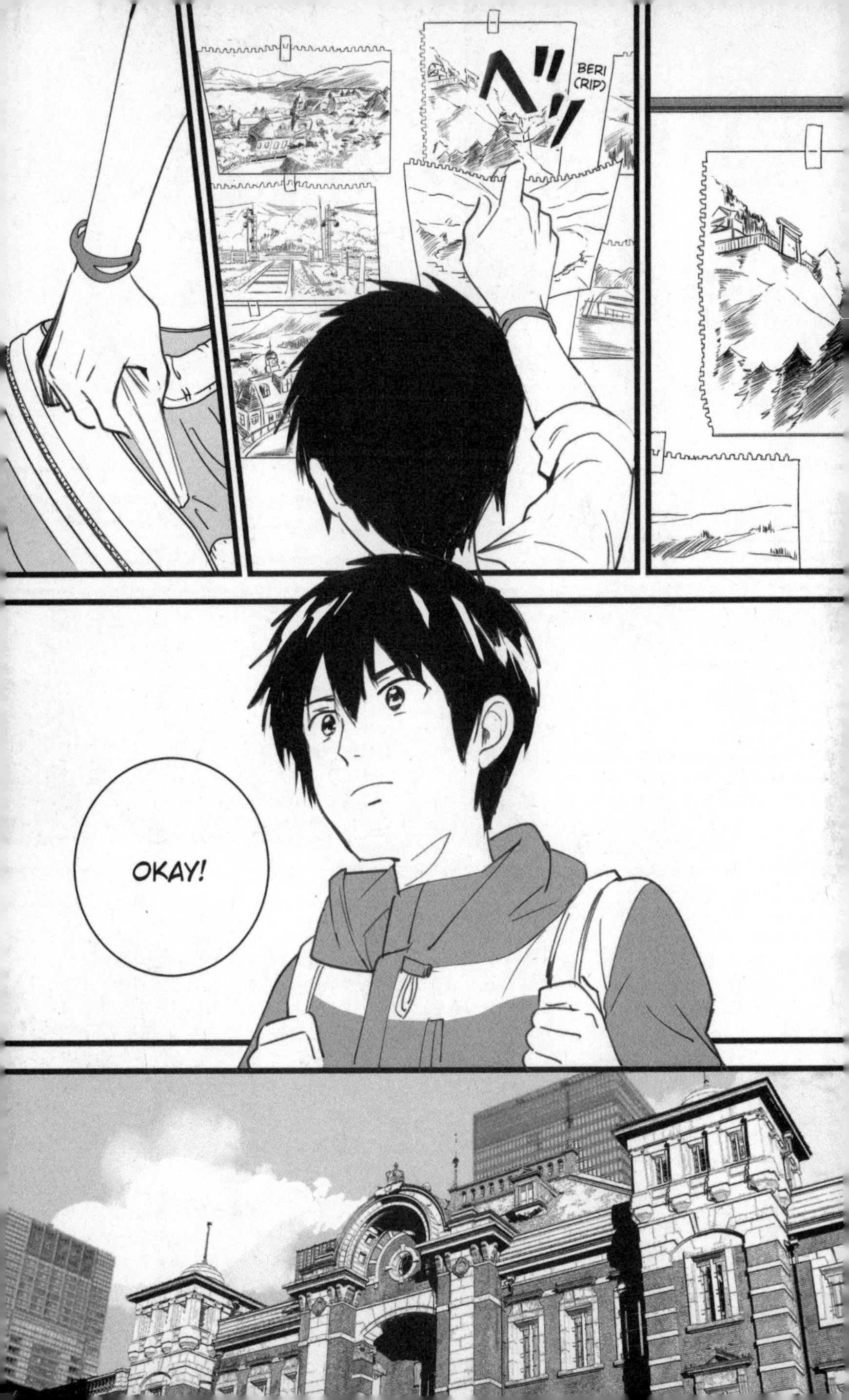
ベリ
BERI (RIP)
OKAY!

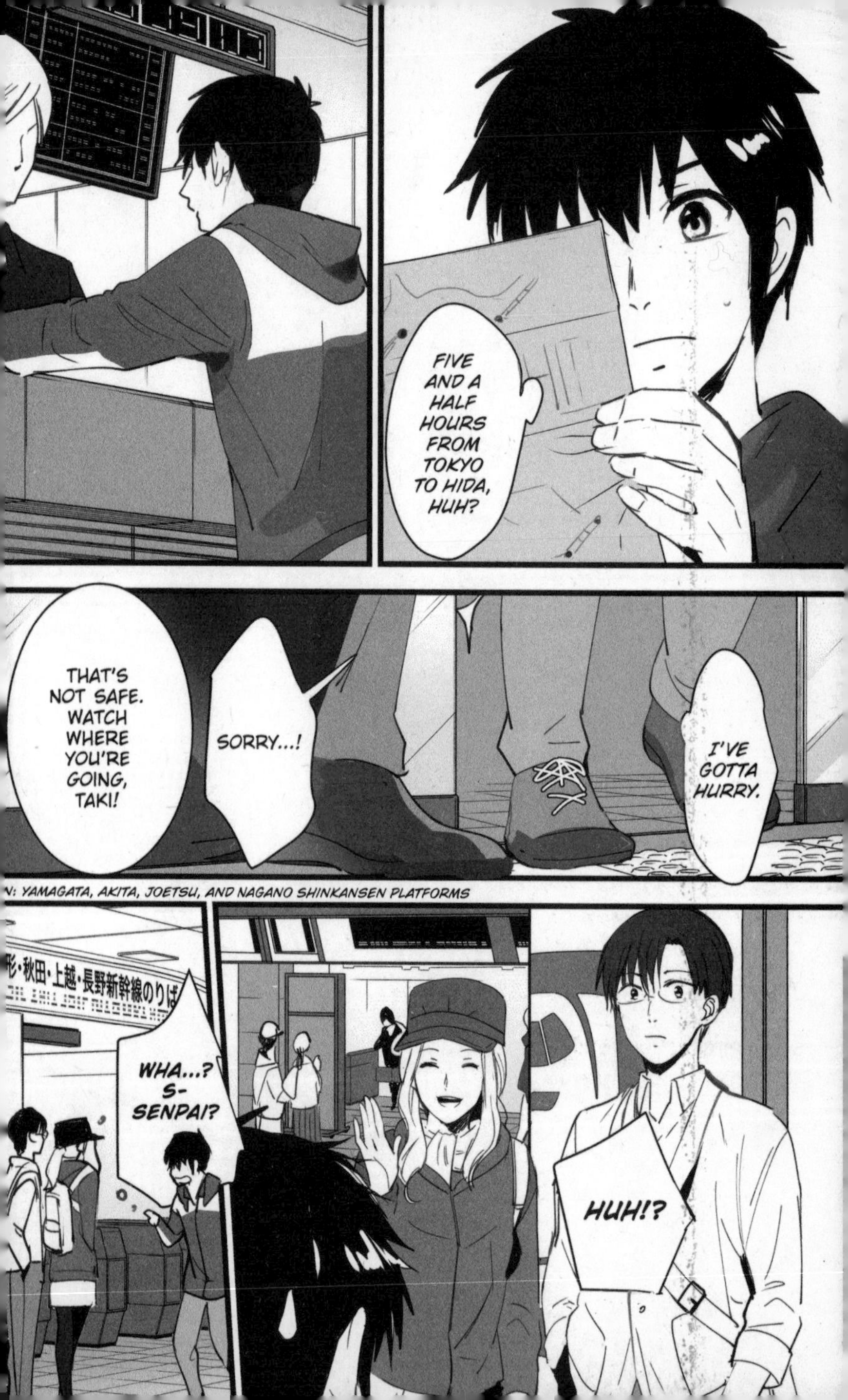
FIVE AND A HALF HOURS FROM TOKYO TO HIDA, HUH?
I'VE GOTTA HURRY.
SORRY...!
THAT'S NOT SAFE. WATCH WHERE YOU'RE GOING, TAKI!
YAMAGATA, AKITA, JOETSU, AND NAGANO SHINKANSEN PLATFORMS
HUH!?
形・秋田・上越・長野新幹線のりば
WHA...? S-SENPAI?

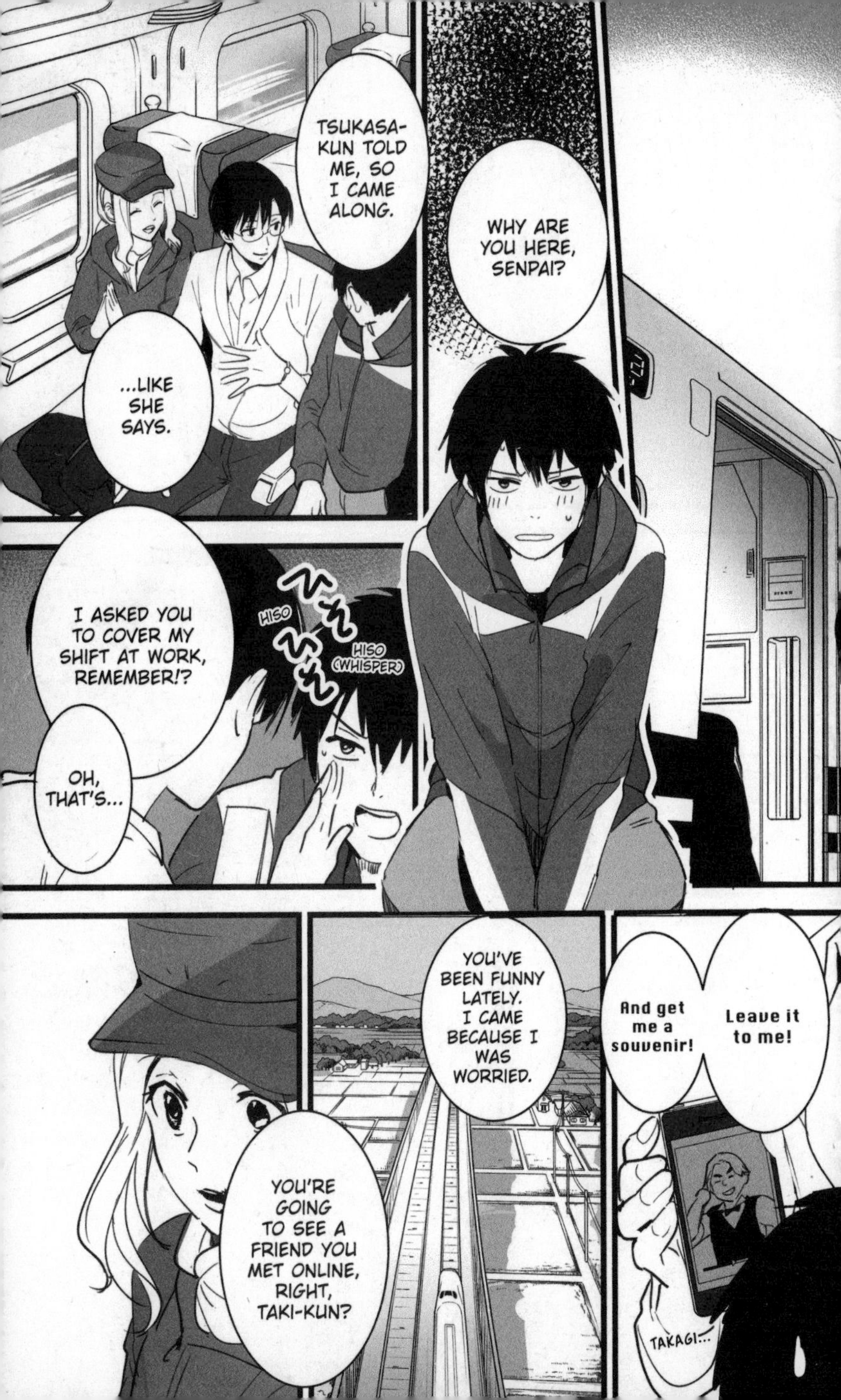
WHY ARE YOU HERE, SENPAI?
TSUKASA-KUN TOLD ME, SO I CAME ALONG.
...LIKE SHE SAYS.
I ASKED YOU TO COVER MY SHIFT AT WORK, REMEMBER!?
HISO
HISO (WHISPER)
OH, THAT'S...
Leave it to me!
And get me a souvenir!
TAKAGI...
YOU'VE BEEN FUNNY LATELY. I CAME BECAUSE I WAS WORRIED.
YOU'RE GOING TO SEE A FRIEND YOU MET ONLINE, RIGHT, TAKI-KUN?

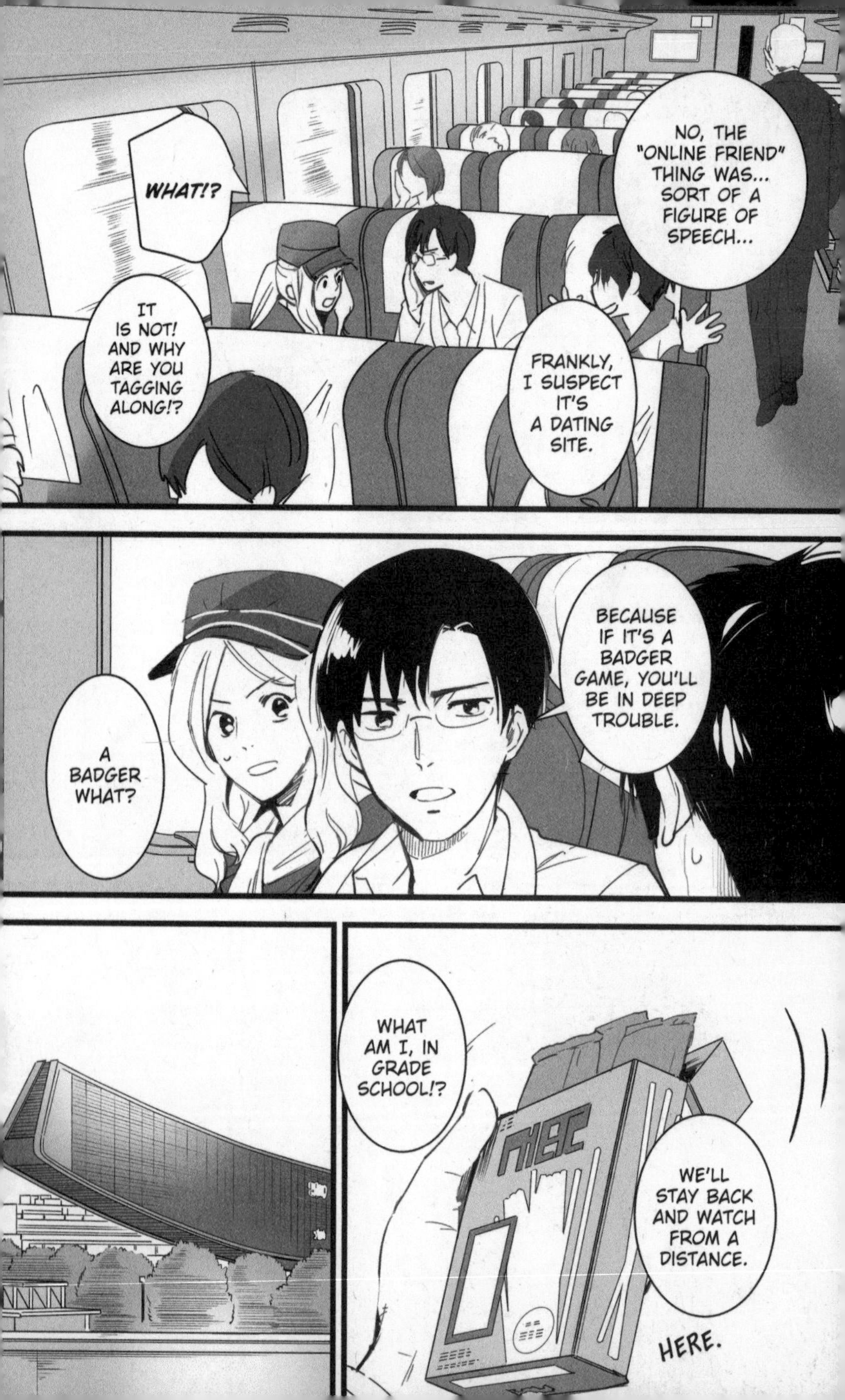
NO, THE "ONLINE FRIEND" THING WAS... SORT OF A FIGURE OF SPEECH...
WHAT!?
FRANKLY, I SUSPECT IT'S A DATING SITE.
IT IS NOT! AND WHY ARE YOU TAGGING ALONG!?
BECAUSE IF IT'S A BADGER GAME, YOU'LL BE IN DEEP TROUBLE.
A BADGER WHAT?
WE'LL STAY BACK AND WATCH FROM A DISTANCE.
HERE.
WHAT AM I, IN GRADE SCHOOL!?

HURRY UP!

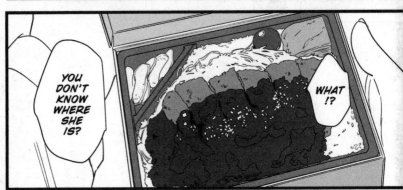

YOU DON'T KNOW WHERE SHE IS?

WHAT!?

BOXES: MISO CUTLET

Y... YEAH.

YOUR ONLY CLUES ARE THOSE DRAWINGS?

ゴッ GOOO (FOOOM)

UM. RIGHT.

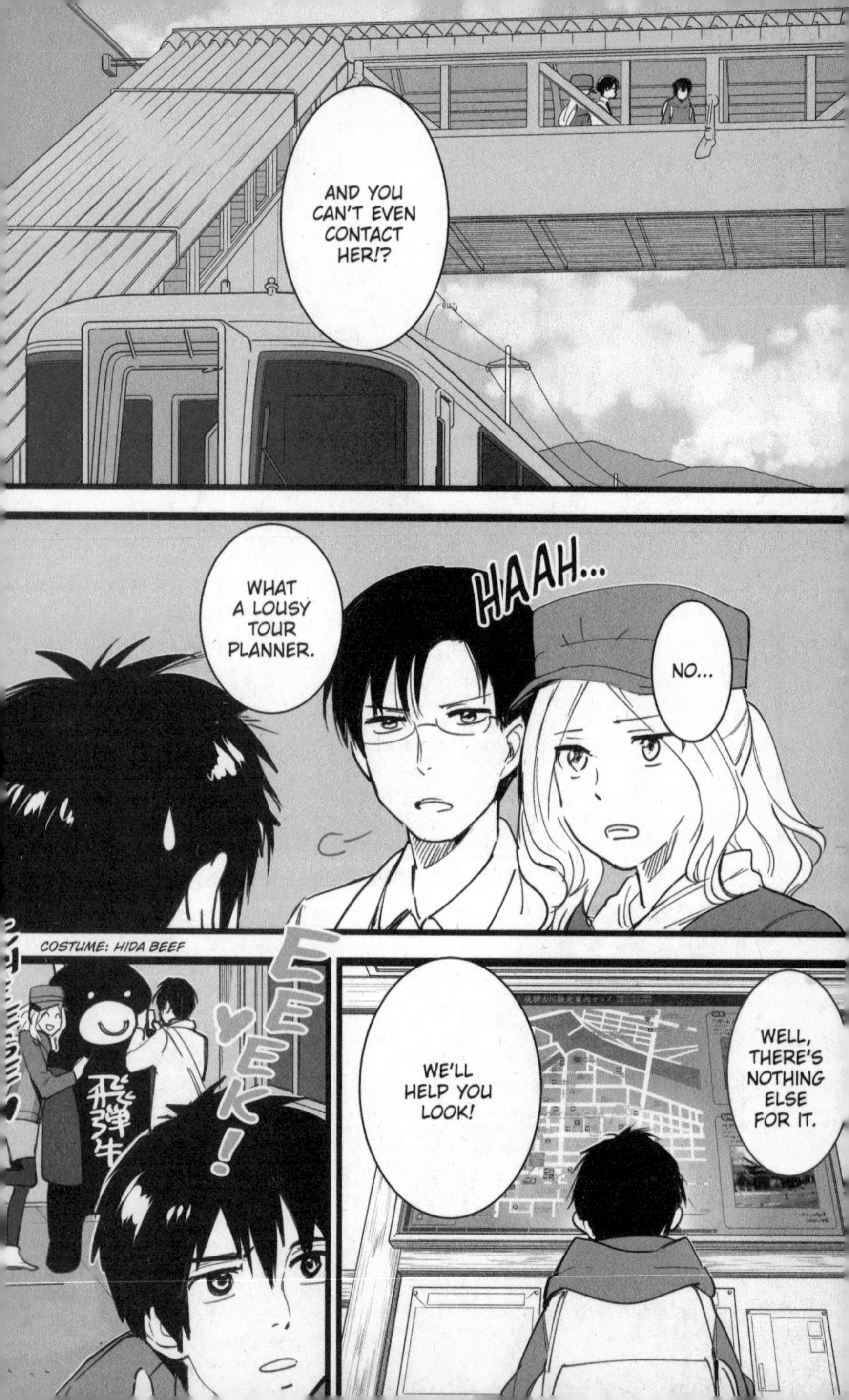
AND YOU CAN'T EVEN CONTACT HER!?
HAAAH...
NO...
WHAT A LOUSY TOUR PLANNER.
WELL, THERE'S NOTHING ELSE FOR IT.
WE'LL HELP YOU LOOK!
COSTUME: HIDA BEEF
EEYEK!
飛弾牛

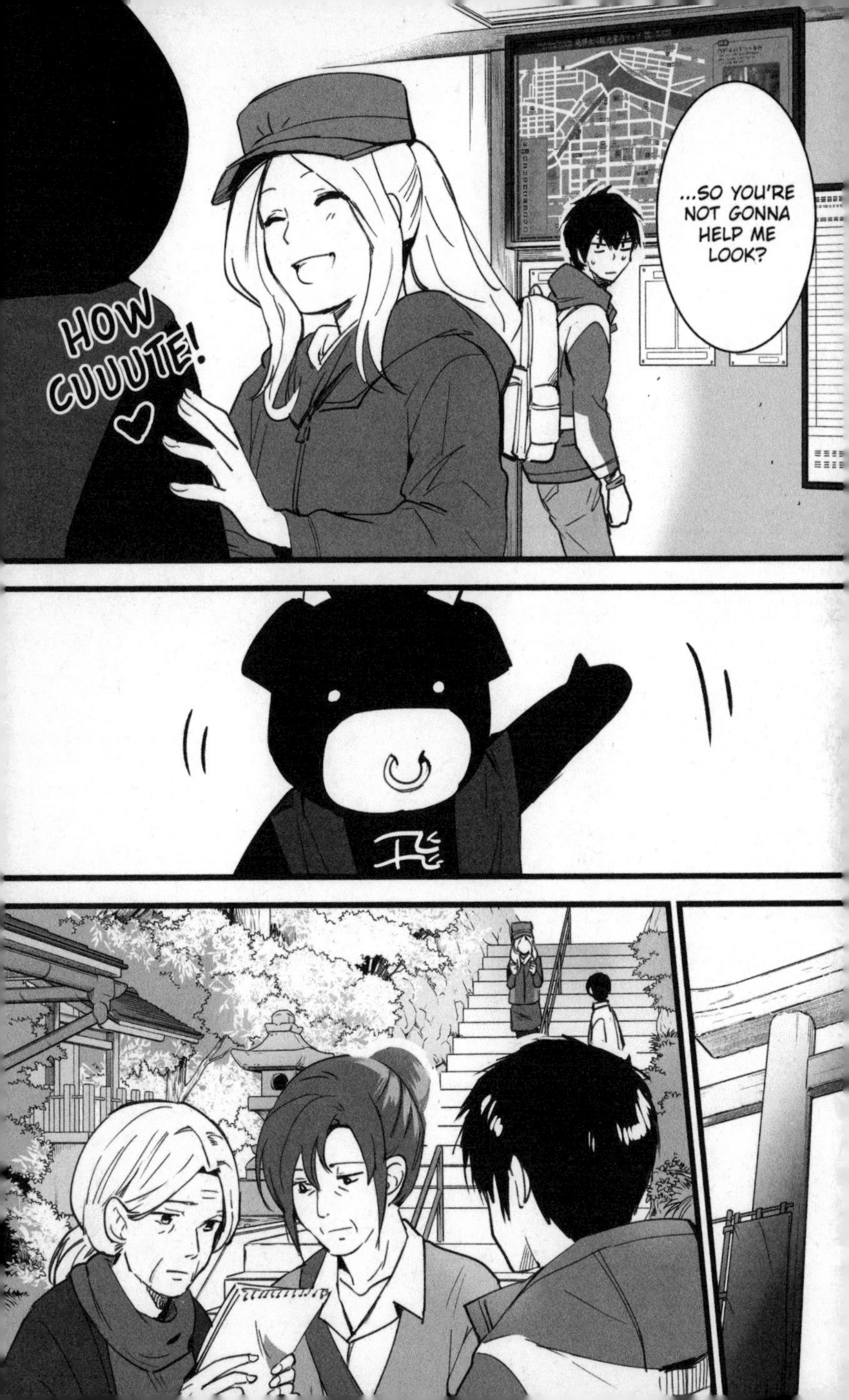
...SO YOU'RE NOT GONNA HELP ME LOOK?
HOW CUUUTE! ♥

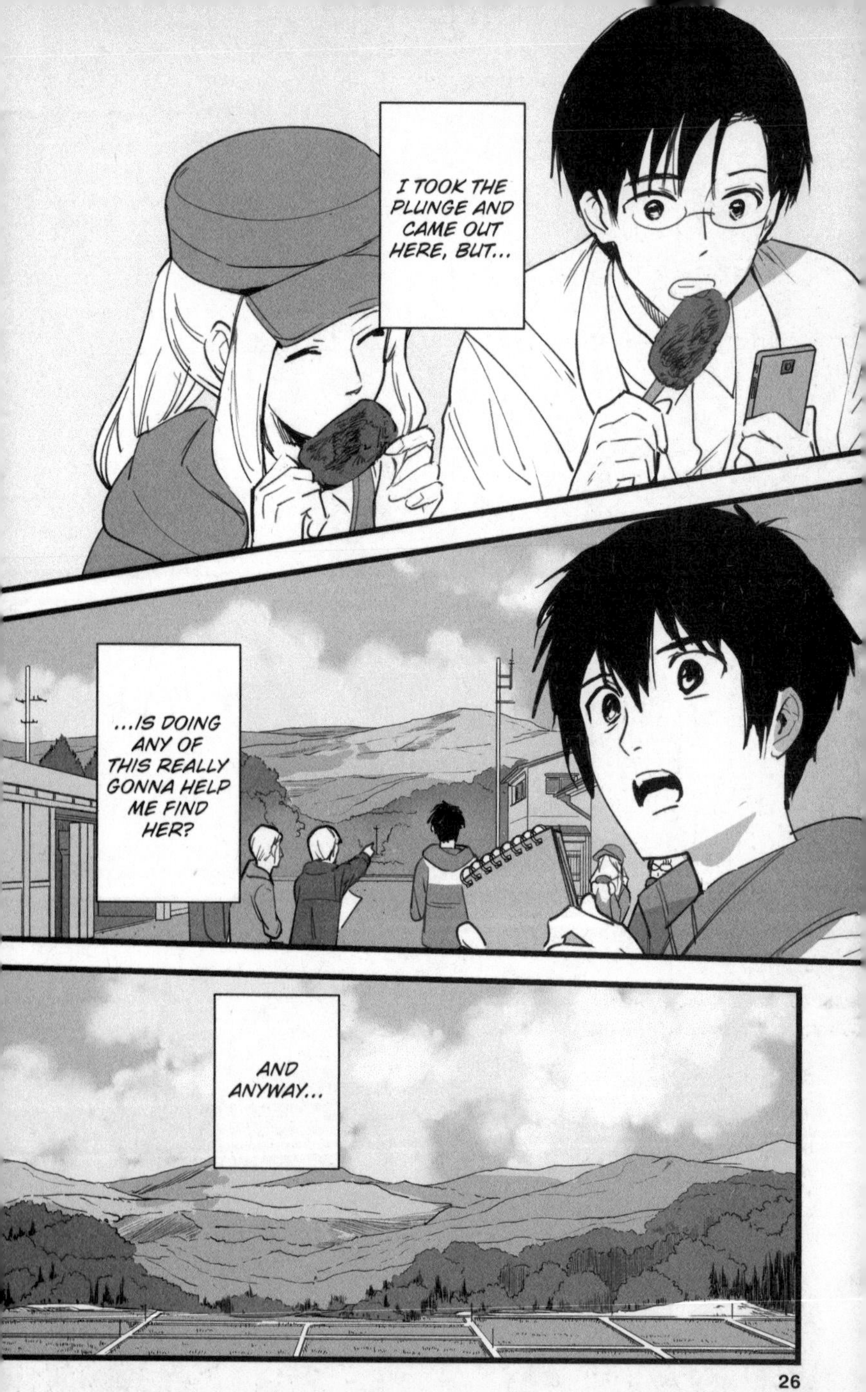
I TOOK THE PLUNGE AND CAME OUT HERE, BUT...
...IS DOING ANY OF THIS REALLY GONNA HELP ME FIND HER?
AND ANYWAY...

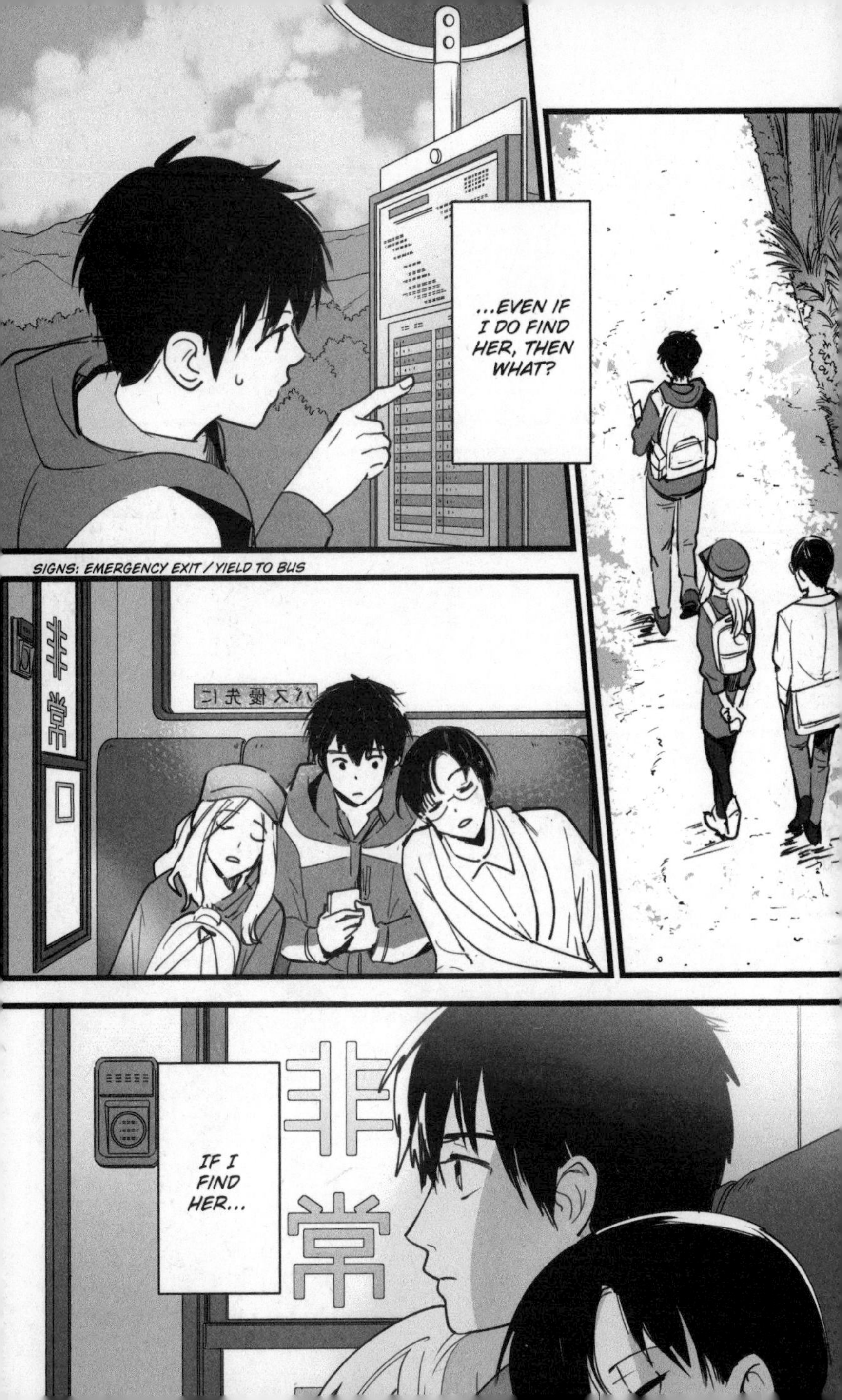
...EVEN IF I DO FIND HER, THEN WHAT?
SIGNS: EMERGENCY EXIT / YIELD TO BUS
非常口
バス優先に
IF I FIND HER...
非常

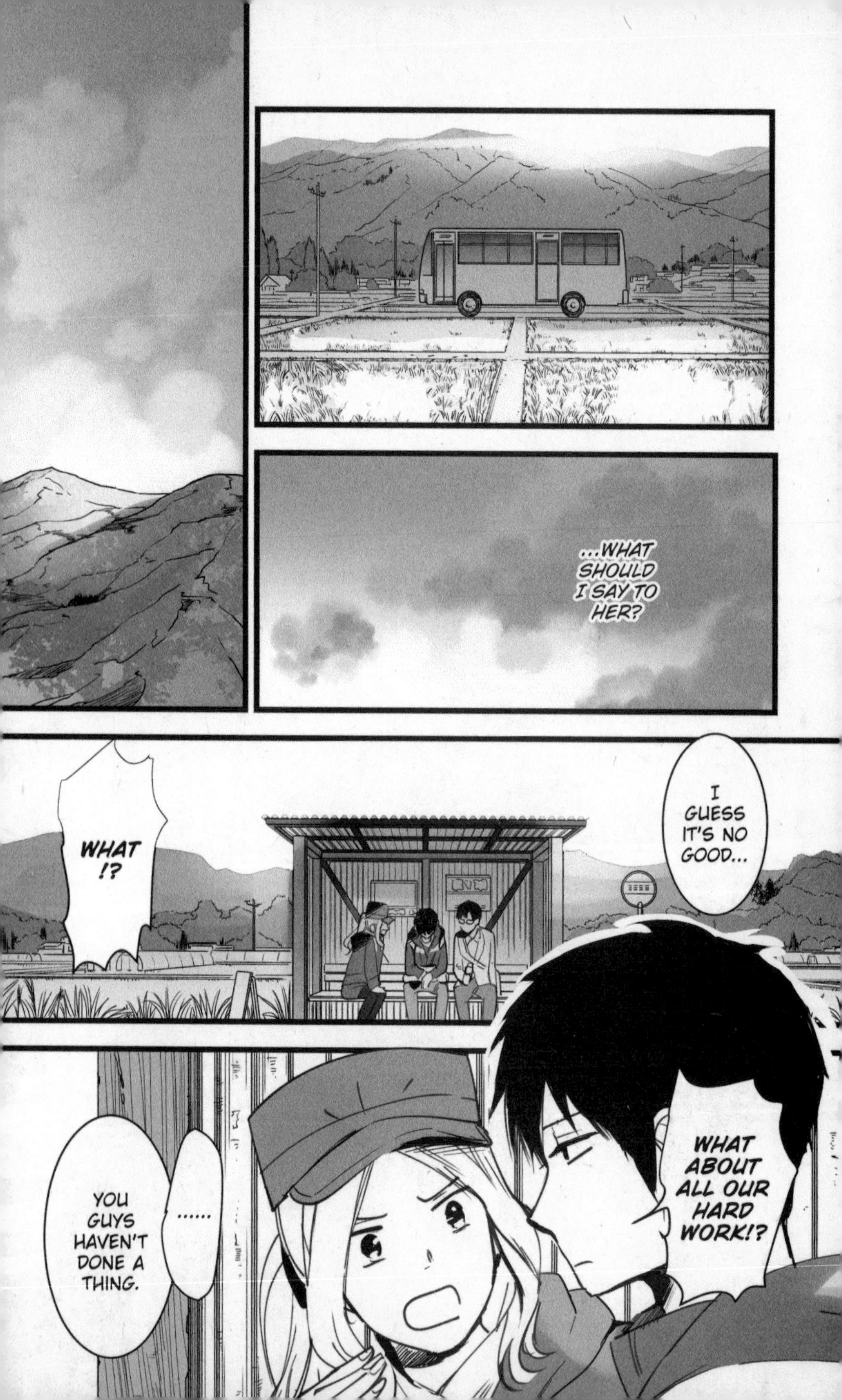
...WHAT SHOULD I SAY TO HER?
I GUESS IT'S NO GOOD...
WHAT!?
WHAT ABOUT ALL OUR HARD WORK!?
......
YOU GUYS HAVEN'T DONE A THING.

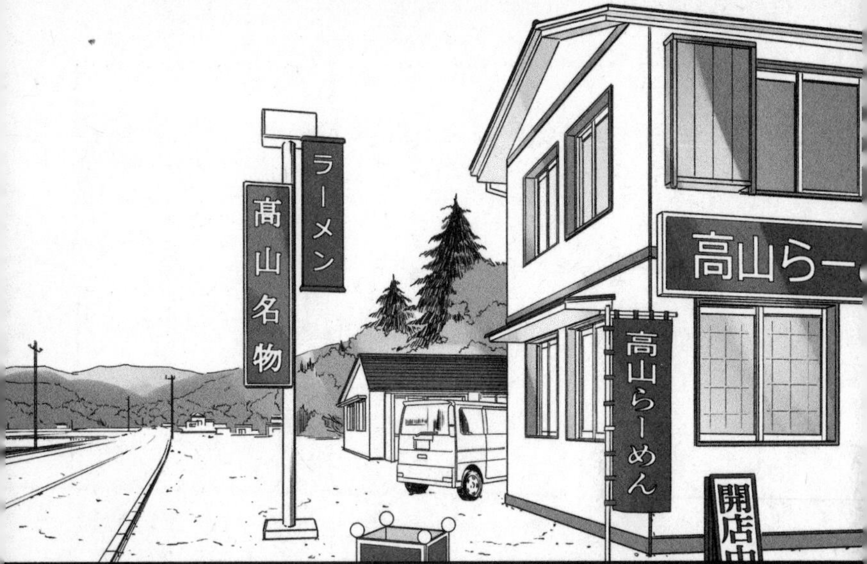
ラーメン
高山名物
高山らーめん
開店

SIGNS: TAKAYAMA RAMEN, A TAKAYAMA SPECIALTY, O

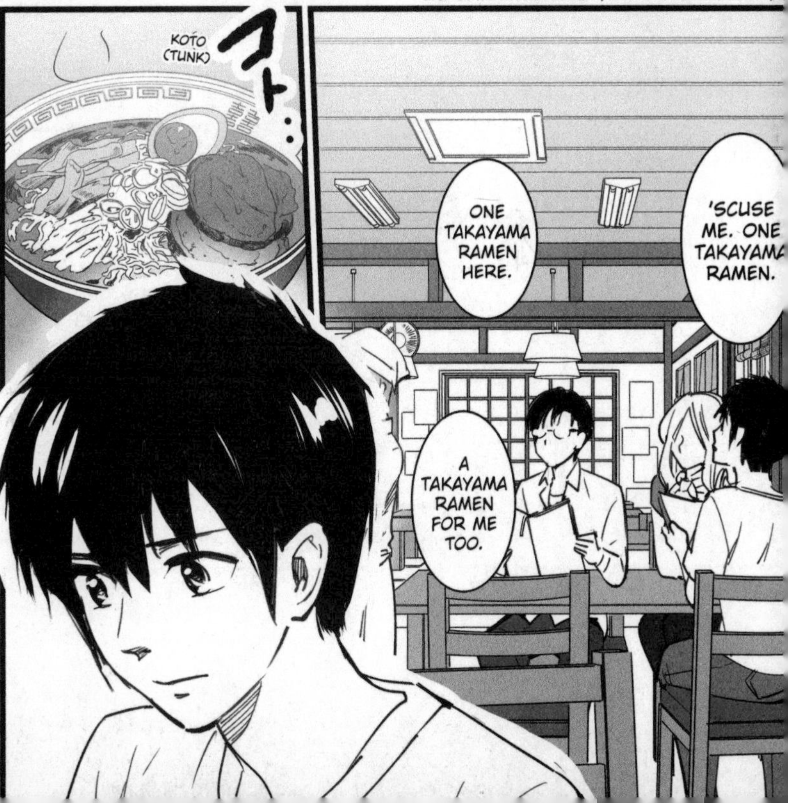
'SCUSE ME. ONE TAKAYAMA RAMEN.
ONE TAKAYAMA RAMEN HERE.
A TAKAYAMA RAMEN FOR ME TOO.
コト…
KOTO (TUNK)

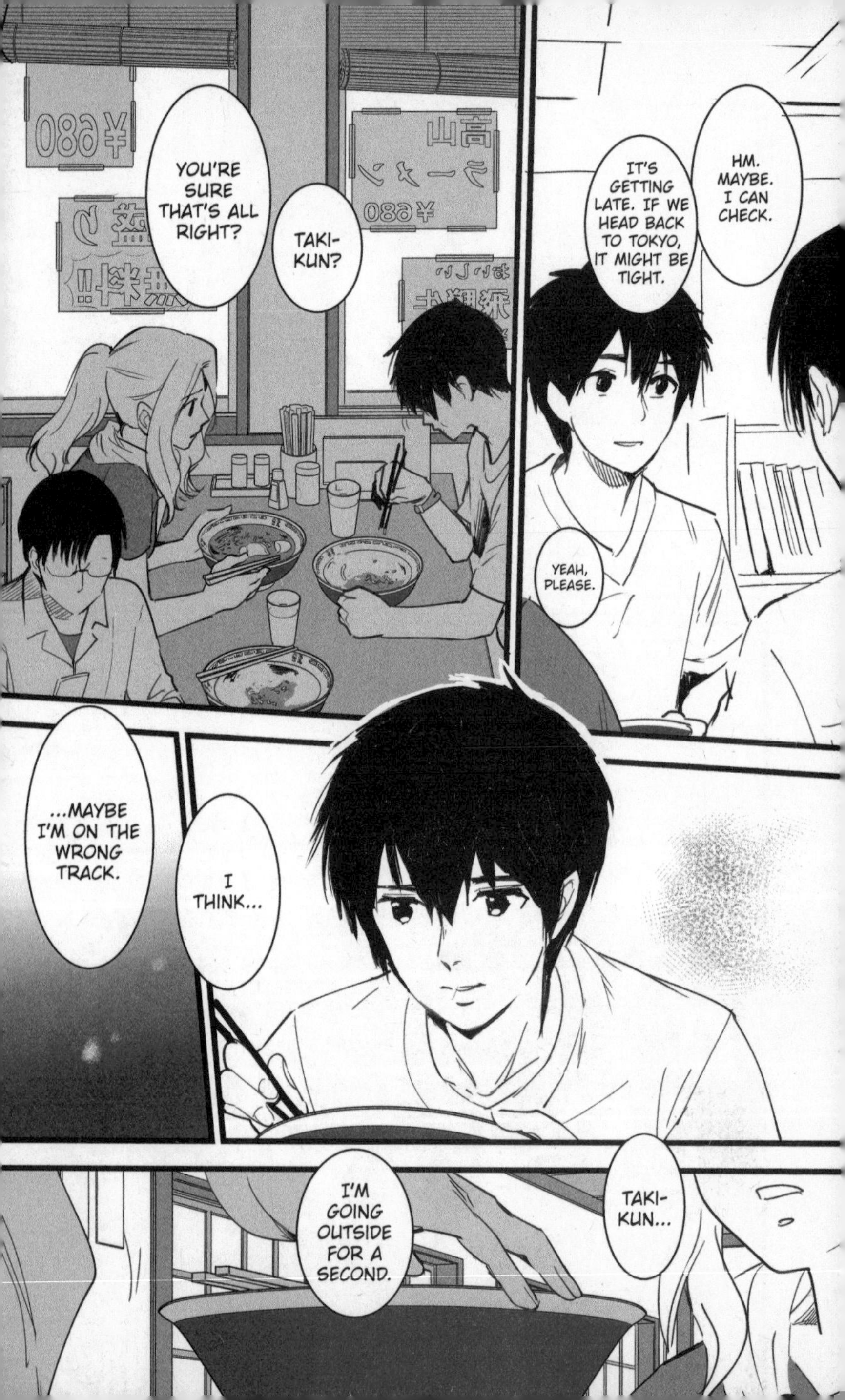
HM. MAYBE. I CAN CHECK.
IT'S GETTING LATE. IF WE HEAD BACK TO TOKYO, IT MIGHT BE TIGHT.
YEAH, PLEASE.
TAKI-KUN?
YOU'RE SURE THAT'S ALL RIGHT?
I THINK...
...MAYBE I'M ON THE WRONG TRACK.
TAKI-KUN...
I'M GOING OUTSIDE FOR A SECOND.

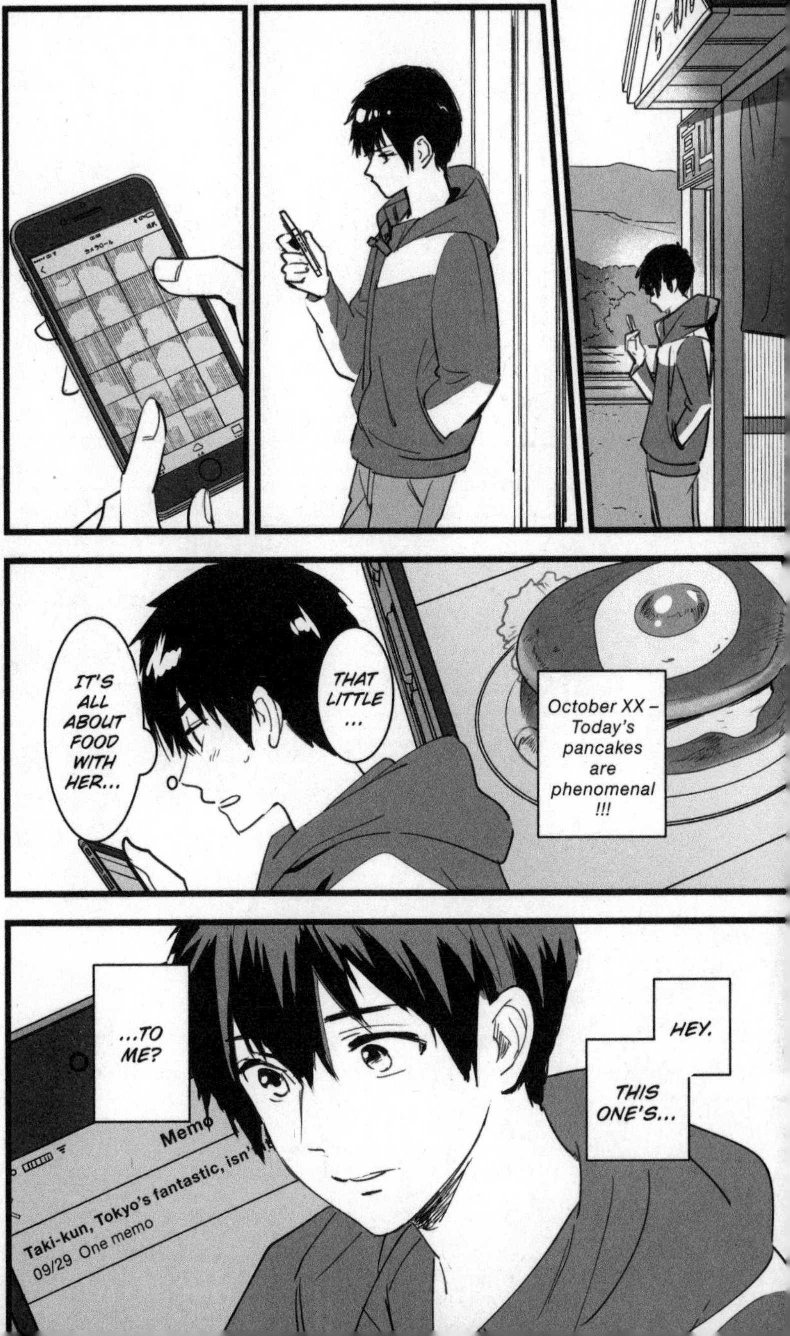
らーめん
October XX – Today's pancakes are phenomenal !!!
THAT LITTLE ...
IT'S ALL ABOUT FOOD WITH HER...
HEY. THIS ONE'S...
...TO ME?
Memo
Taki-kun, Tokyo's fantastic, isn'
09/29 One memo

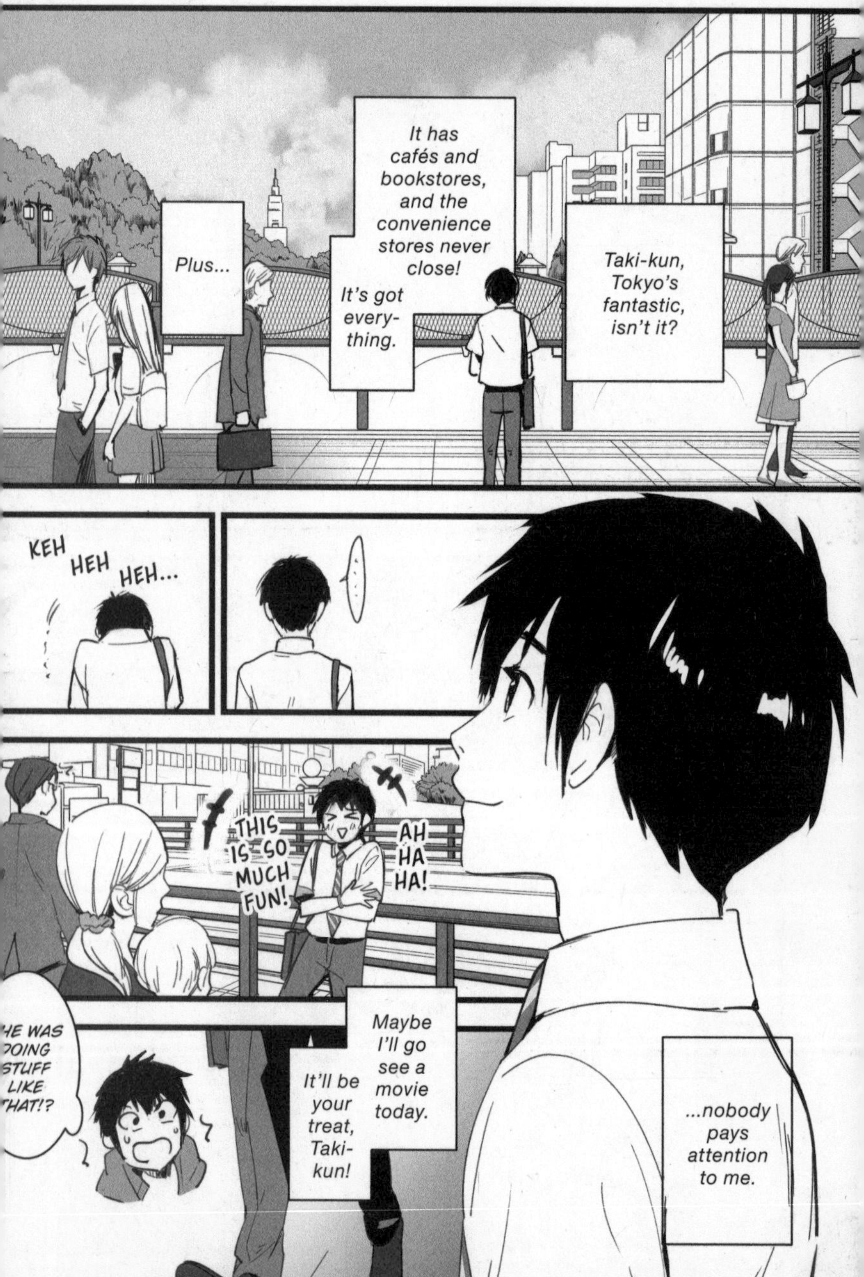
Taki-kun, Tokyo's fantastic, isn't it?
It has cafés and bookstores, and the convenience stores never close!
It's got every-thing.
Plus...
...nobody pays attention to me.
...
KEH HEH HEH...
AH HA HA!
THIS IS SO MUCH FUN!
Maybe I'll go see a movie today.
It'll be your treat, Taki-kun!
HE WAS OING STUFF LIKE HAT!?

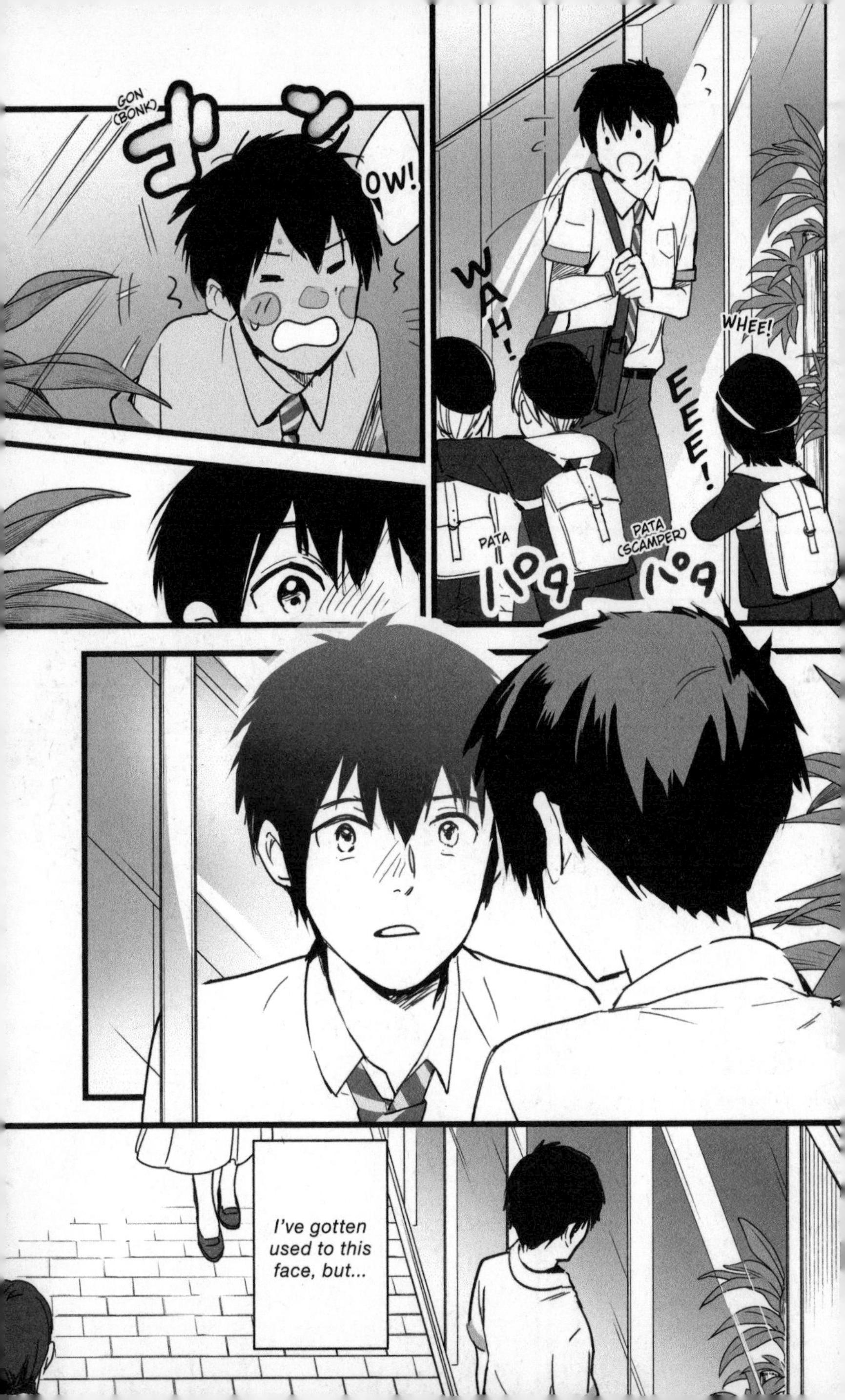
WAH!
WHEE!
EEE!
PATA (SCAMPER)
PATA
GON (BONK)
OW!
I've gotten used to this face, but...

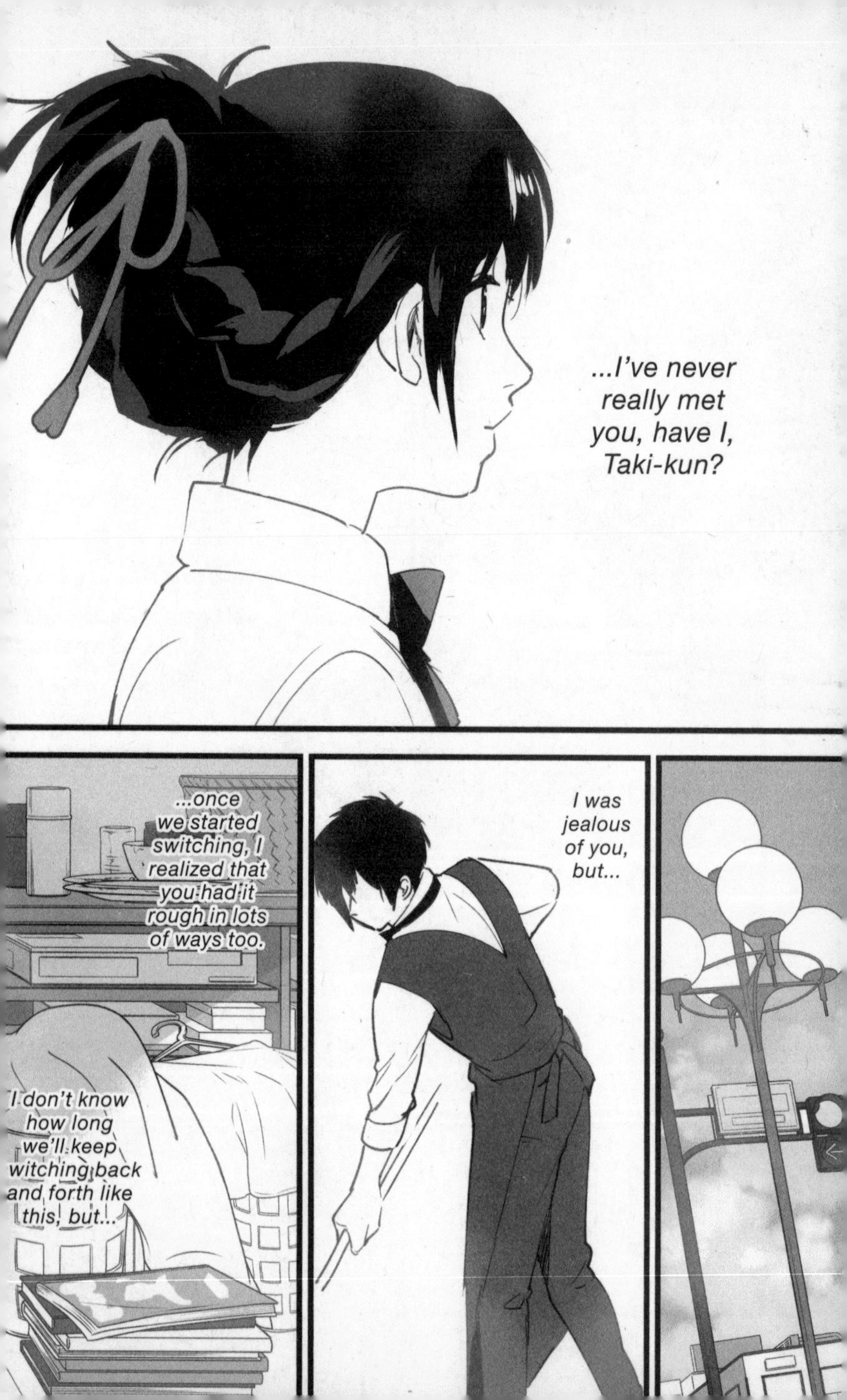
...I've never really met you, have I, Taki-kun?
I was jealous of you, but...
...once we started switching, I realized that you had it rough in lots of ways too.
I don't know how long we'll keep witching back and forth like this, but...

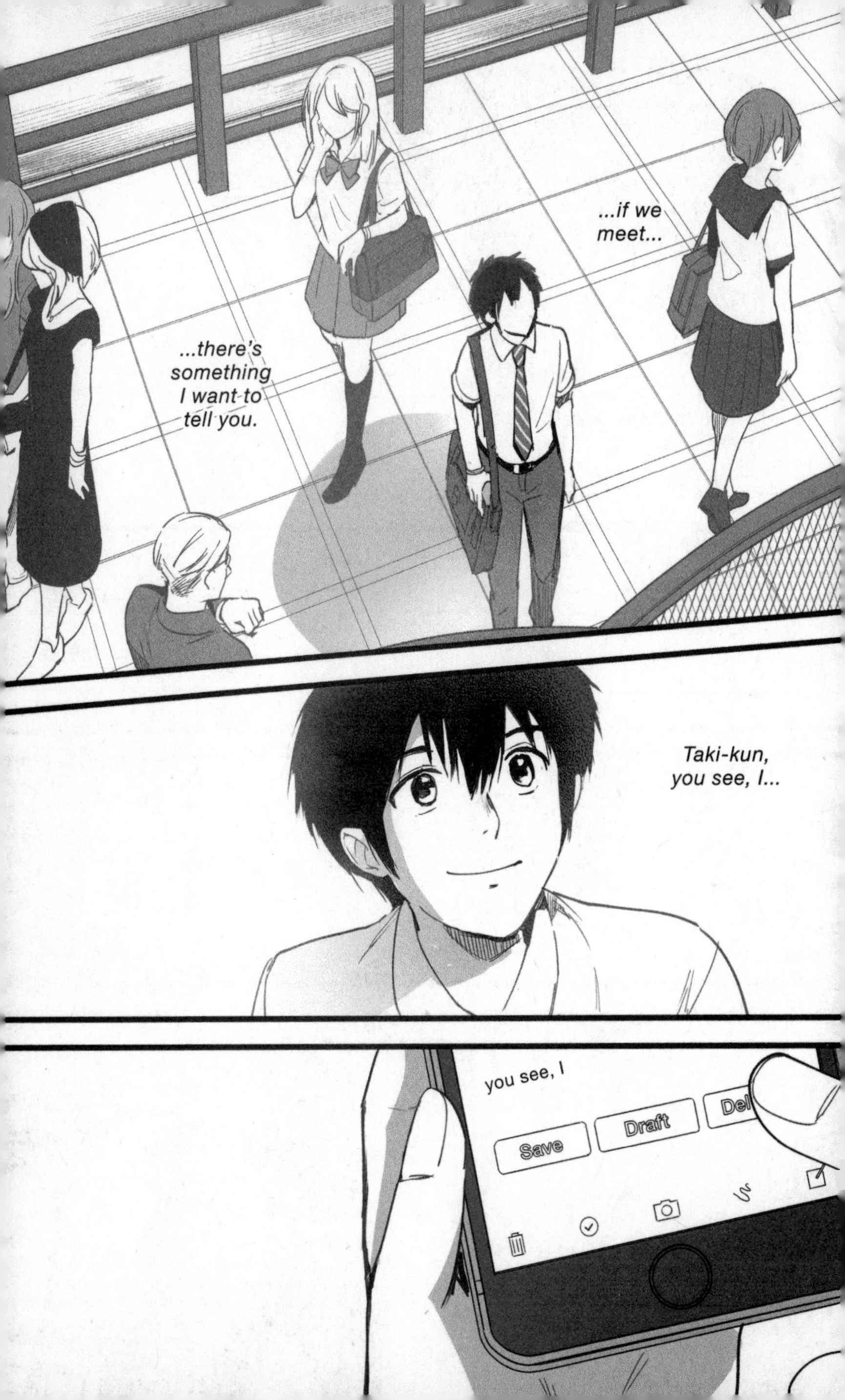
...if we meet...
...there's something I want to tell you.
Taki-kun, you see, I...
you see, I
Del
Draft
Save

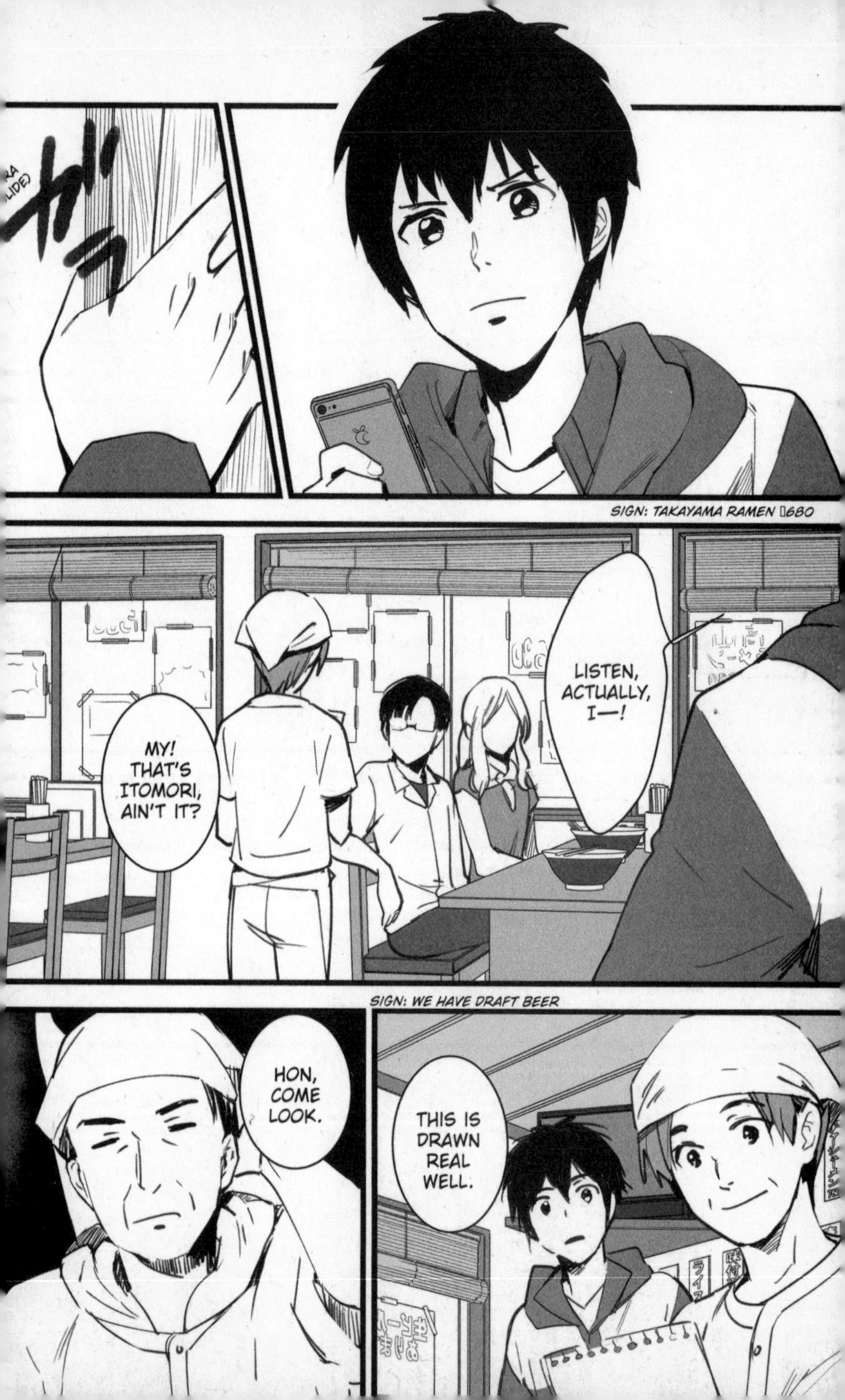
SIGN: TAKAYAMA RAMEN ¥680
LISTEN, ACTUALLY, I—!
MY! THAT'S ITOMORI, AIN'T IT?
SIGN: WE HAVE DRAFT BEER
THIS IS DRAWN REAL WELL.
HON, COME LOOK.

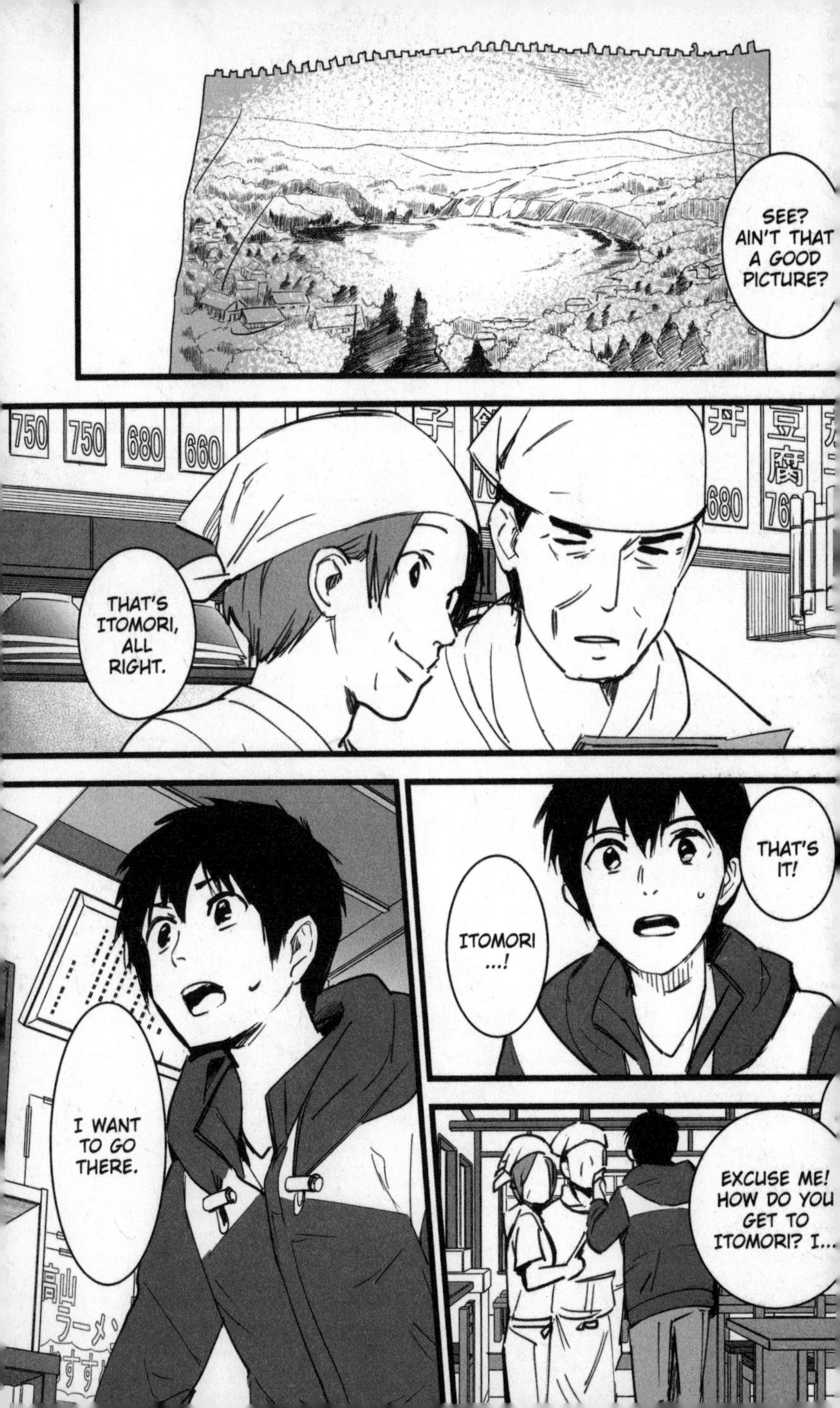
SEE? AIN'T THAT A GOOD PICTURE?
THAT'S ITOMORI, ALL RIGHT.
THAT'S IT!
ITOMORI ...!
EXCUSE ME! HOW DO YOU GET TO ITOMORI? I...
I WANT TO GO THERE.

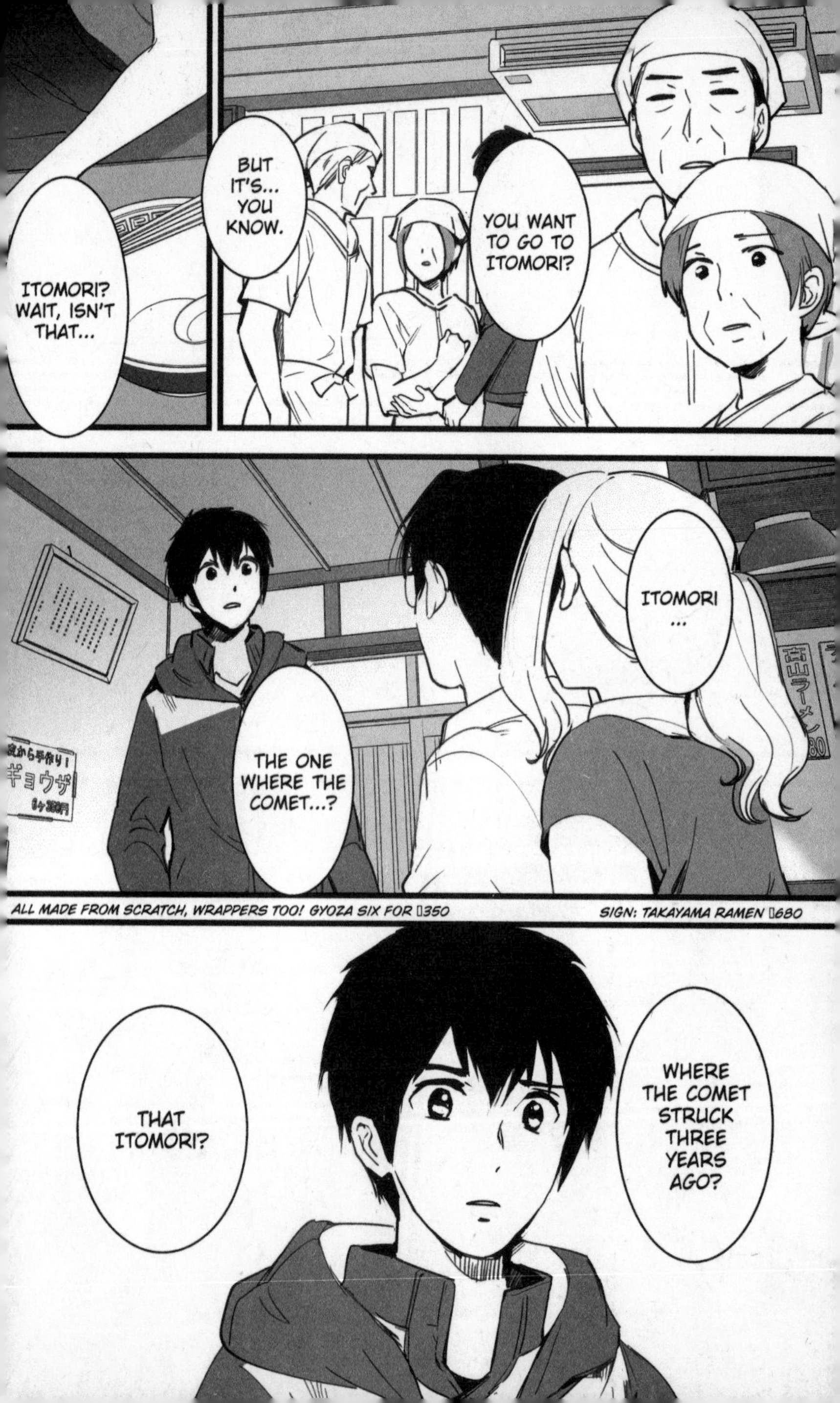
YOU WANT TO GO TO ITOMORI?
BUT IT'S... YOU KNOW.
ITOMORI? WAIT, ISN'T THAT...
ITOMORI ...
THE ONE WHERE THE COMET...?
ALL MADE FROM SCRATCH, WRAPPERS TOO! GYOZA SIX FOR ¥350
SIGN: TAKAYAMA RAMEN ¥680
WHERE THE COMET STRUCK THREE YEARS AGO?
THAT ITOMORI?

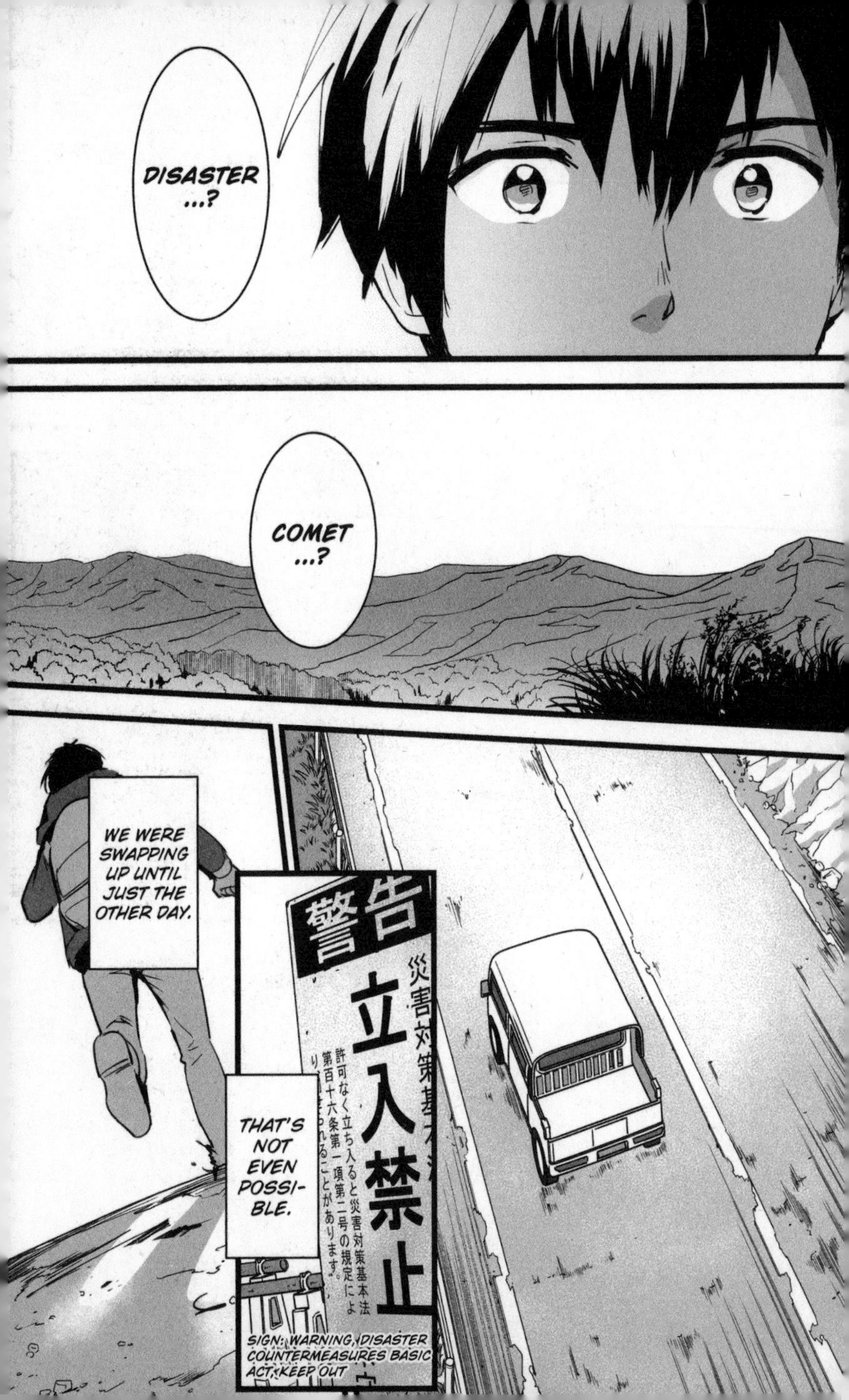
DISASTER ...?
COMET ...?
WE WERE SWAPPING UP UNTIL JUST THE OTHER DAY.
警告
立入禁止
許可なく立ち入ると災害対策基本法
第百十六条第一項第二号の規定によ
ることがあります。
THAT'S NOT EVEN POSSI-BLE.
SIGN: WARNING, DISASTER COUNTERMEASURES BASIC ACT, KEEP OUT

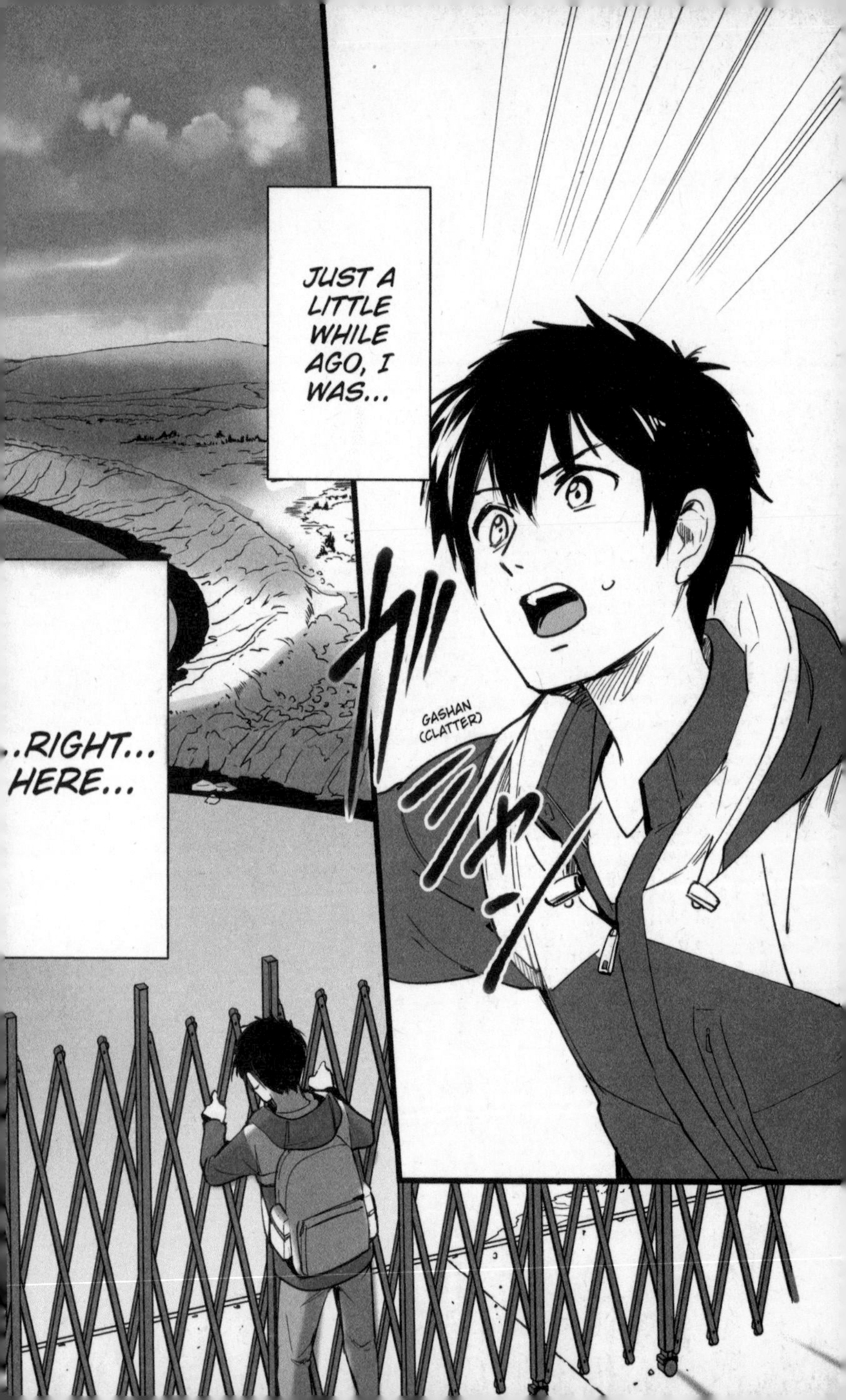
JUST A LITTLE WHILE AGO, I WAS...
GASHAN (CLATTER)
..RIGHT... HERE...

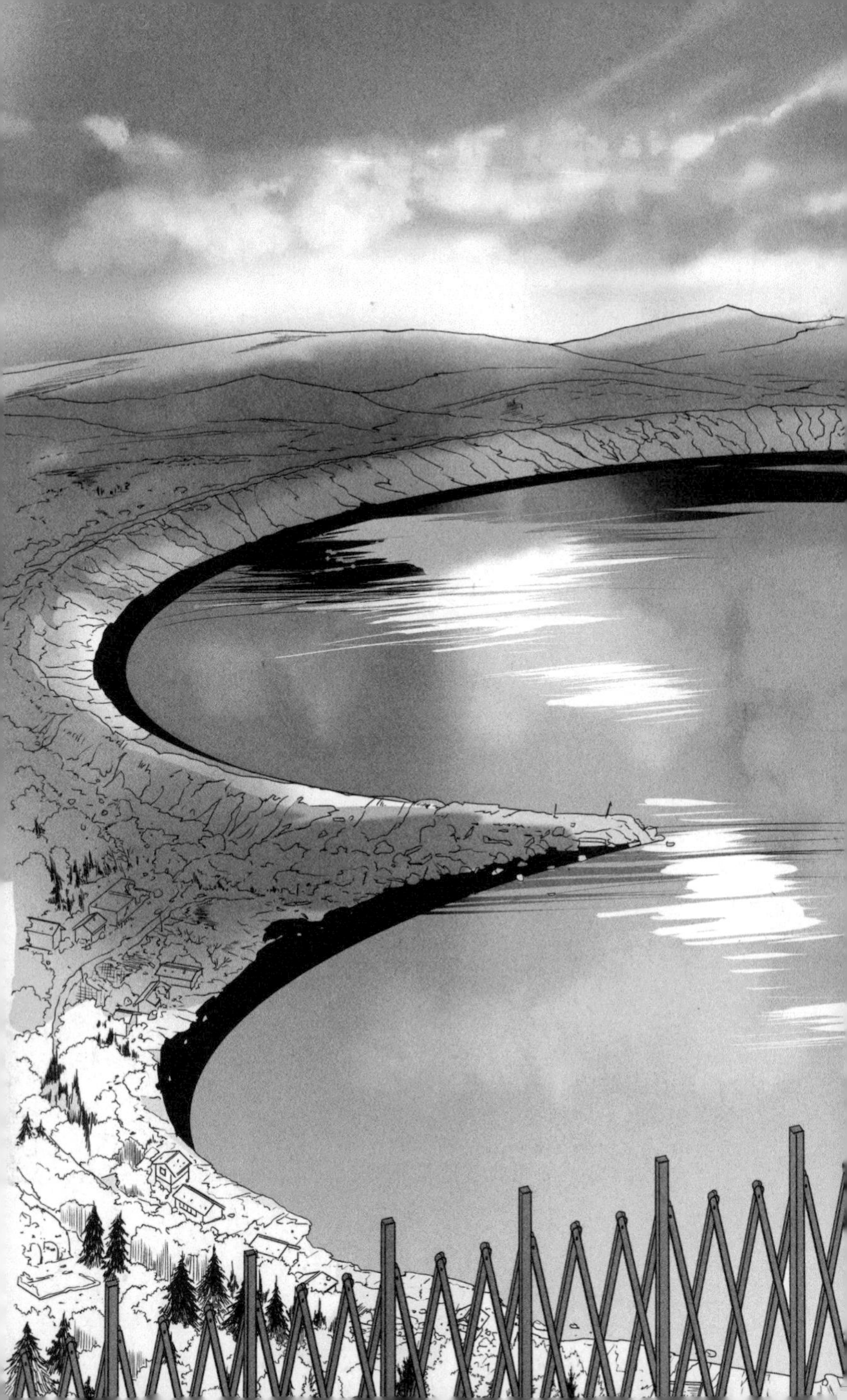

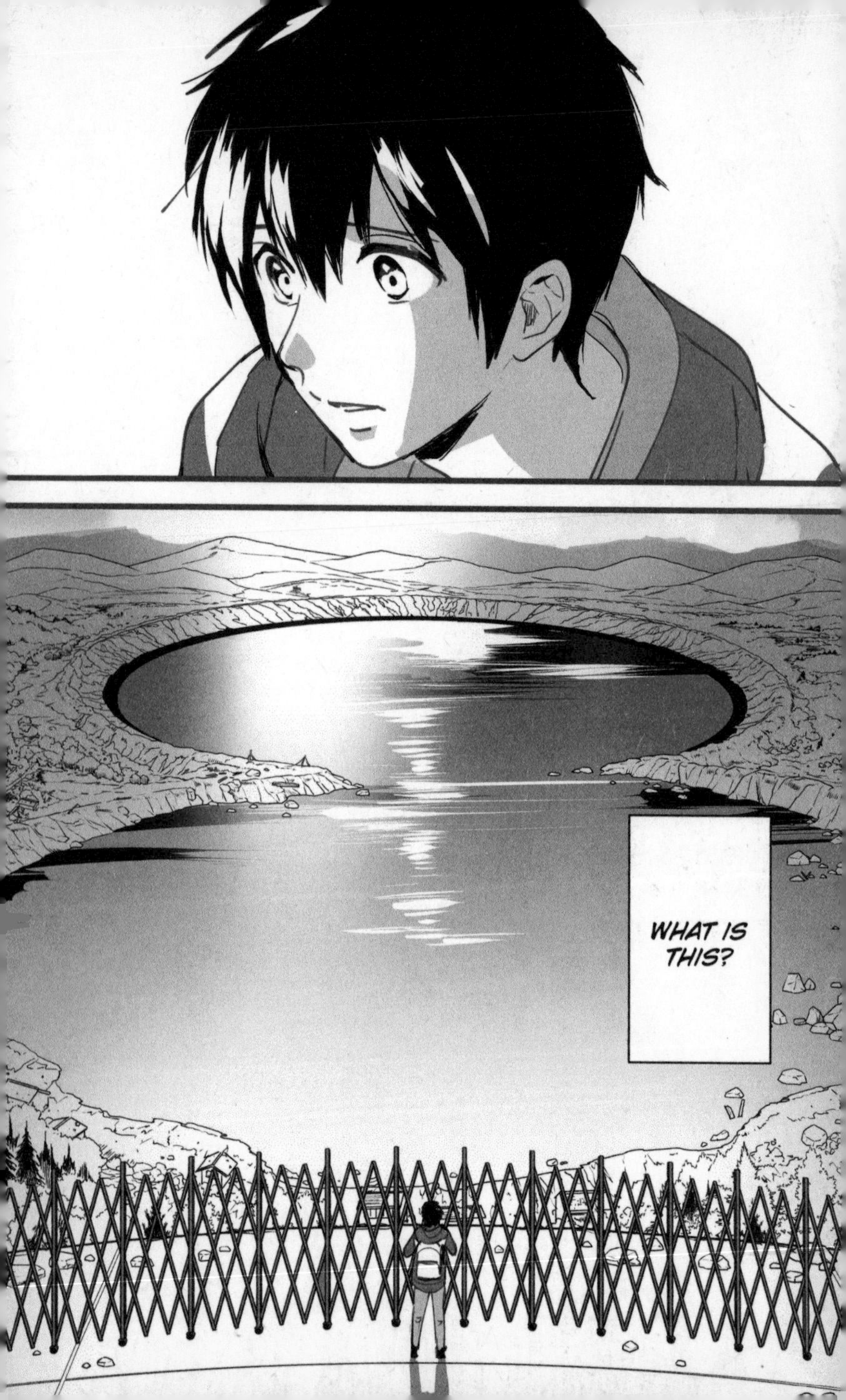
WHAT IS THIS?

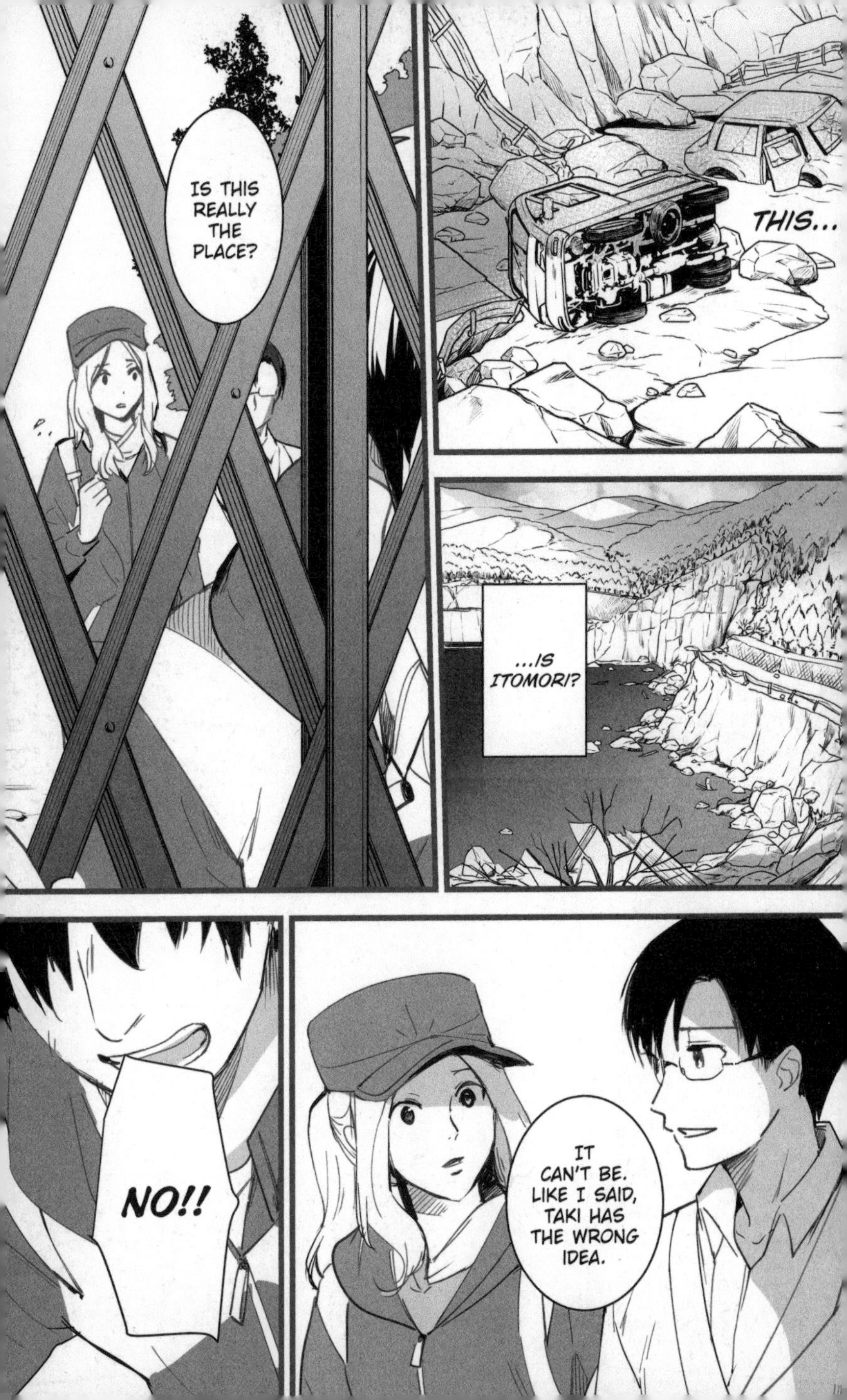
THIS...
...IS ITOMORI?
IS THIS REALLY THE PLACE?
IT CAN'T BE. LIKE I SAID, TAKI HAS THE WRONG IDEA.
NO!!

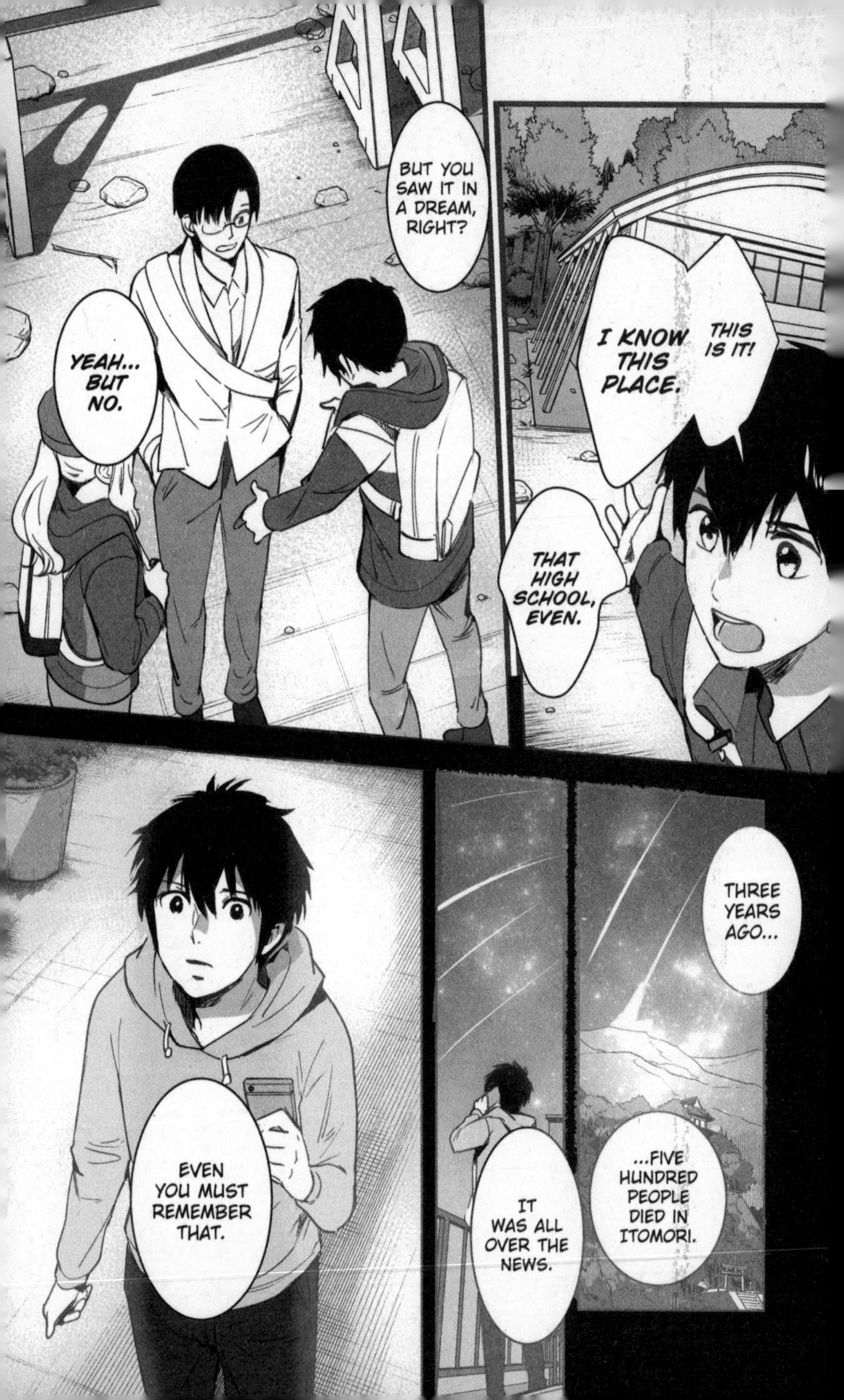

THIS IS IT!
I KNOW THIS PLACE.
THAT HIGH SCHOOL, EVEN.
BUT YOU SAW IT IN A DREAM, RIGHT?
YEAH... BUT NO.
THREE YEARS AGO...
...FIVE HUNDRED PEOPLE DIED IN ITOMORI.
IT WAS ALL OVER THE NEWS.
EVEN YOU MUST REMEMBER THAT.

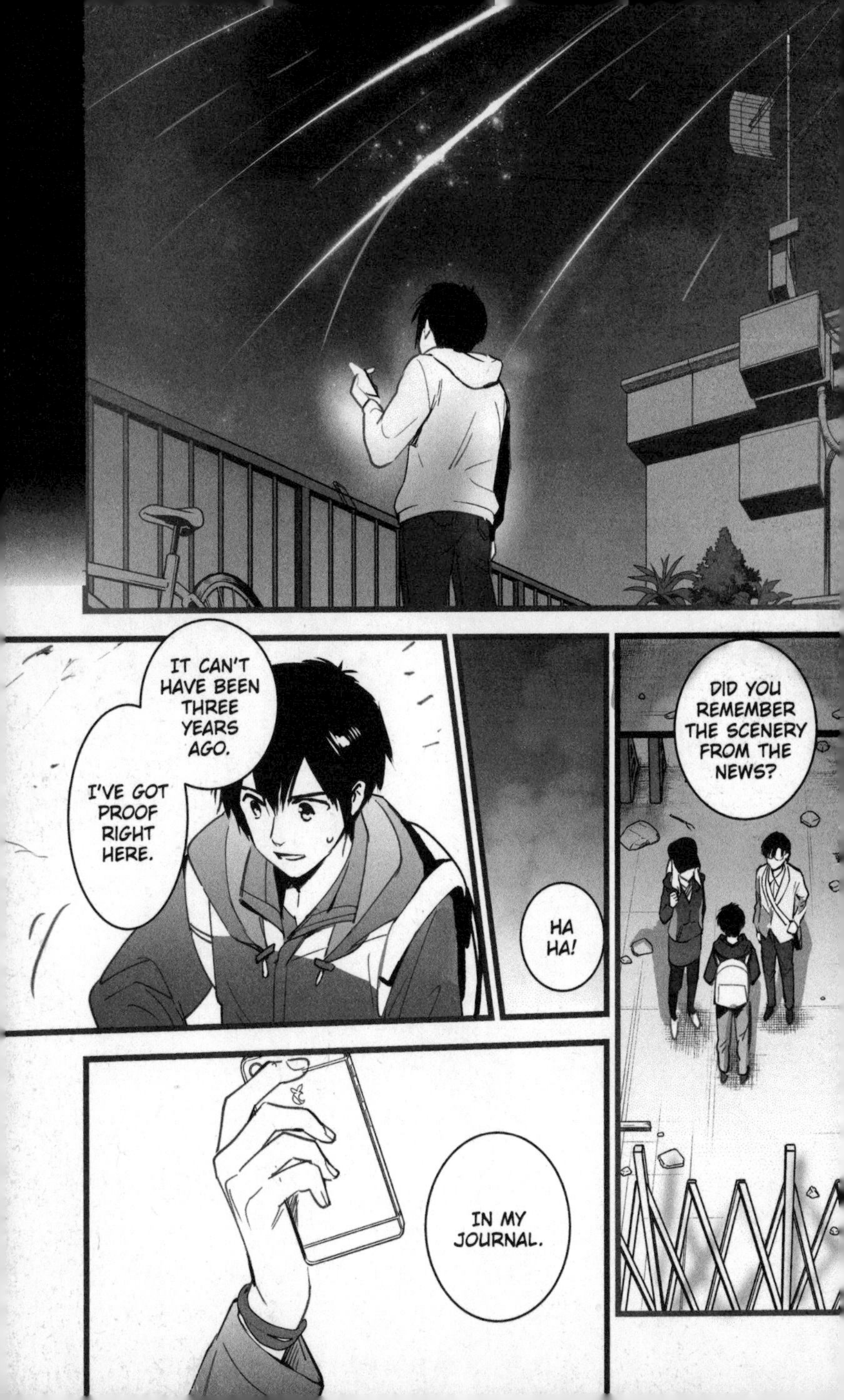
DID YOU REMEMBER THE SCENERY FROM THE NEWS?
HA HA!
IT CAN'T HAVE BEEN THREE YEARS AGO.
I'VE GOT PROOF RIGHT HERE.
IN MY JOURNAL.

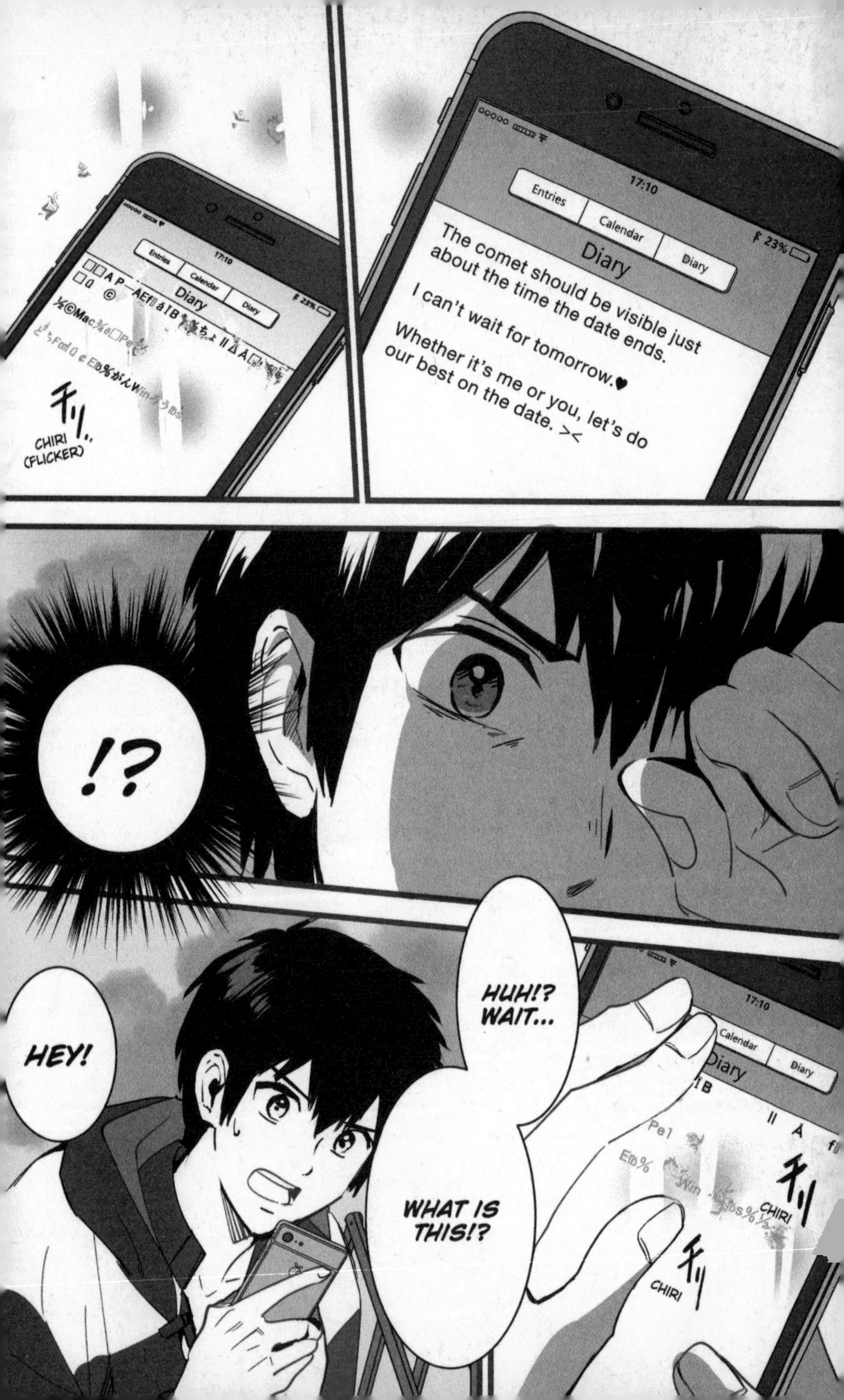
17:10
Entries
Calendar
Diary
23%
Diary
The comet should be visible just about the time the date ends.
I can't wait for tomorrow.♥
Whether it's me or you, let's do our best on the date. ><
17:10
Entries
Calendar
Diary
23%
Diary
チリ
CHIRI (FLICKER)
!?
チリ
CHIRI
チリ
CHIRI
HUH!? WAIT...
WHAT IS THIS!?
HEY!

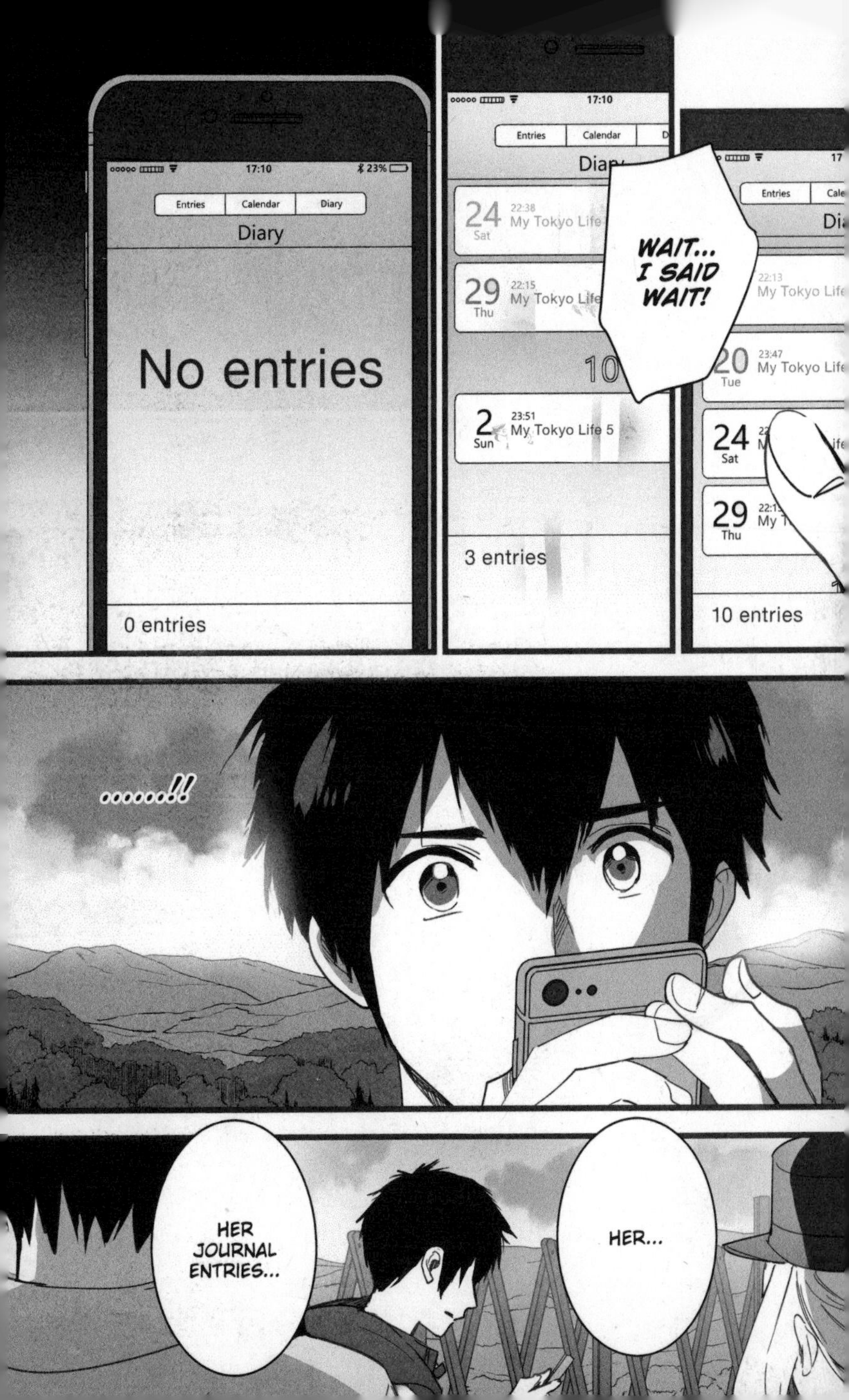

Entries
22:13 My Tokyo Life
20 23:47 My Tokyo Life Tue
24 Sat
29 Thu
10 entries
WAIT... I SAID WAIT!
17:10
Entries Calendar
24 22:38 My Tokyo Life Sat
29 22:15 My Tokyo Life Thu
10
2 23:51 My Tokyo Life 5 Sun
3 entries
17:10 23%
Entries Calendar Diary
Diary
No entries
0 entries
......!!
HER...
HER JOURNAL ENTRIES...

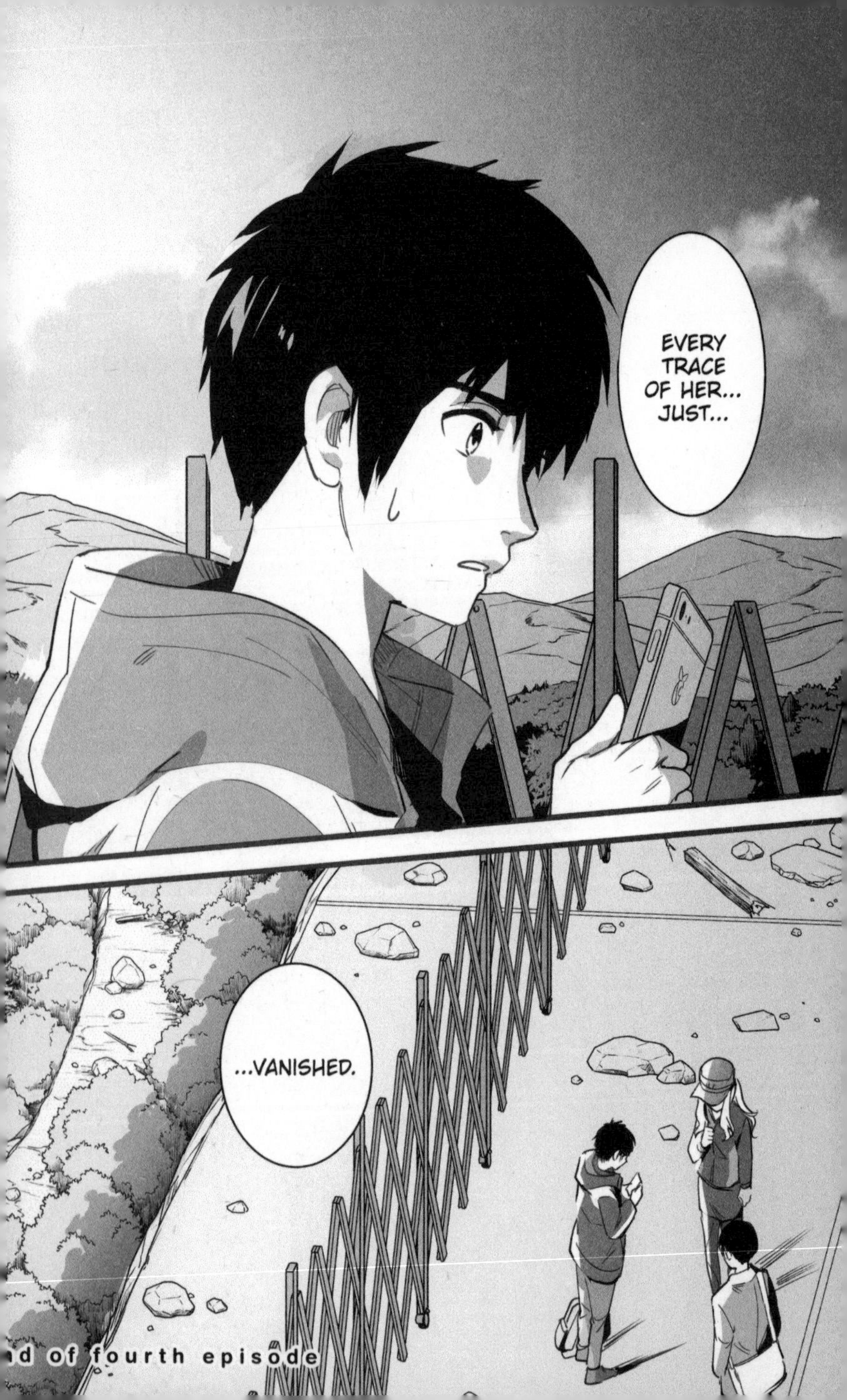
EVERY TRACE OF HER... JUST...
...VANISHED.
nd of fourth episode

your name.

your name.

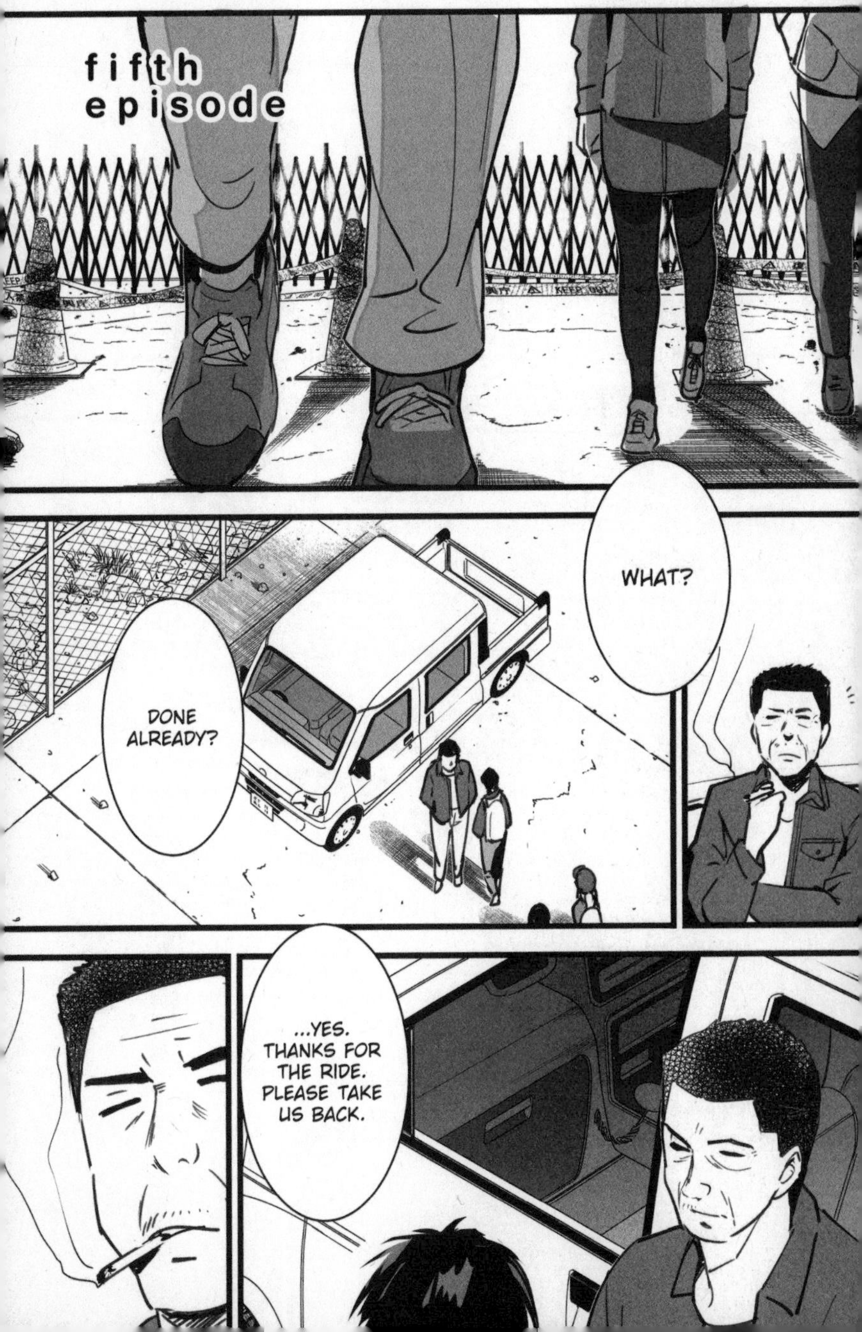
fifth episode
WHAT?
DONE ALREADY?
...YES. THANKS FOR THE RIDE. PLEASE TAKE US BACK.

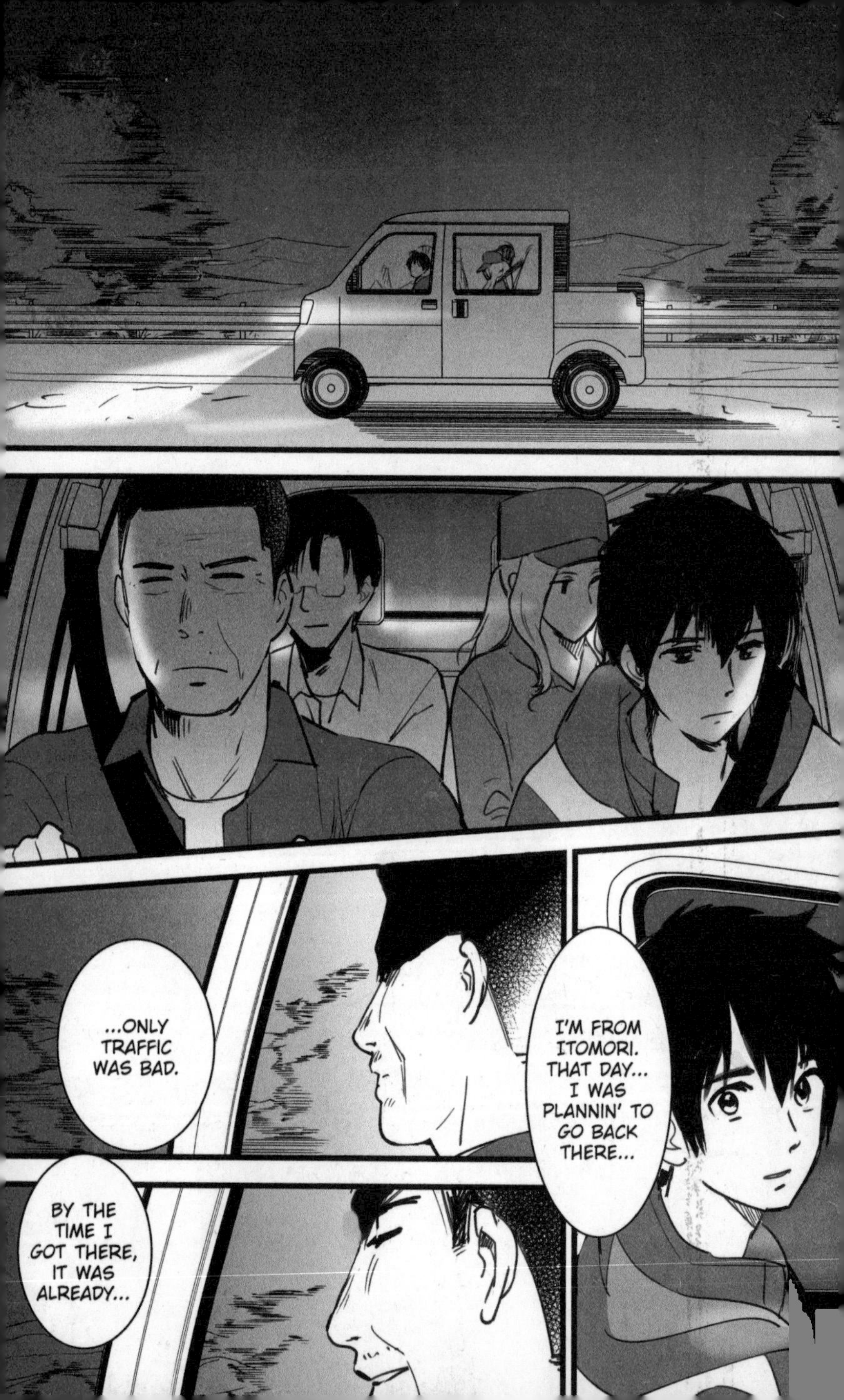
I'M FROM ITOMORI. THAT DAY... I WAS PLANNIN' TO GO BACK THERE...
...ONLY TRAFFIC WAS BAD.
BY THE TIME I GOT THERE, IT WAS ALREADY...

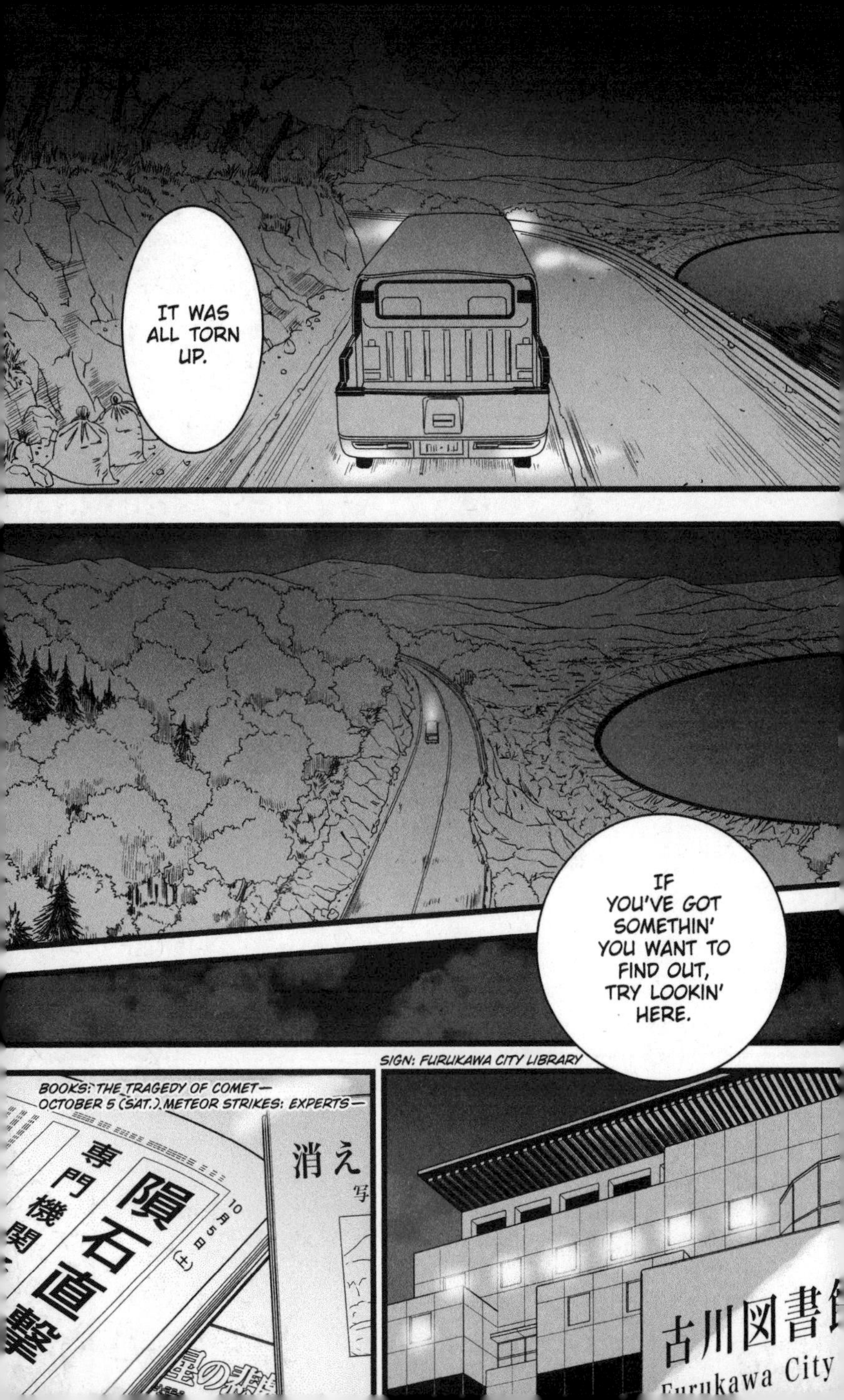
IT WAS ALL TORN UP.
IF YOU'VE GOT SOMETHIN' YOU WANT TO FIND OUT, TRY LOOKIN' HERE.
SIGN: FURUKAWA CITY LIBRARY
古川図書
Furukawa City
BOOKS: THE TRAGEDY OF COMET—
OCTOBER 5 (SAT.) METEOR STRIKES: EXPERTS—
隕石直撃
専門機関
10月5日(土)
消え

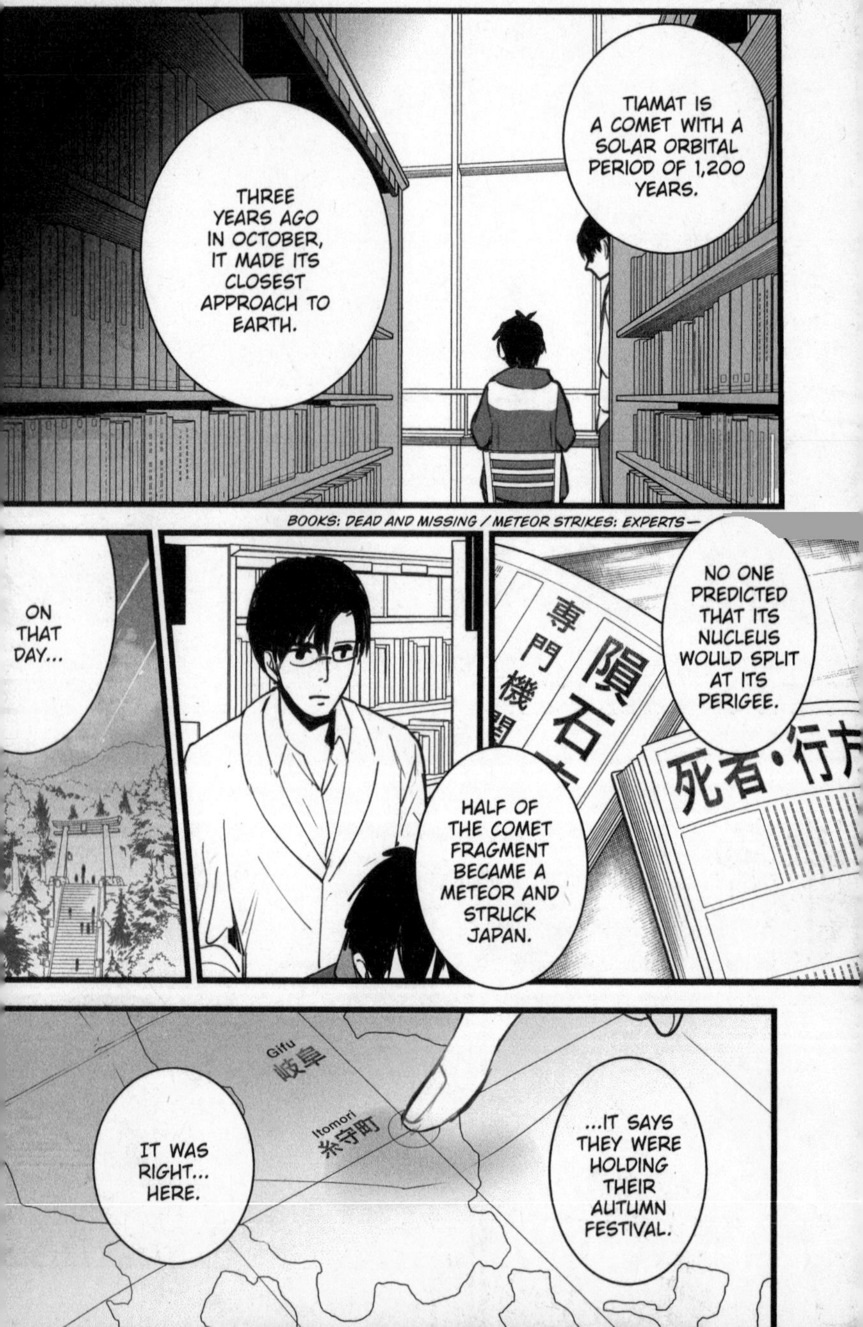

TIAMAT IS A COMET WITH A SOLAR ORBITAL PERIOD OF 1,200 YEARS.
THREE YEARS AGO IN OCTOBER, IT MADE ITS CLOSEST APPROACH TO EARTH.
BOOKS: DEAD AND MISSING / METEOR STRIKES: EXPERTS—
NO ONE PREDICTED THAT ITS NUCLEUS WOULD SPLIT AT ITS PERIGEE.
HALF OF THE COMET FRAGMENT BECAME A METEOR AND STRUCK JAPAN.
ON THAT DAY...
...IT SAYS THEY WERE HOLDING THEIR AUTUMN FESTIVAL.
Gifu
岐阜
Itomori
糸守町
IT WAS RIGHT... HERE.

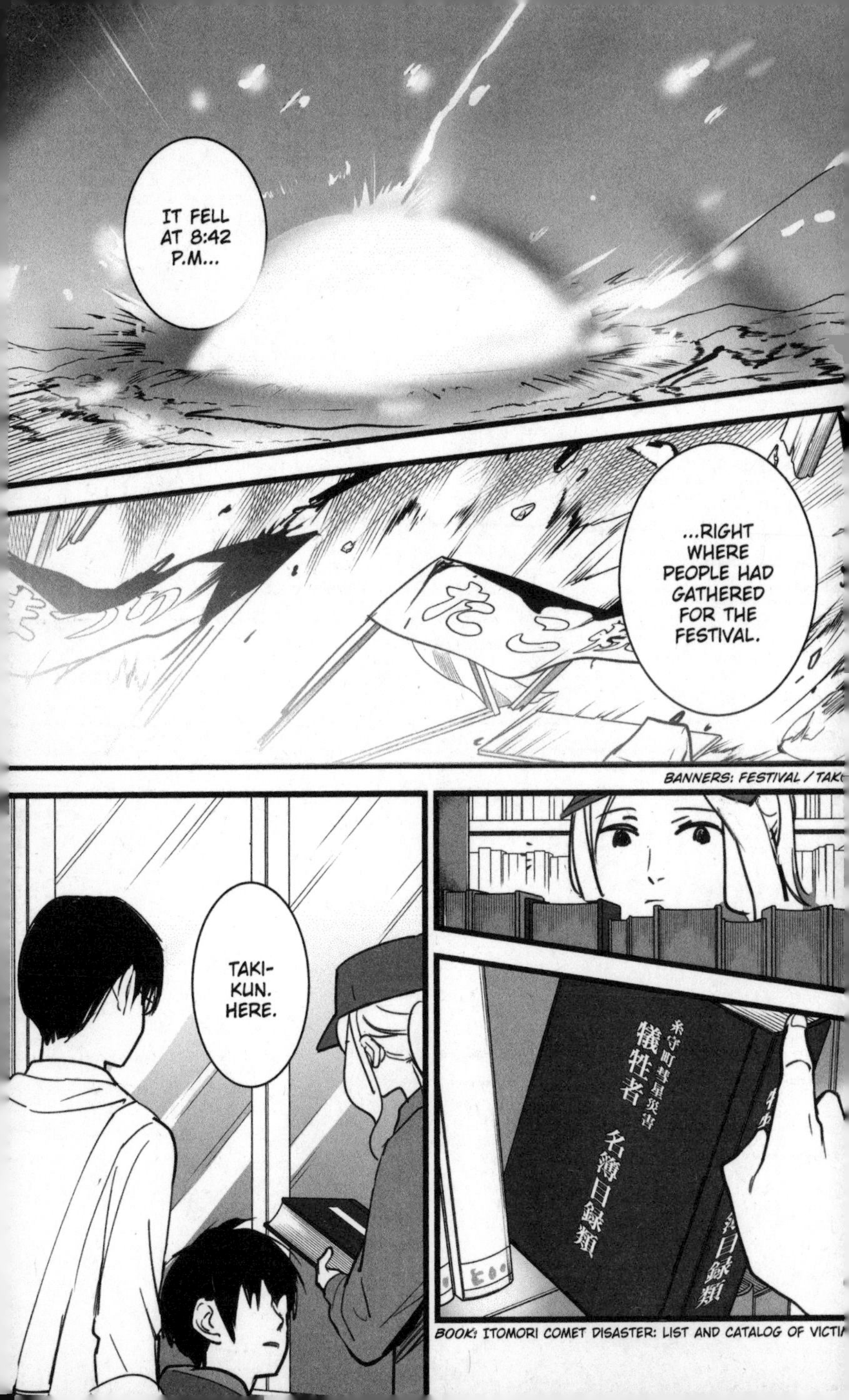
IT FELL AT 8:42 P.M...
...RIGHT WHERE PEOPLE HAD GATHERED FOR THE FESTIVAL.
BANNERS: FESTIVAL / TAK
糸守町彗星災害
犠牲者
名簿目録類
BOOK: ITOMORI COMET DISASTER: LIST AND CATALOG OF VICTI
TAKI-KUN. HERE.

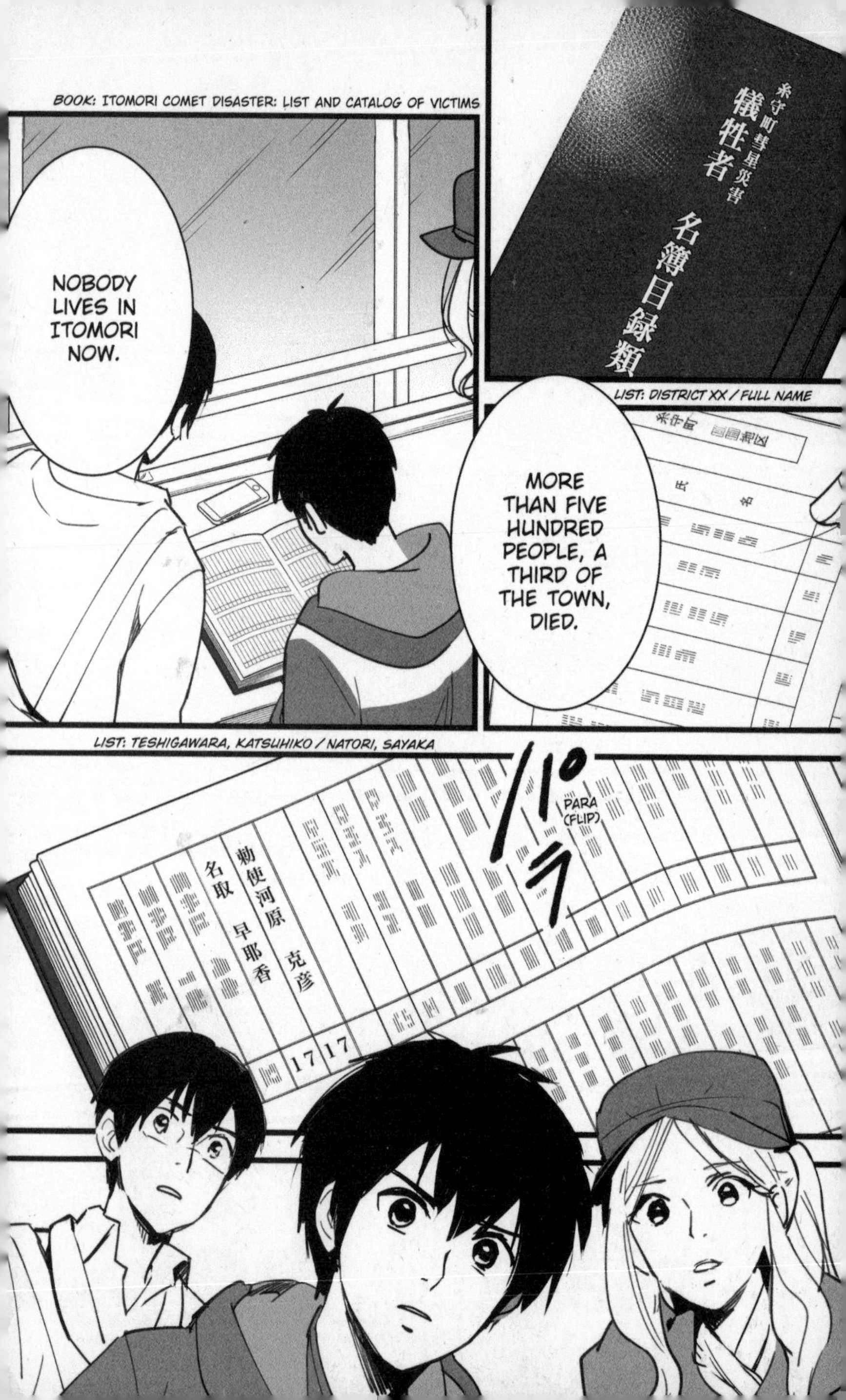
BOOK: ITOMORI COMET DISASTER: LIST AND CATALOG OF VICTIMS
糸守町彗星災害
犠牲者
名簿目録類
LIST: DISTRICT XX / FULL NAME
MORE THAN FIVE HUNDRED PEOPLE, A THIRD OF THE TOWN, DIED.
NOBODY LIVES IN ITOMORI NOW.
LIST: TESHIGAWARA, KATSUHIKO / NATORI, SAYAKA
パラ
PARA (FLIP)
勅使河原 克彦
名取 早耶香
17
17

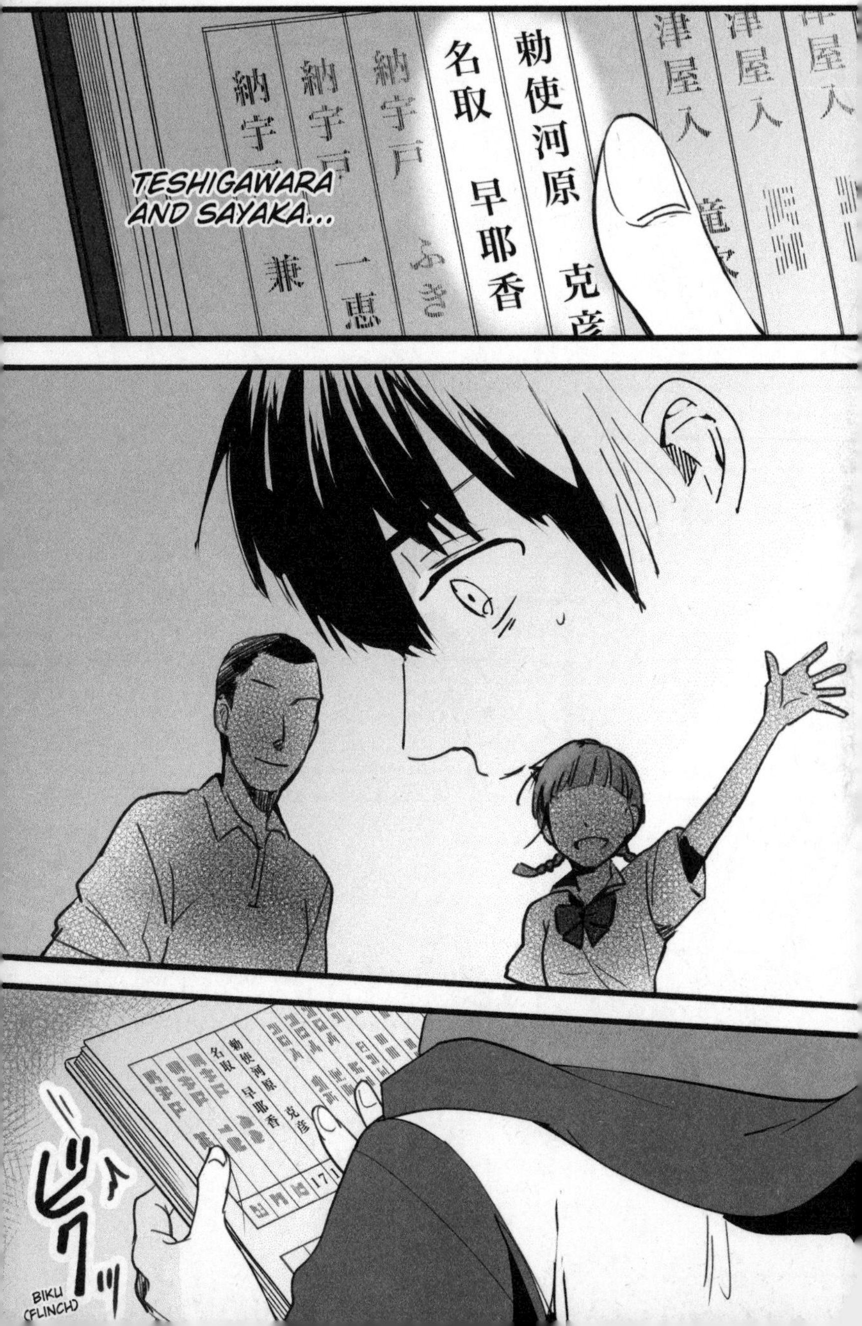
勅使河原　克彦
名取　早耶香
TESHIGAWARA AND SAYAKA...
ビクッ
BIKU (FLINCH)

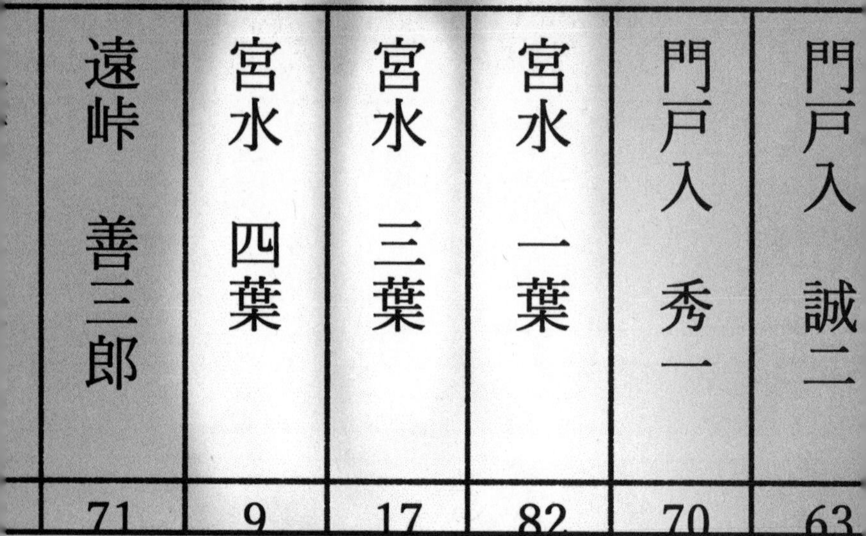
門戸入 誠二 63
門戸入 秀一 70
宮水 一葉 82
宮水 三葉 17
宮水 四葉 9
遠峠 善三郎 71
LIST (L-R): MIYAMIZU, YOTSUHA (9) / MIYAMIZU, MITSUHA (17) / MIYAMIZU, HITOHA (82)

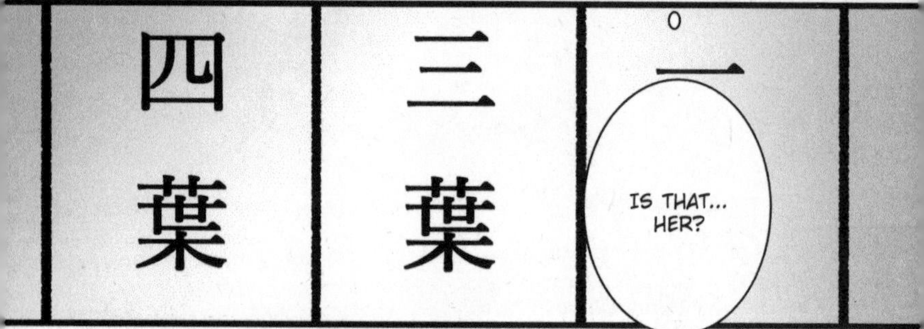
一
三葉
四葉
IS THAT... HER?
MITSUHA

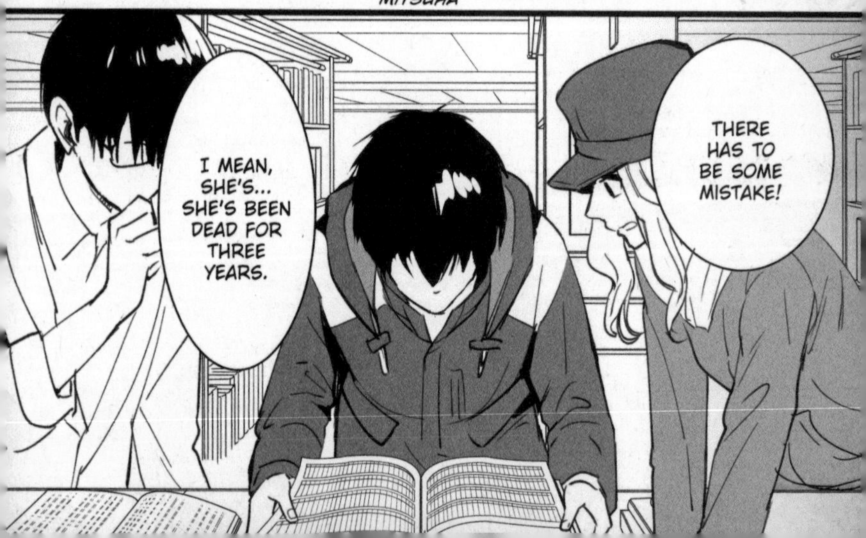
THERE HAS TO BE SOME MISTAKE!
I MEAN, SHE'S... SHE'S BEEN DEAD FOR THREE YEARS.

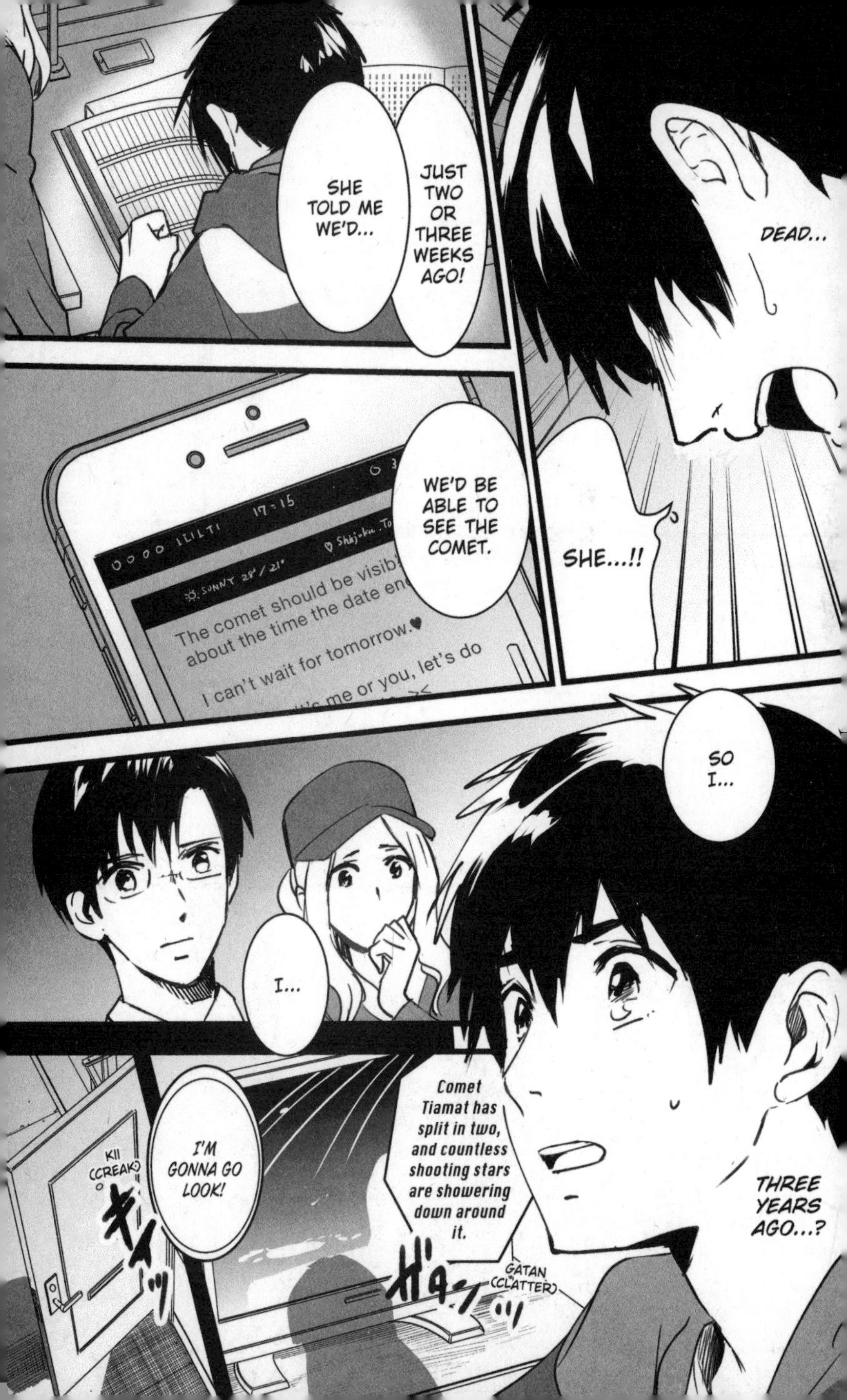
DEAD...
SHE...!!
JUST TWO OR THREE WEEKS AGO!
SHE TOLD ME WE'D...
WE'D BE ABLE TO SEE THE COMET.
17:15
SUNNY 28°/21°
The comet should be visib
about the time the date en
I can't wait for tomorrow.♥
SO I...
THREE YEARS AGO...?
I...
Comet Tiamat has split in two, and countless shooting stars are showering down around it.
GATAN (CLATTER)
I'M GONNA GO LOOK!
KII (CREAK)

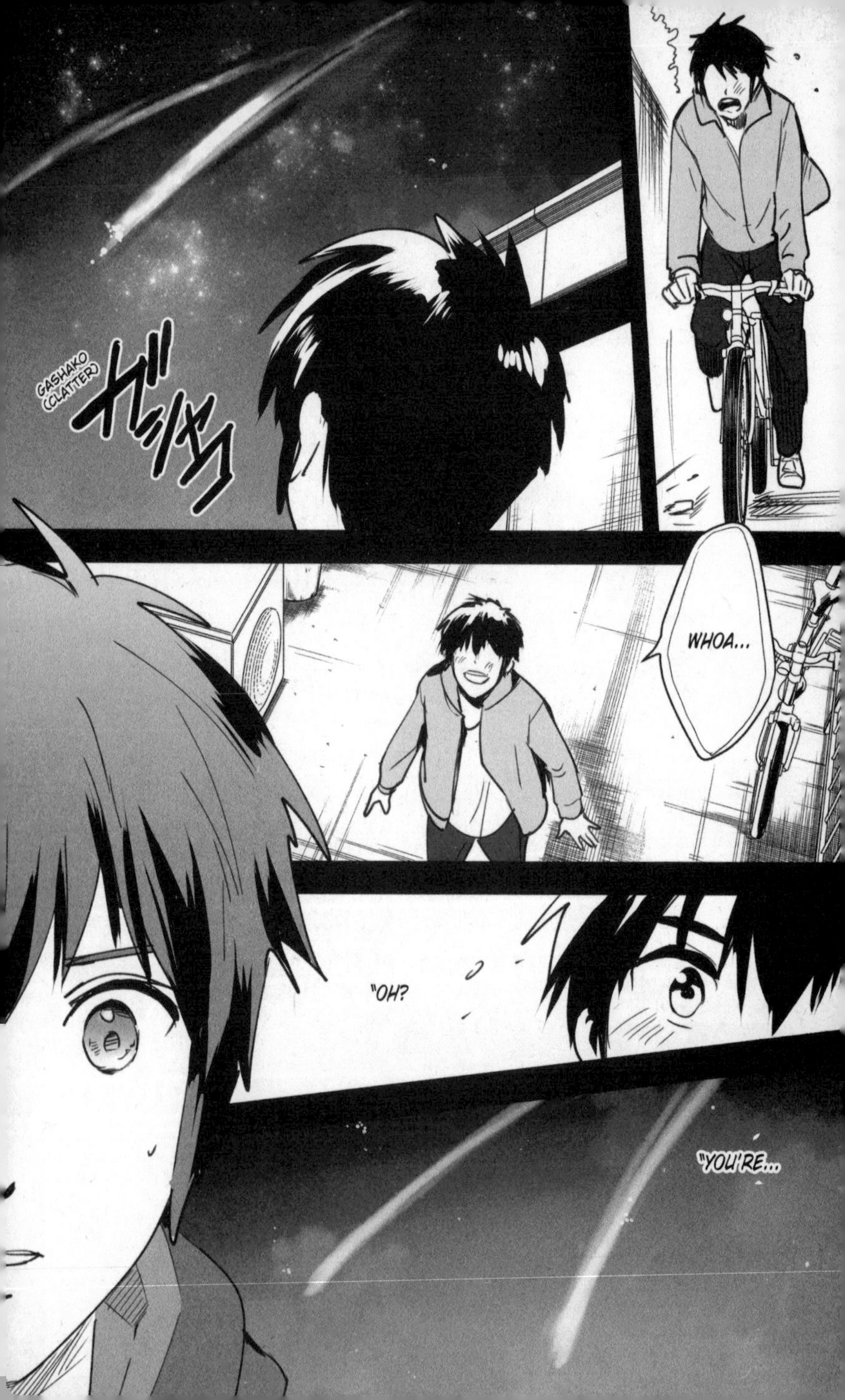
GASHAKO (CLATTER)
WHOA...
"OH?
"YOU'RE...

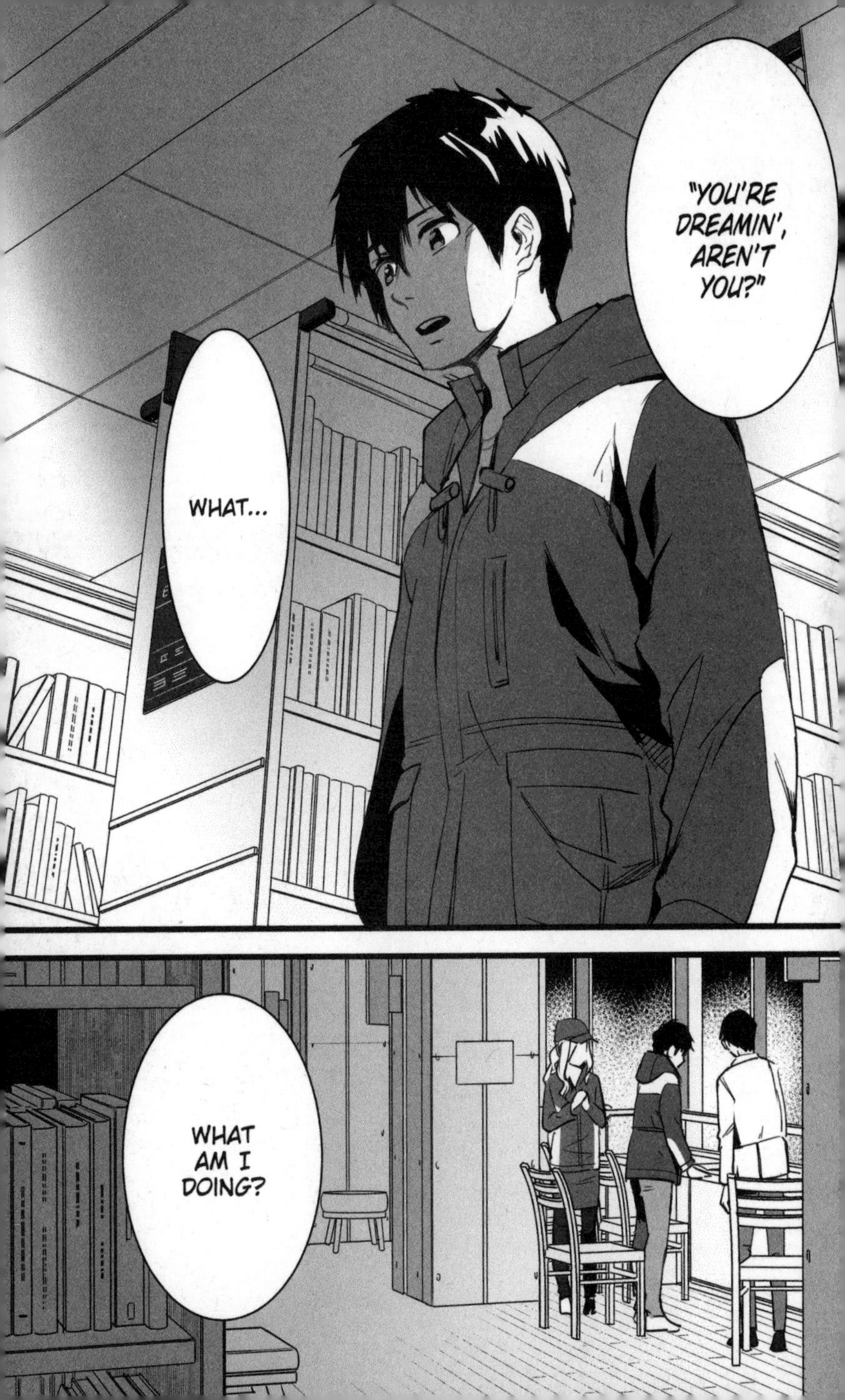
"YOU'RE DREAMIN', AREN'T YOU?"
WHAT...
WHAT AM I DOING?

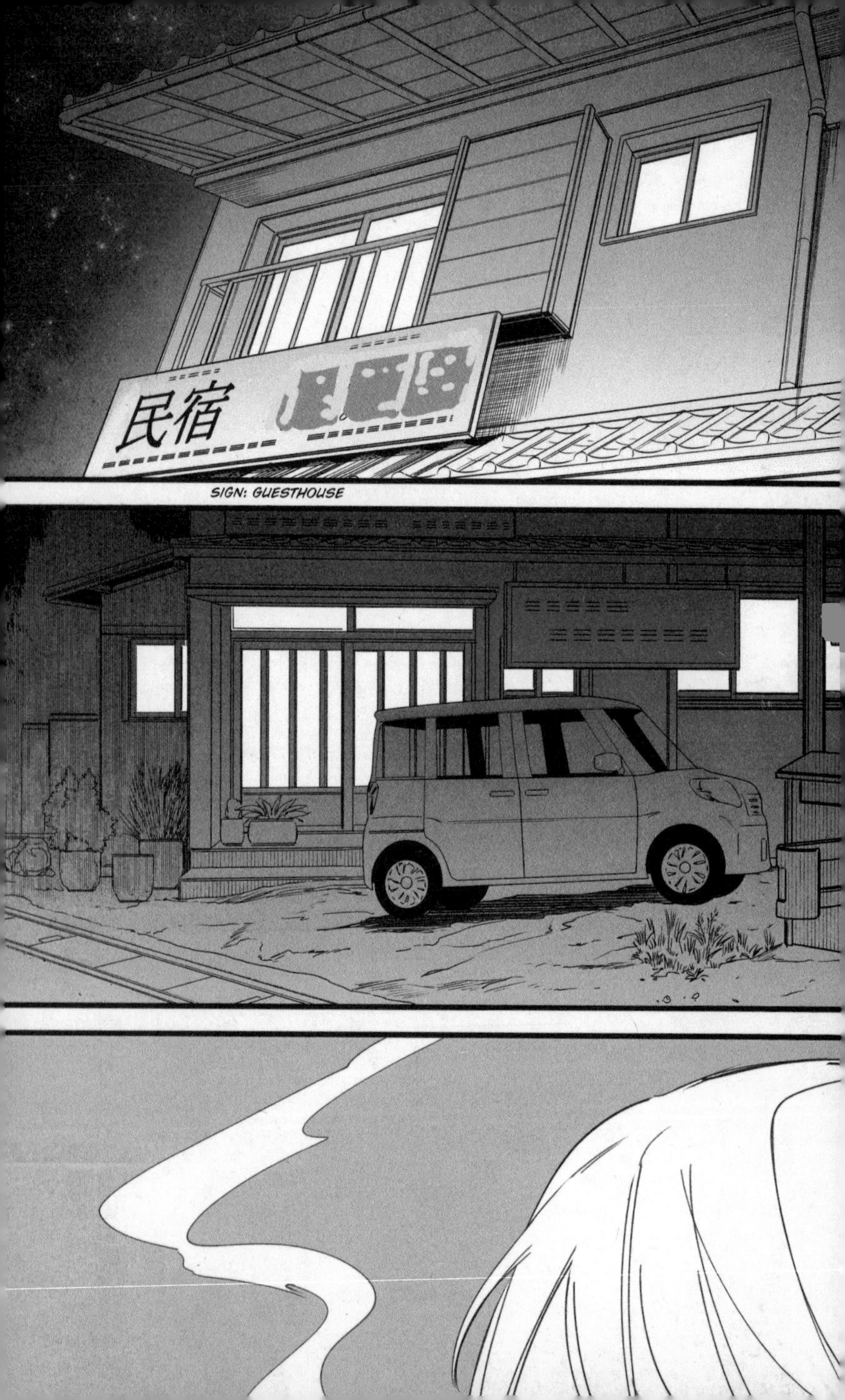
民宿
SIGN: GUESTHOUSE

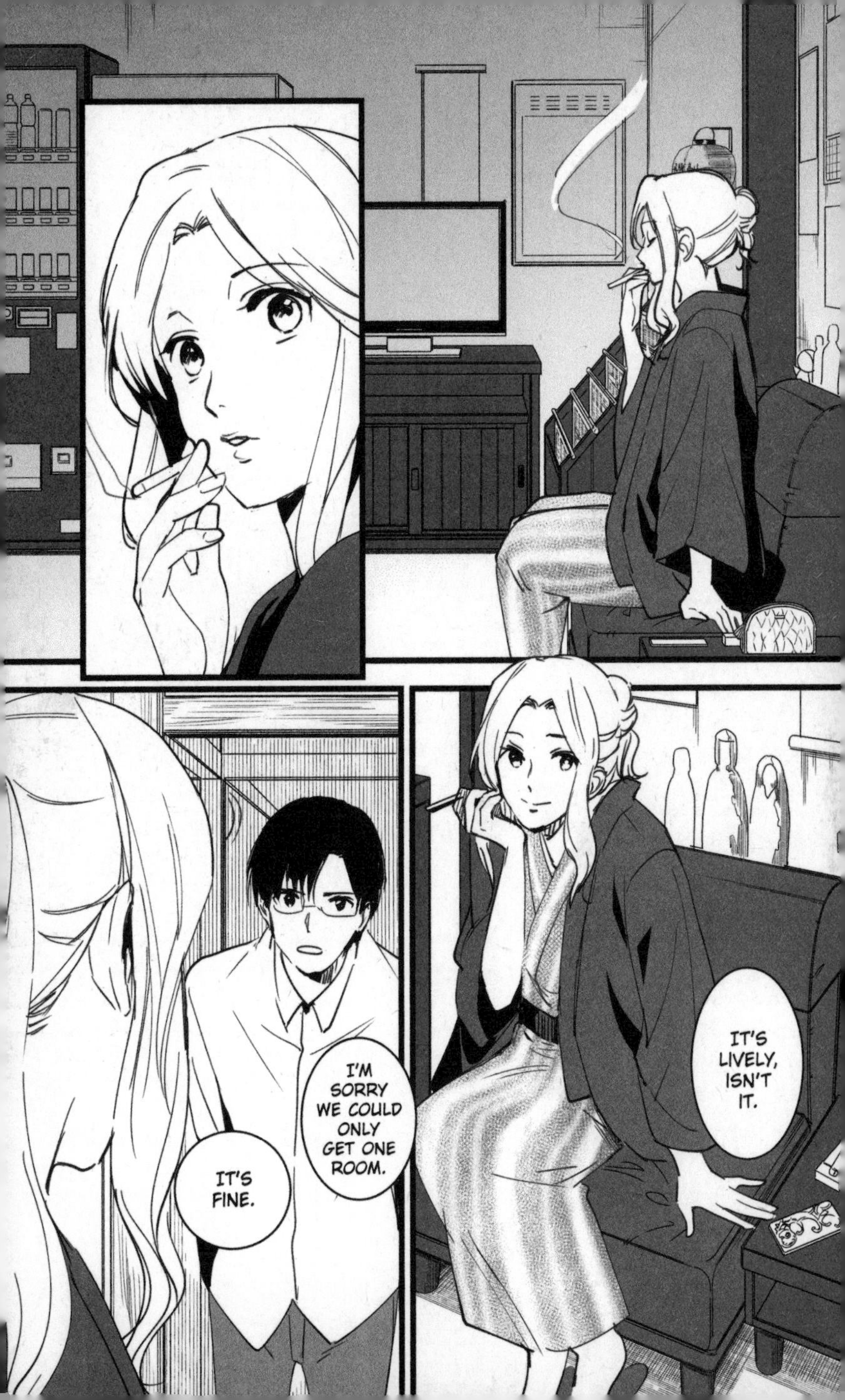
IT'S LIVELY, ISN'T IT.
I'M SORRY WE COULD ONLY GET ONE ROOM.
IT'S FINE.

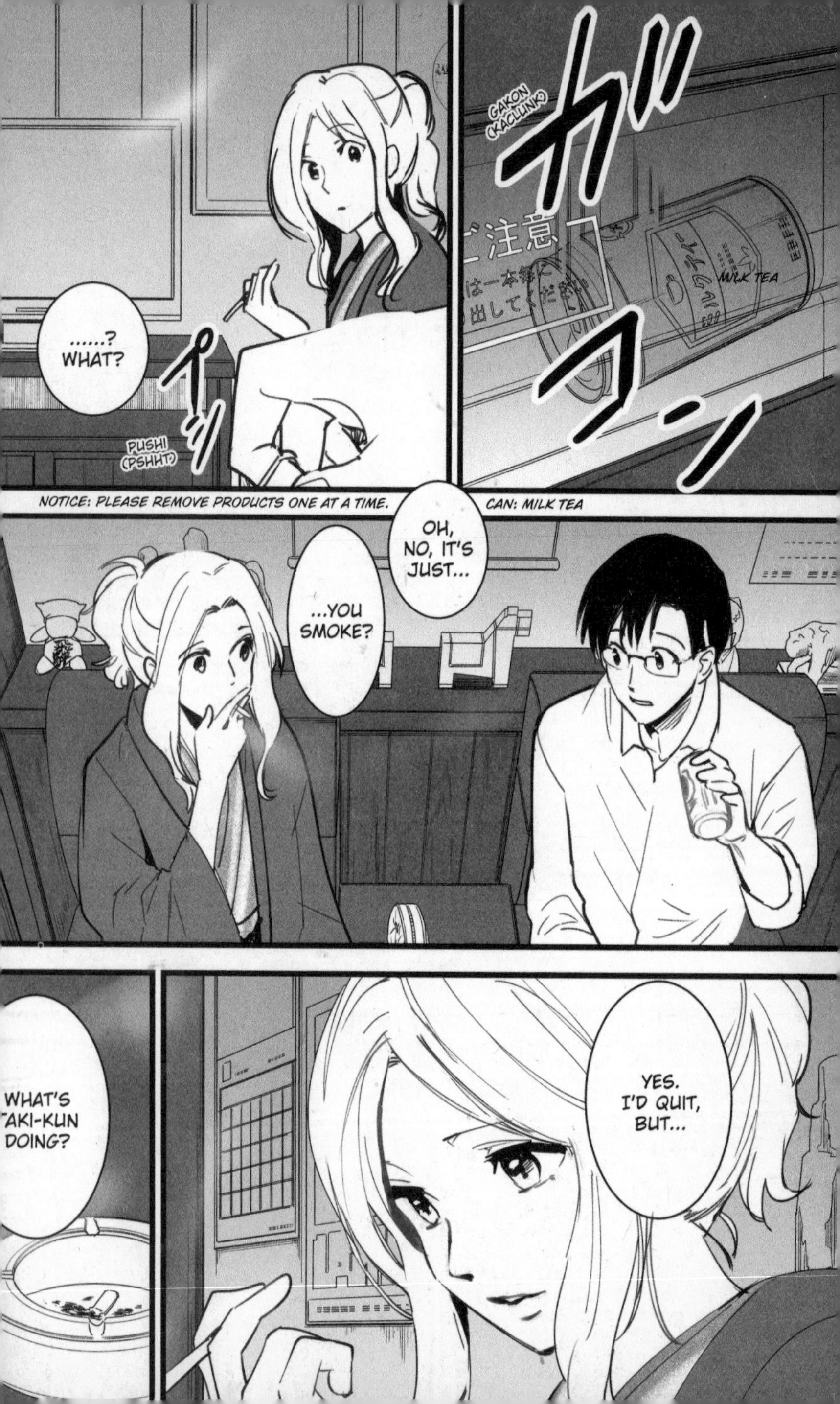
GAKON (KACLUNK)
ご注意
MILK TEA
PUSHI (PSHHT)
......? WHAT?
NOTICE: PLEASE REMOVE PRODUCTS ONE AT A TIME.
CAN: MILK TEA
OH, NO, IT'S JUST...
...YOU SMOKE?
YES. I'D QUIT, BUT...
WHAT'S TAKI-KUN DOING?

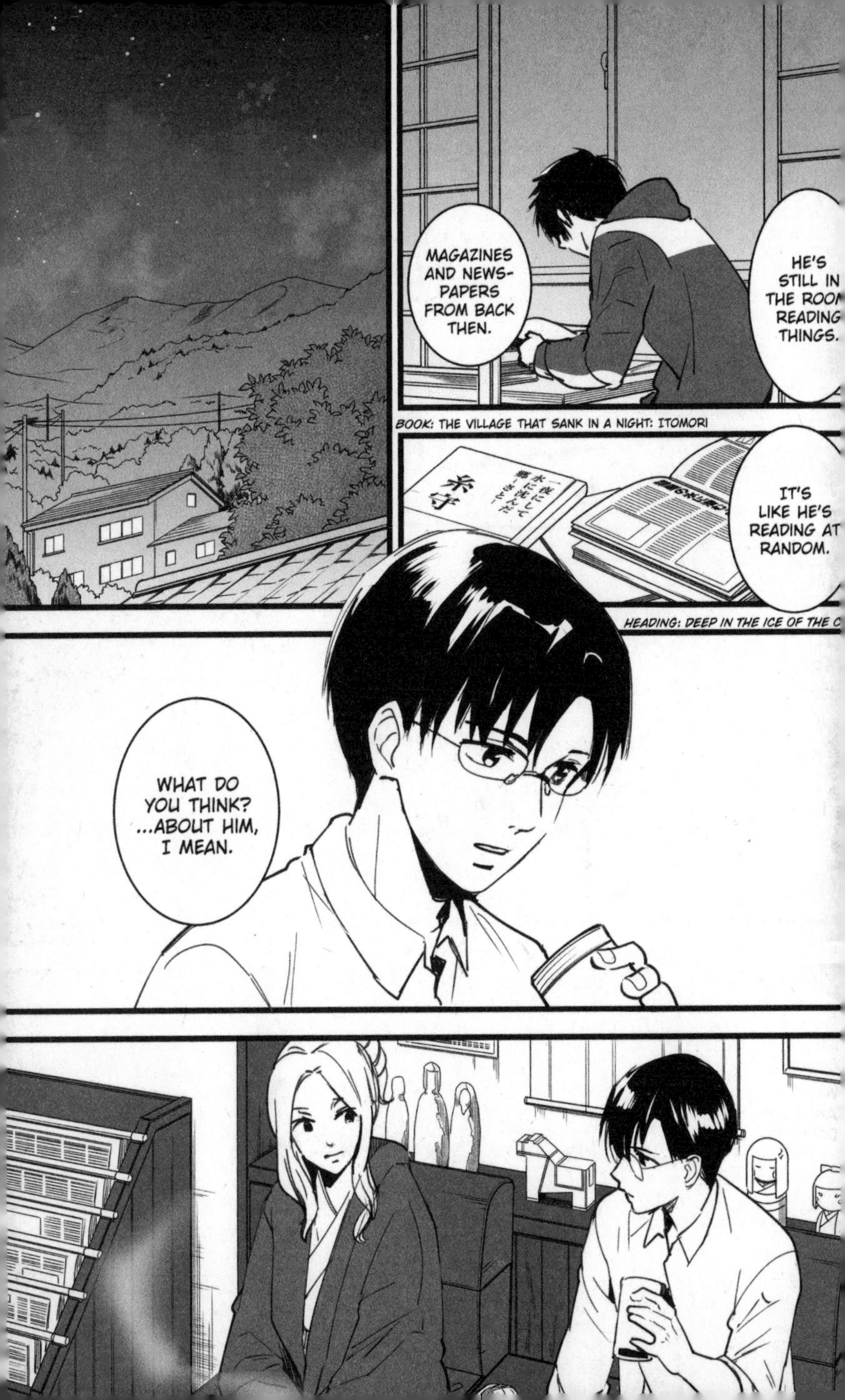
HE'S STILL IN THE ROOM READING THINGS.
MAGAZINES AND NEWS-PAPERS FROM BACK THEN.
BOOK: THE VILLAGE THAT SANK IN A NIGHT: ITOMORI
IT'S LIKE HE'S READING AT RANDOM.
HEADING: DEEP IN THE ICE OF THE C
WHAT DO YOU THINK? ...ABOUT HIM, I MEAN.

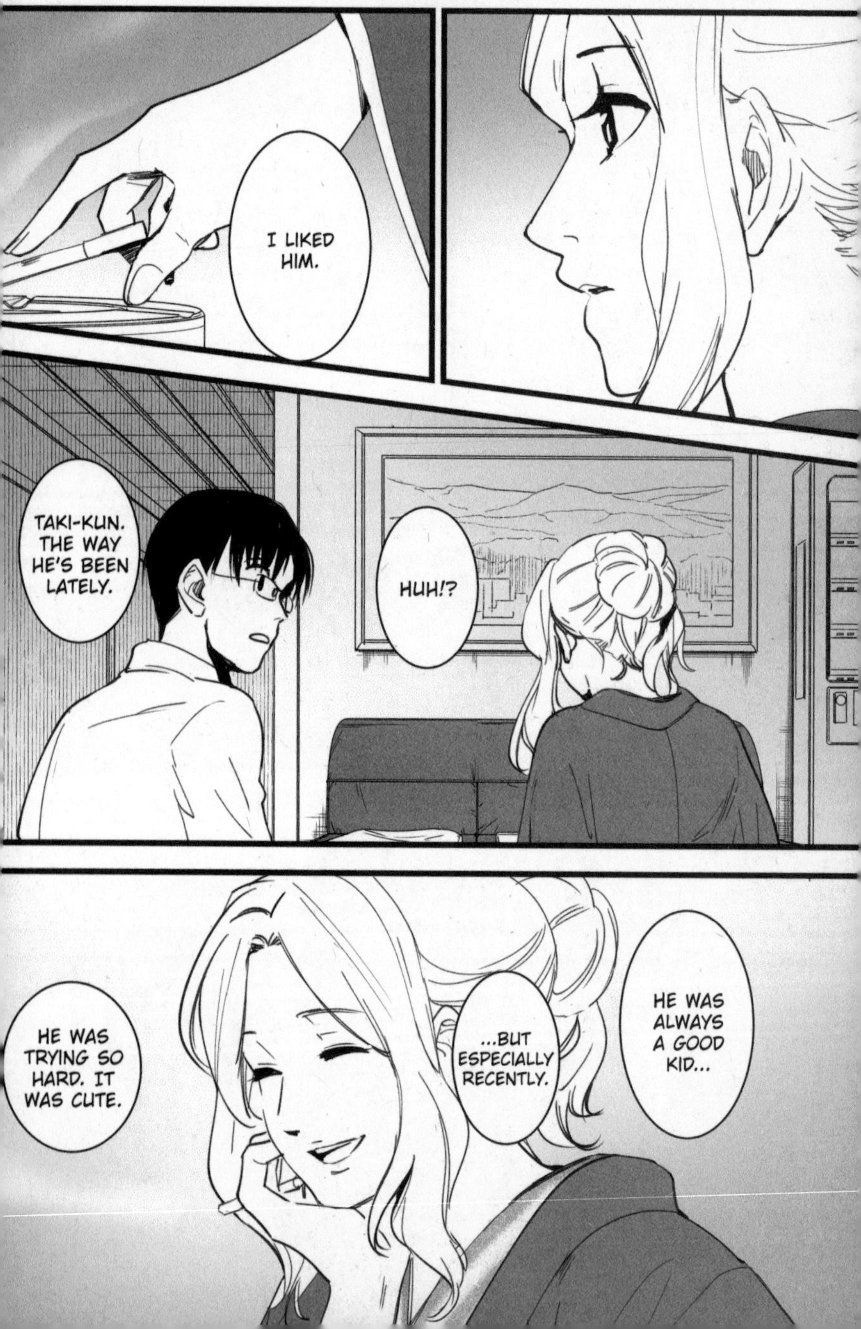
I LIKED HIM.
HUH!?
TAKI-KUN. THE WAY HE'S BEEN LATELY.
HE WAS ALWAYS A GOOD KID...
...BUT ESPECIALLY RECENTLY.
HE WAS TRYING SO HARD. IT WAS CUTE.

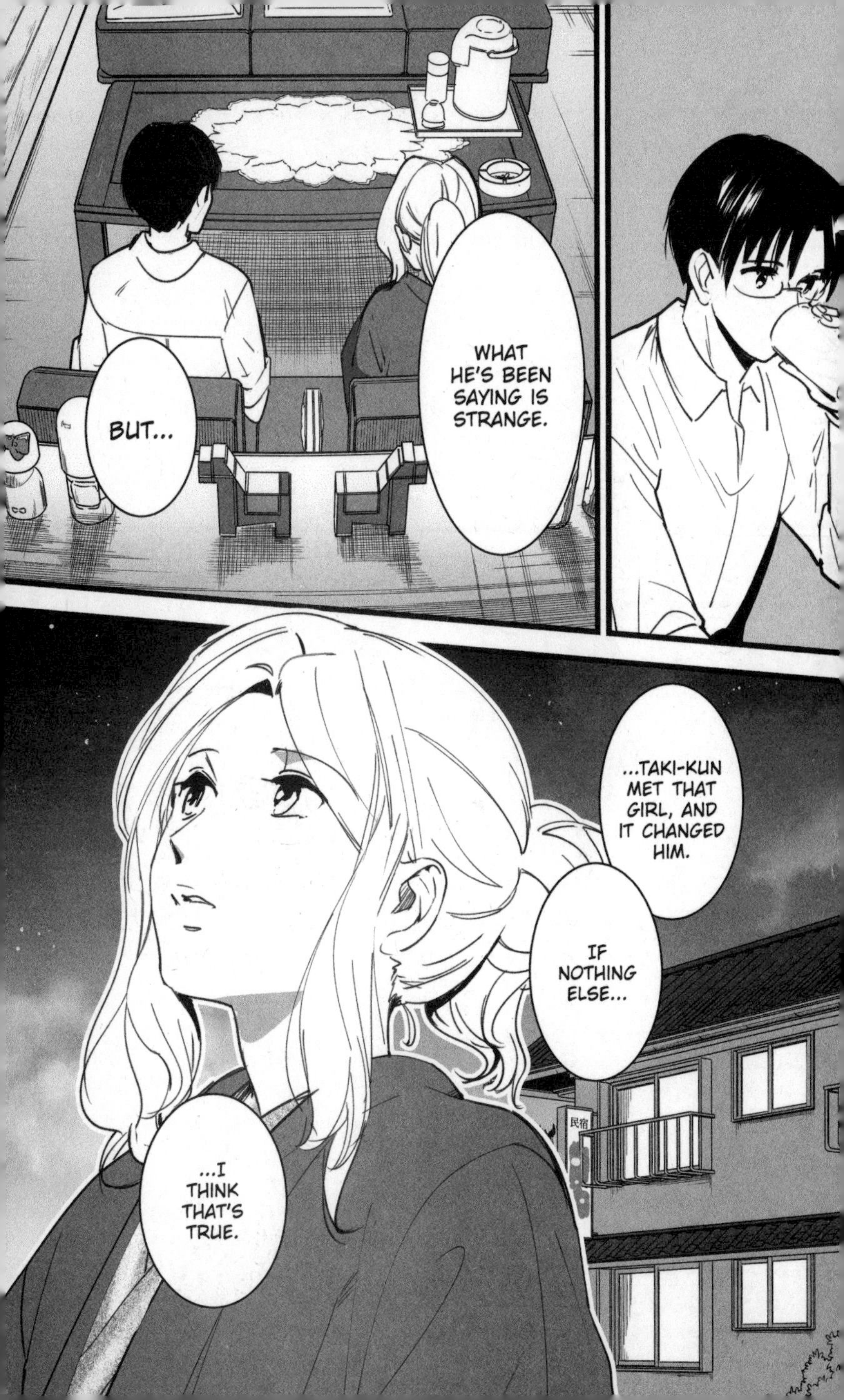
WHAT HE'S BEEN SAYING IS STRANGE.
BUT...
...TAKI-KUN MET THAT GIRL, AND IT CHANGED HIM.
IF NOTHING ELSE...
...I THINK THAT'S TRUE.
民宿

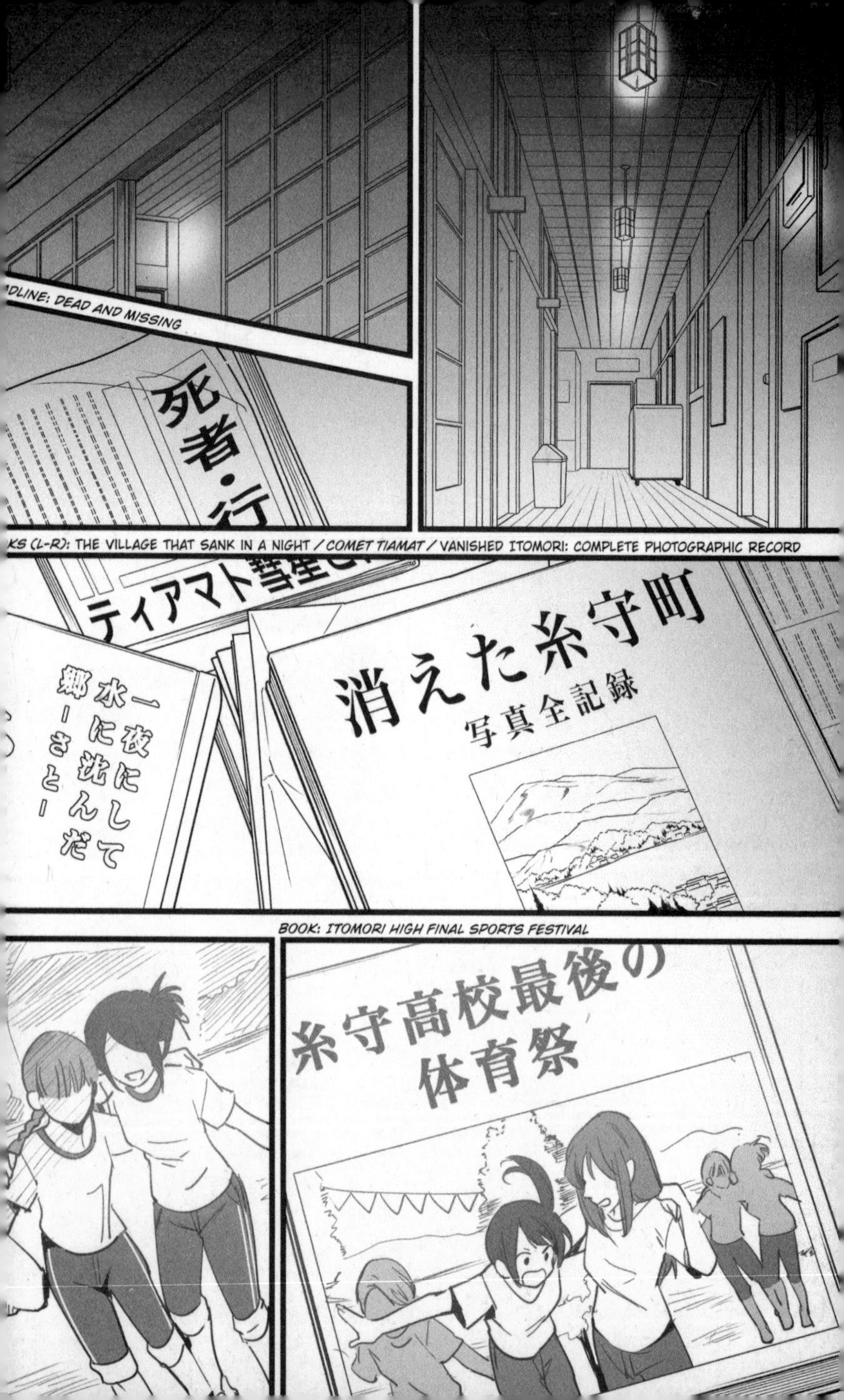
DLINE: DEAD AND MISSING
死者・行
KS (L-R): THE VILLAGE THAT SANK IN A NIGHT / COMET TIAMAT / VANISHED ITOMORI: COMPLETE PHOTOGRAPHIC RECORD
消えた糸守町
写真全記録
ティアマト彗星
一夜にして水に沈んだ郷ーさとー
BOOK: ITOMORI HIGH FINAL SPORTS FESTIVAL
糸守高校最後の体育祭

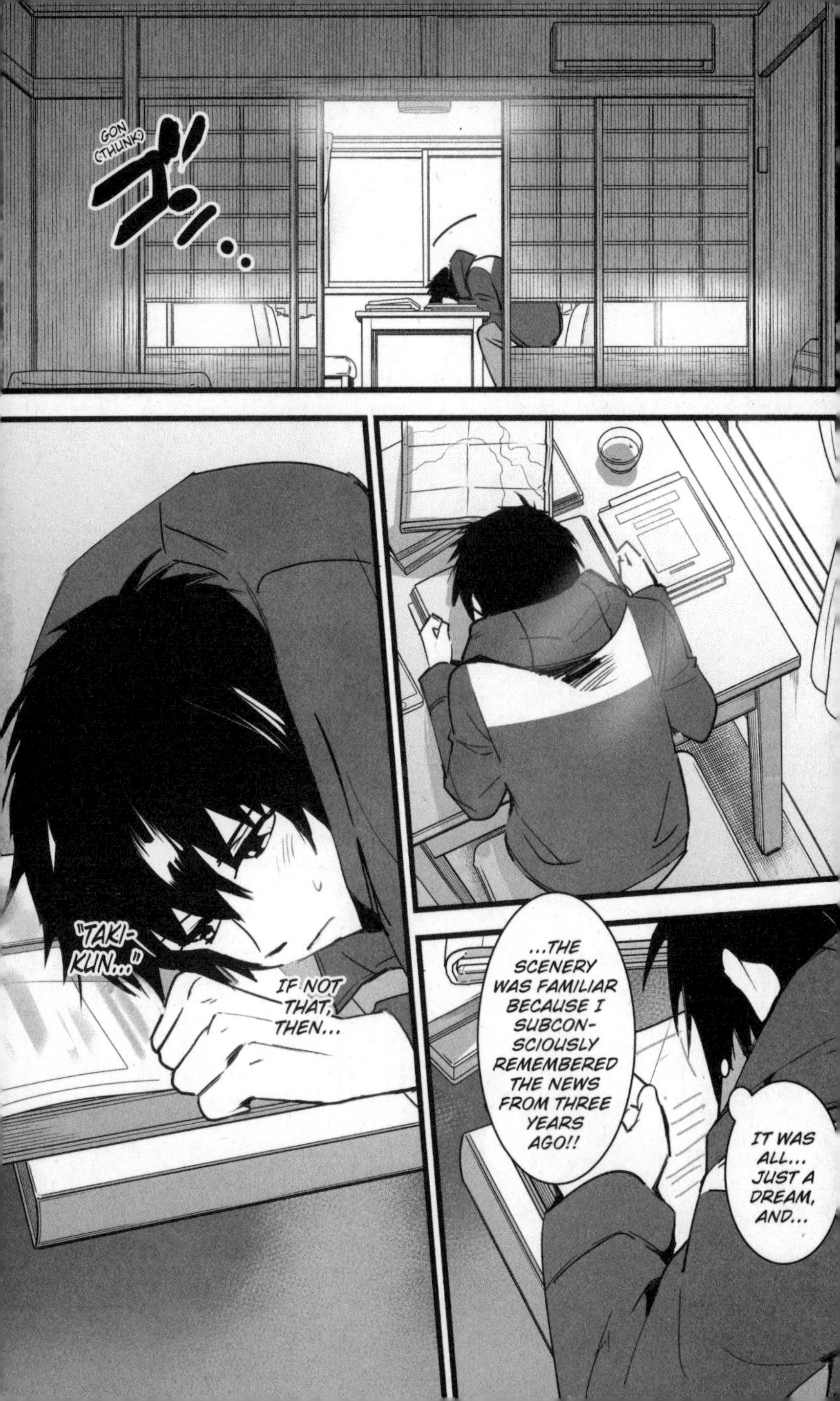
GON (THUNK)
IT WAS ALL... JUST A DREAM, AND...
...THE SCENERY WAS FAMILIAR BECAUSE I SUBCONSCIOUSLY REMEMBERED THE NEWS FROM THREE YEARS AGO!!
"TAKI-KUN..."
IF NOT THAT, THEN...

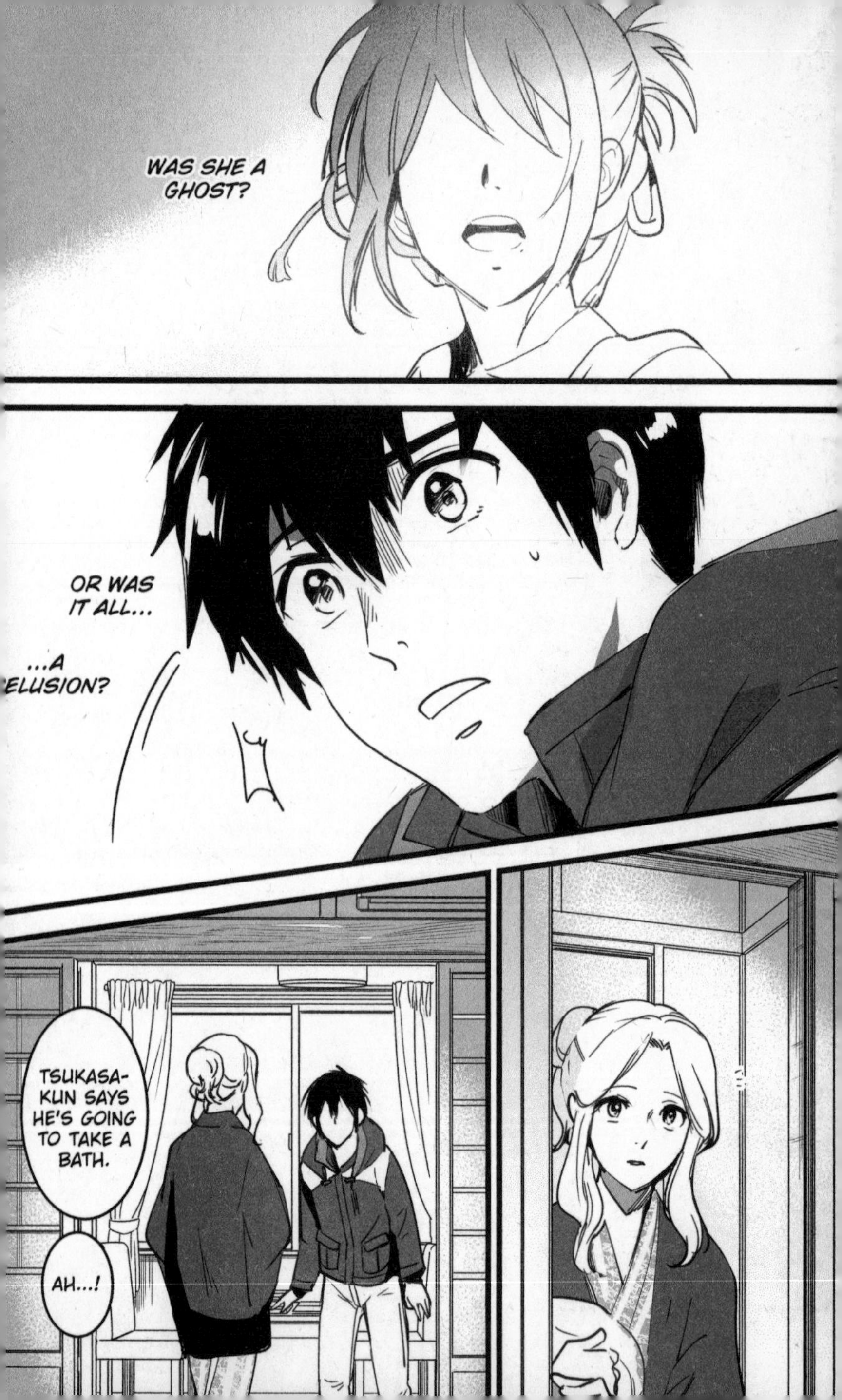
WAS SHE A GHOST?
OR WAS IT ALL...
...A DELUSION?
TSUKASA-KUN SAYS HE'S GOING TO TAKE A BATH.
AH...!

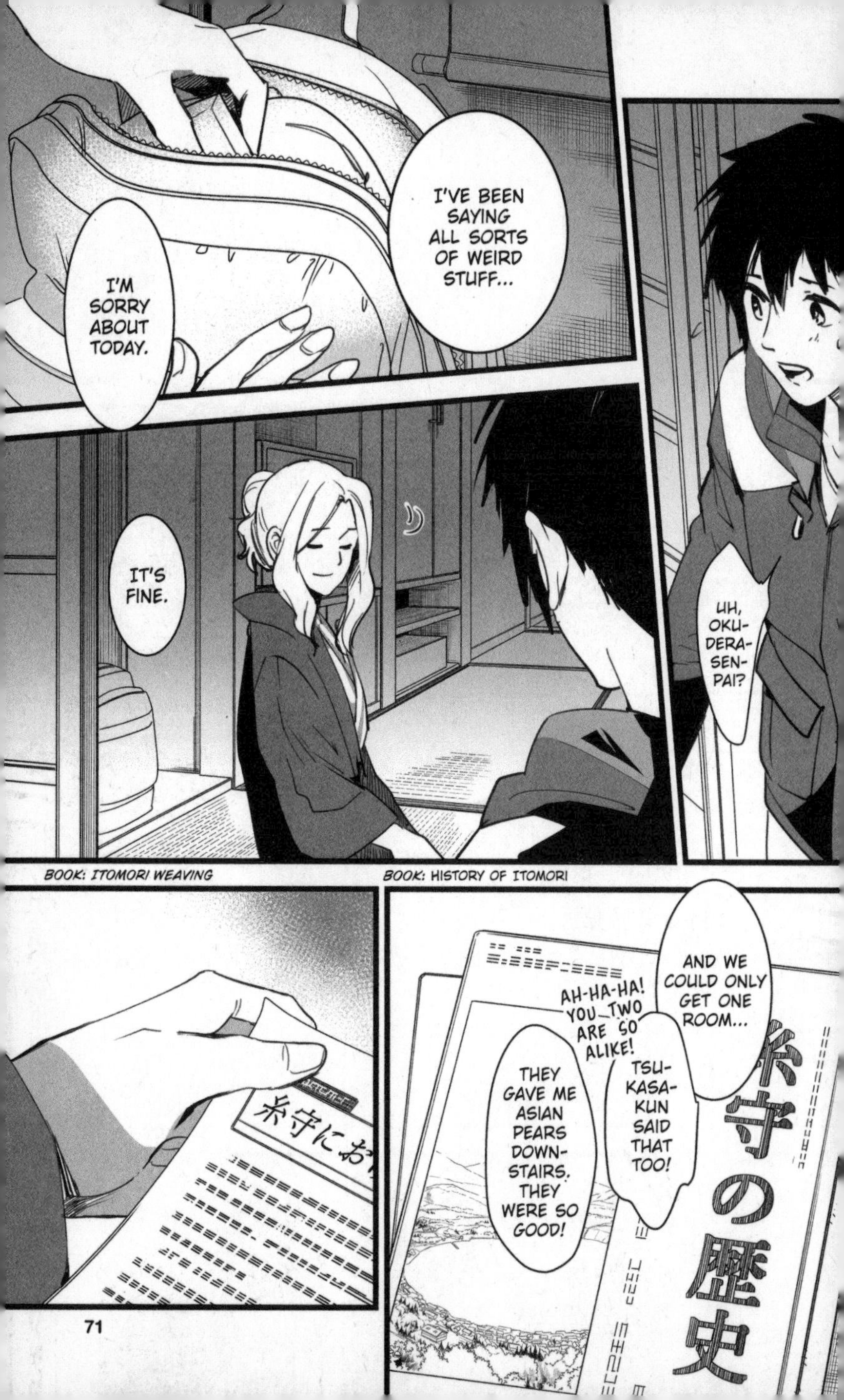
UH, OKU-DERA-SEN-PAI?
I'VE BEEN SAYING ALL SORTS OF WEIRD STUFF...
I'M SORRY ABOUT TODAY.
IT'S FINE.
BOOK: HISTORY OF ITOMORI
BOOK: ITOMORI WEAVING
糸守の歴史
AND WE COULD ONLY GET ONE ROOM...
TSU-KASA-KUN SAID THAT TOO!
AH-HA-HA! YOU TWO ARE SO ALIKE!
THEY GAVE ME ASIAN PEARS DOWN-STAIRS. THEY WERE SO GOOD!

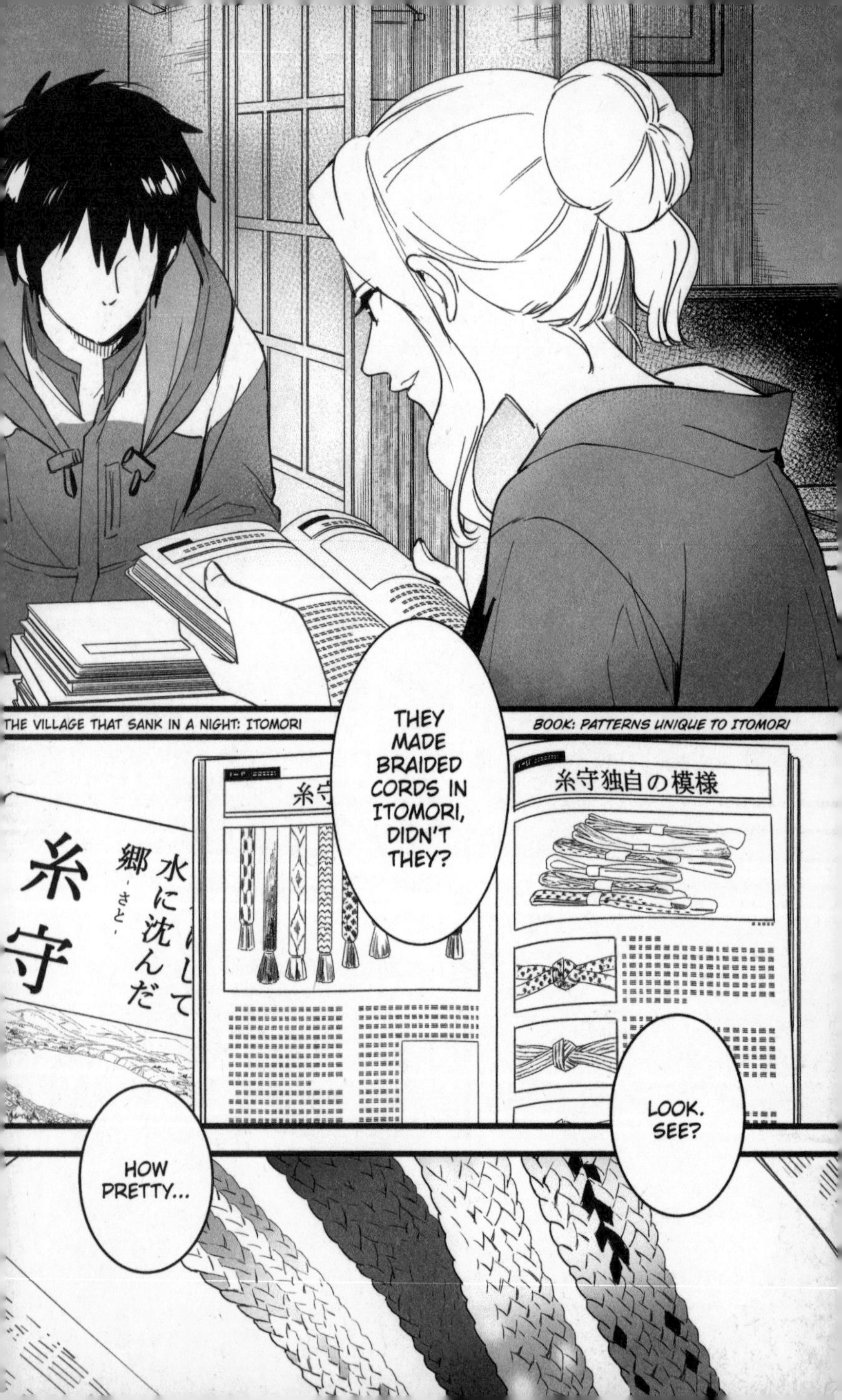

THEY MADE BRAIDED CORDS IN ITOMORI, DIDN'T THEY?
BOOK: PATTERNS UNIQUE TO ITOMORI
糸守独自の模様
THE VILLAGE THAT SANK IN A NIGHT: ITOMORI
糸守
水に沈んだ
郷
さと
LOOK. SEE?
HOW PRETTY...

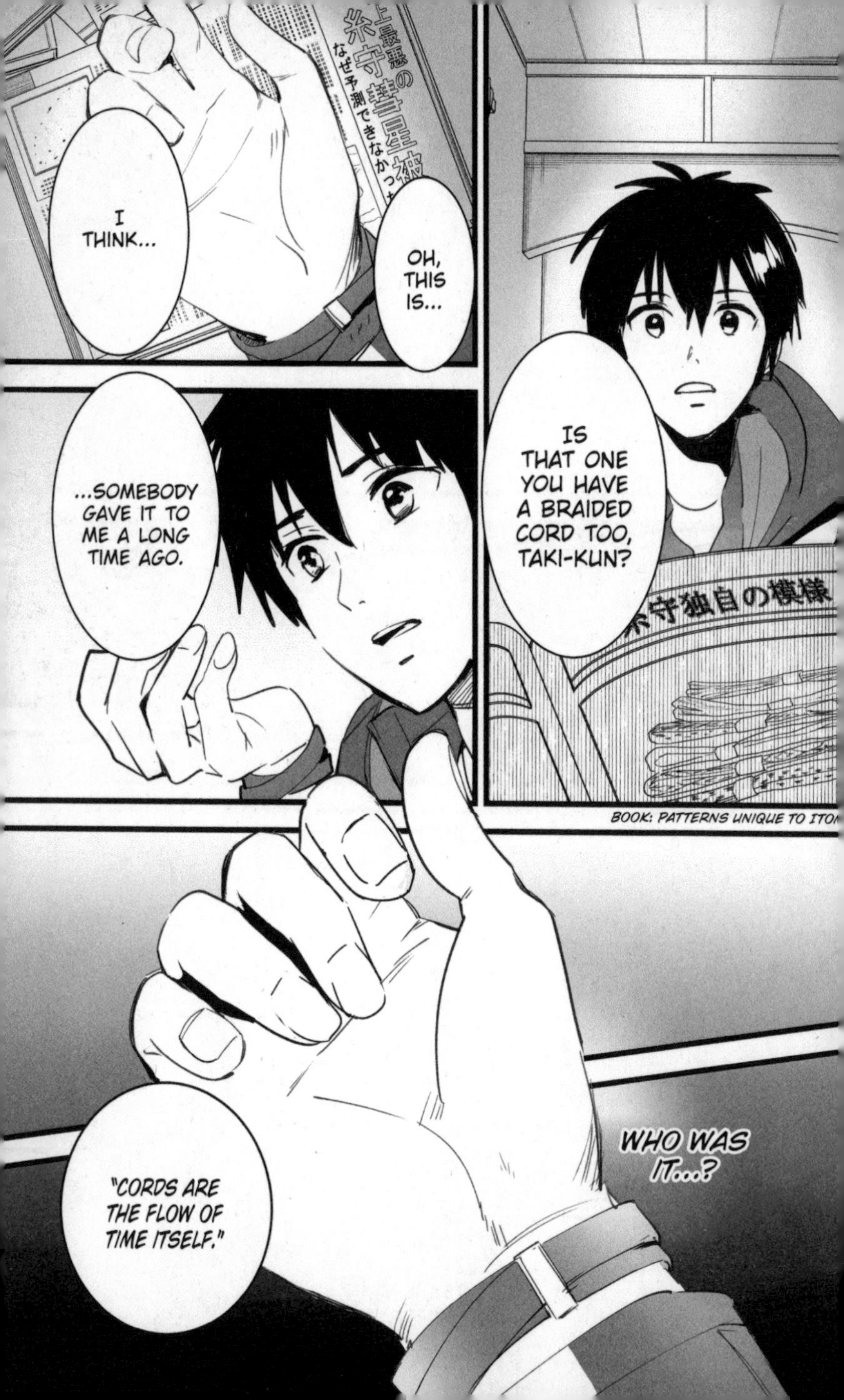

IS THAT ONE YOU HAVE A BRAIDED CORD TOO, TAKI-KUN?
BOOK: PATTERNS UNIQUE TO ITOM
OH, THIS IS...
I THINK...
...SOMEBODY GAVE IT TO ME A LONG TIME AGO.
WHO WAS IT...?
"CORDS ARE THE FLOW OF TIME ITSELF."

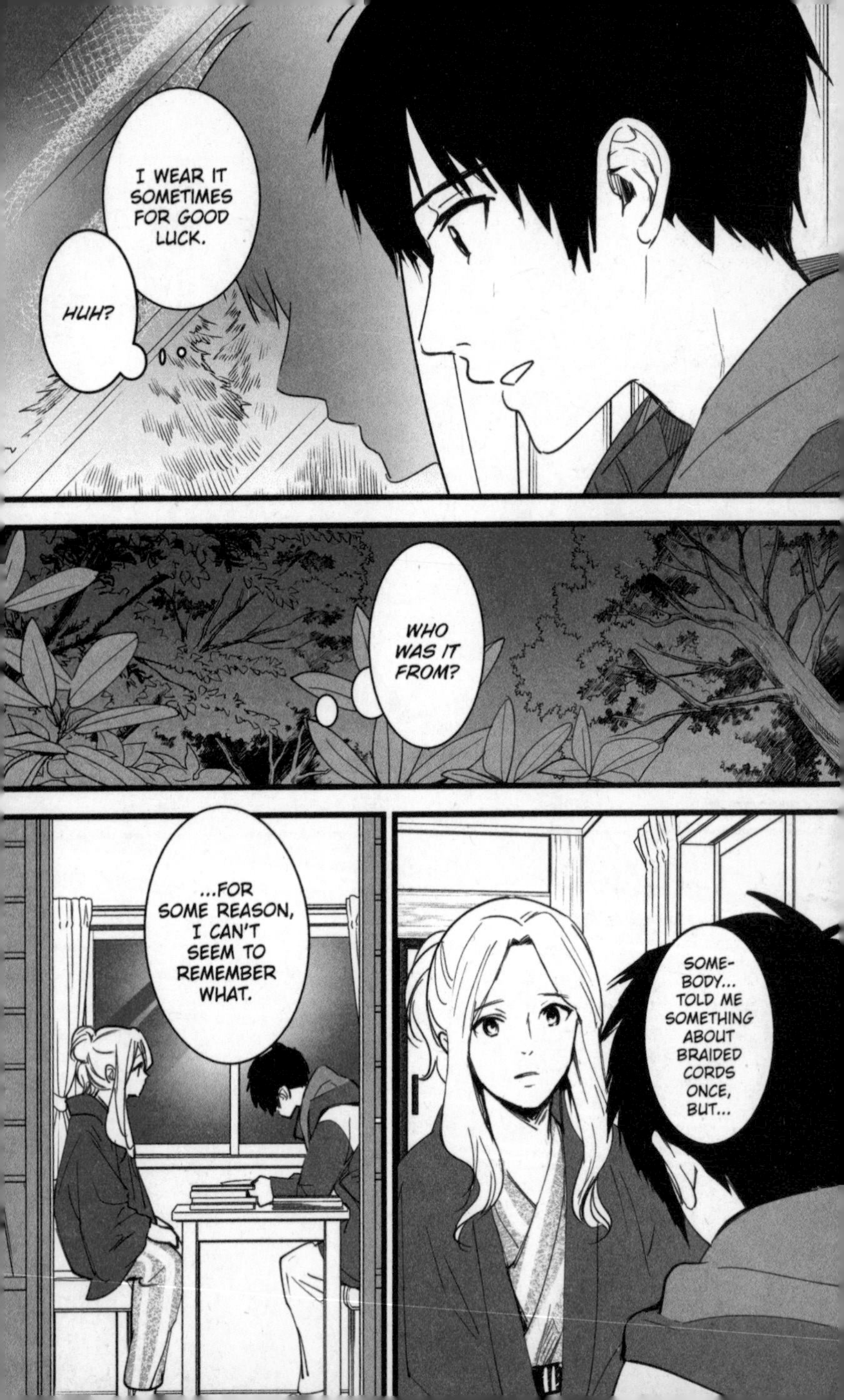
I WEAR IT SOMETIMES FOR GOOD LUCK.
HUH?
WHO WAS IT FROM?
SOME-BODY... TOLD ME SOMETHING ABOUT BRAIDED CORDS ONCE, BUT...
...FOR SOME REASON, I CAN'T SEEM TO REMEMBER WHAT.

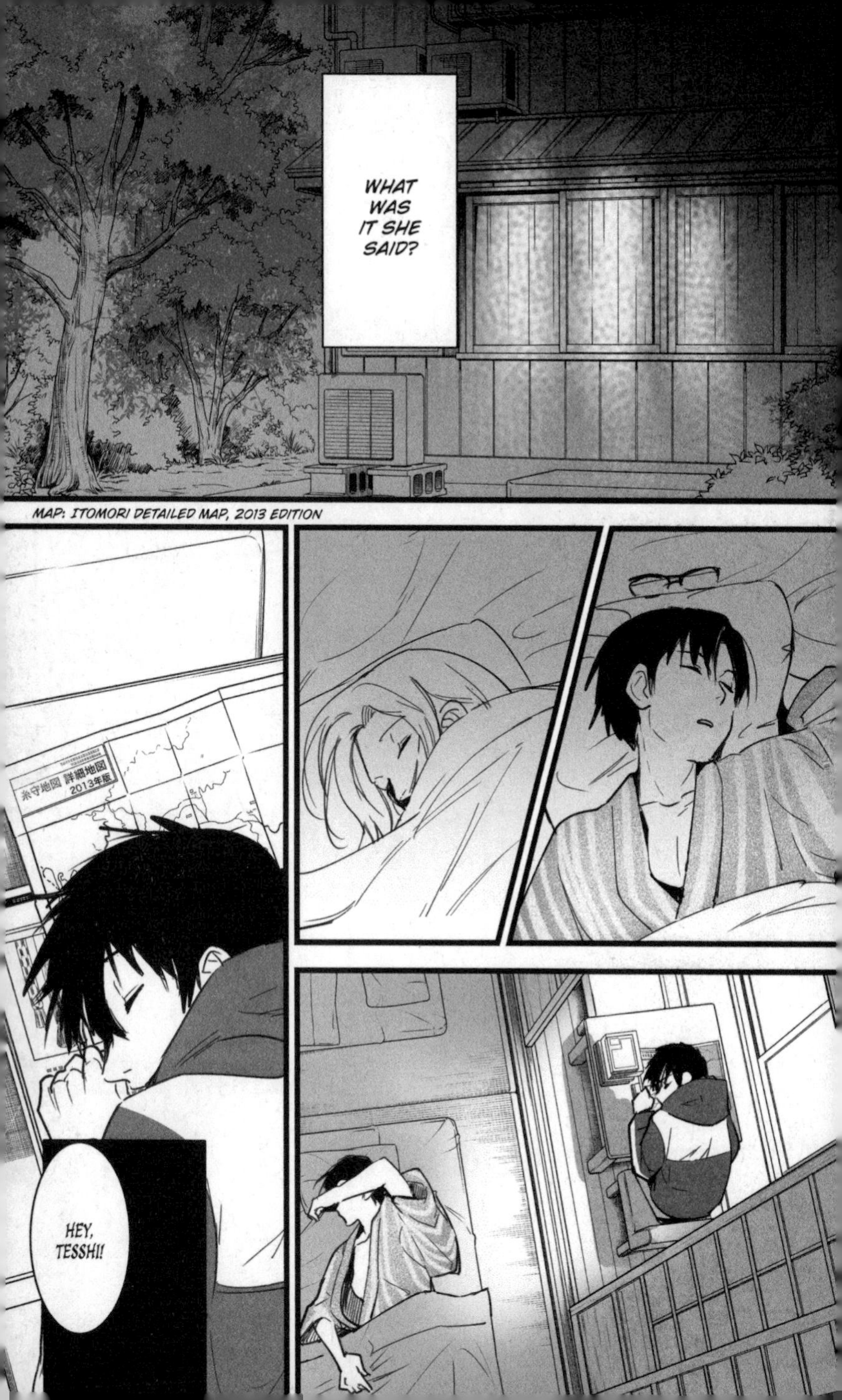
WHAT WAS IT SHE SAID?
MAP: ITOMORI DETAILED MAP, 2013 EDITION
糸守地図 詳細地図
2013年版
HEY, TESSHI!

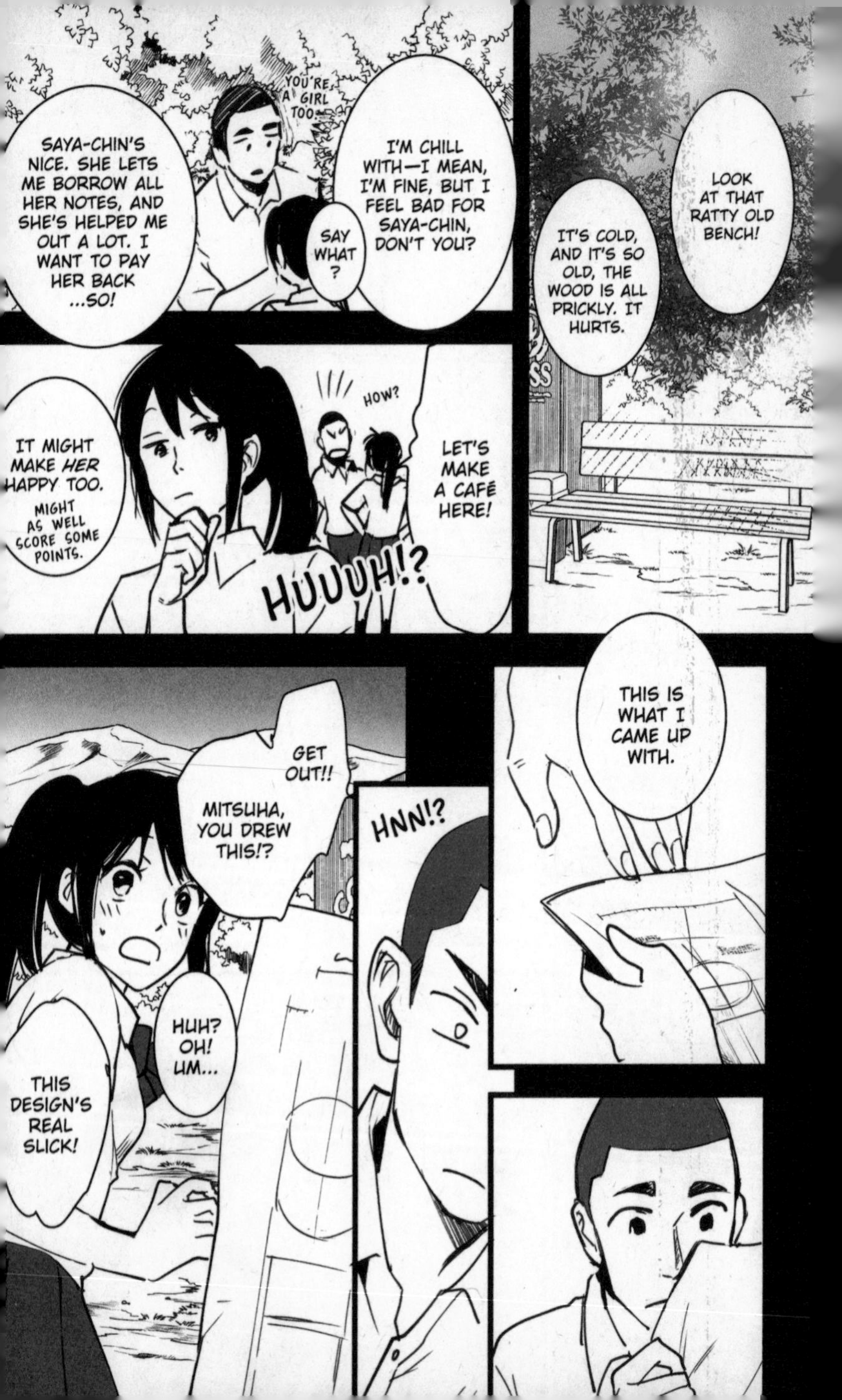
LOOK AT THAT RATTY OLD BENCH!
IT'S COLD, AND IT'S SO OLD, THE WOOD IS ALL PRICKLY. IT HURTS.
I'M CHILL WITH—I MEAN, I'M FINE, BUT I FEEL BAD FOR SAYA-CHIN, DON'T YOU?
YOU'RE A GIRL TOO.
SAY WHAT?
SAYA-CHIN'S NICE. SHE LETS ME BORROW ALL HER NOTES, AND SHE'S HELPED ME OUT A LOT. I WANT TO PAY HER BACK ...SO!
LET'S MAKE A CAFÉ HERE!
HOW?
HUUUH!?
IT MIGHT MAKE *HER* HAPPY TOO.
MIGHT AS WELL SCORE SOME POINTS.
THIS IS WHAT I CAME UP WITH.
HNN!?
GET OUT!!
MITSUHA, YOU DREW THIS!?
HUH? OH! UM...
THIS DESIGN'S REAL SLICK!

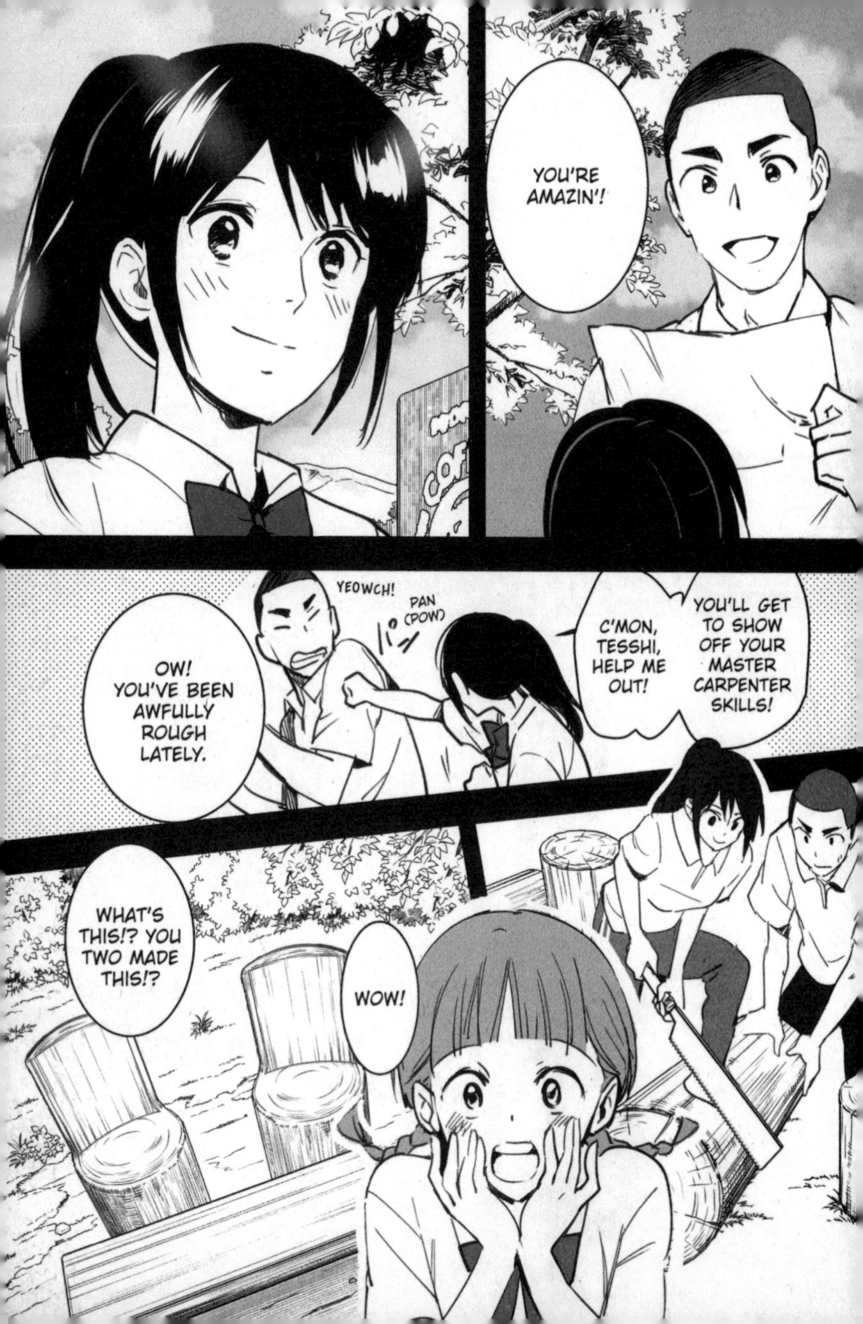
YOU'RE AMAZIN'!
YOU'LL GET TO SHOW OFF YOUR MASTER CARPENTER SKILLS!
C'MON, TESSHI, HELP ME OUT!
YEOWCH!
PAN (POW)
OW! YOU'VE BEEN AWFULLY ROUGH LATELY.
WOW!
WHAT'S THIS!? YOU TWO MADE THIS!?

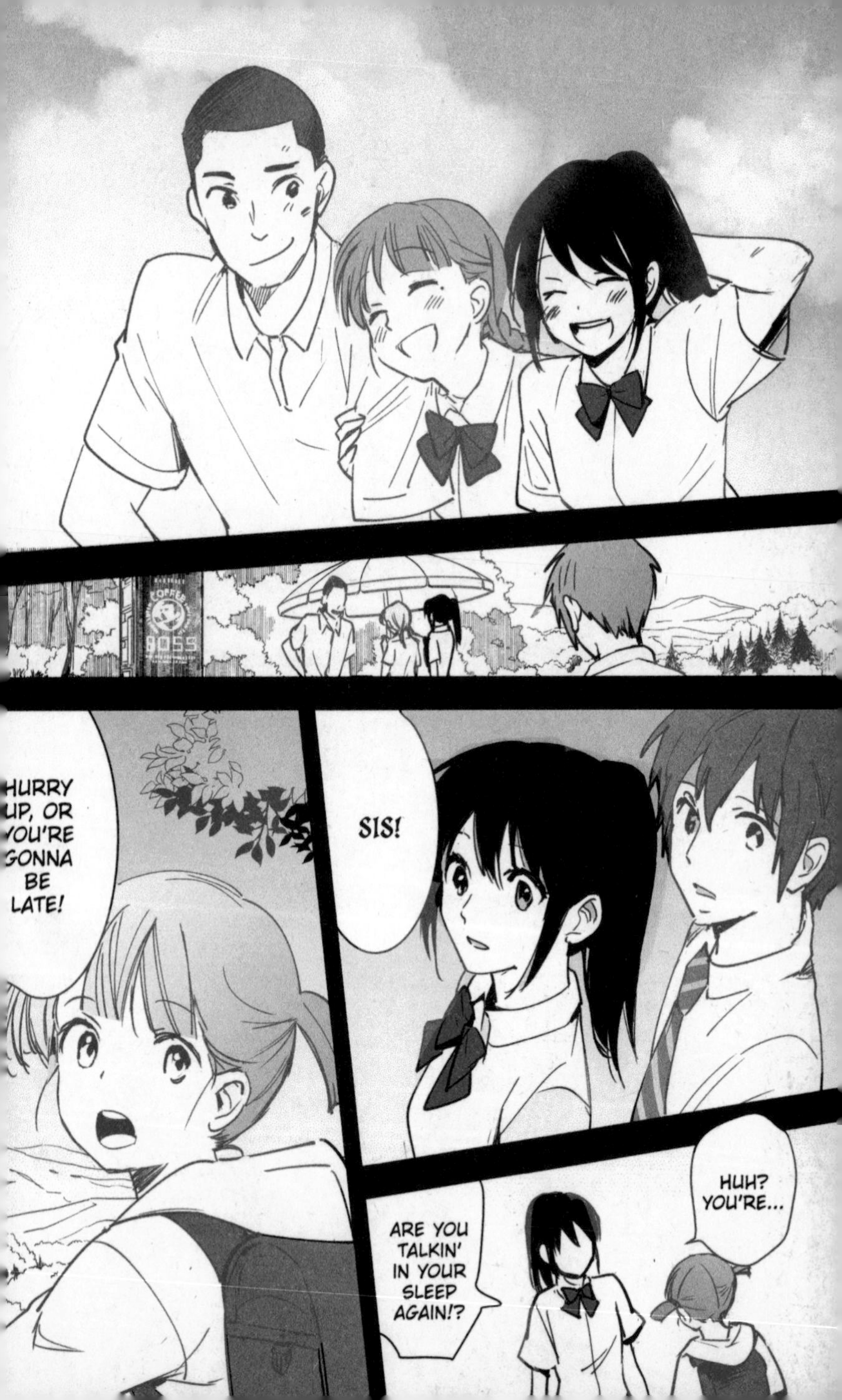
COFFEE
BOSS
SIS!
HUH? YOU'RE...
ARE YOU TALKIN' IN YOUR SLEEP AGAIN!?
HURRY UP, OR YOU'RE GONNA BE LATE!

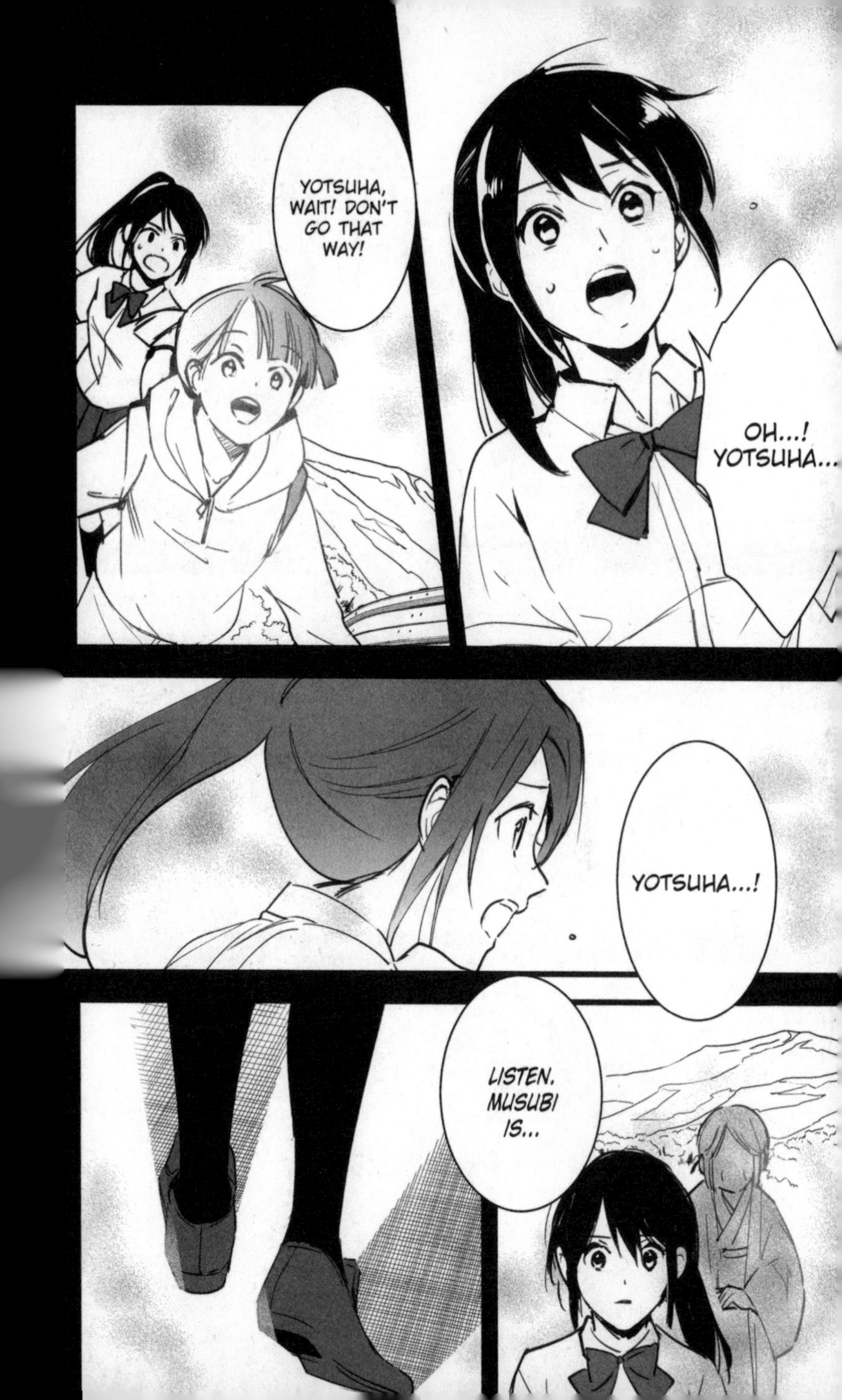
OH...! YOTSUHA...
YOTSUHA, WAIT! DON'T GO THAT WAY!
YOTSUHA...!
LISTEN. MUSUBI IS...

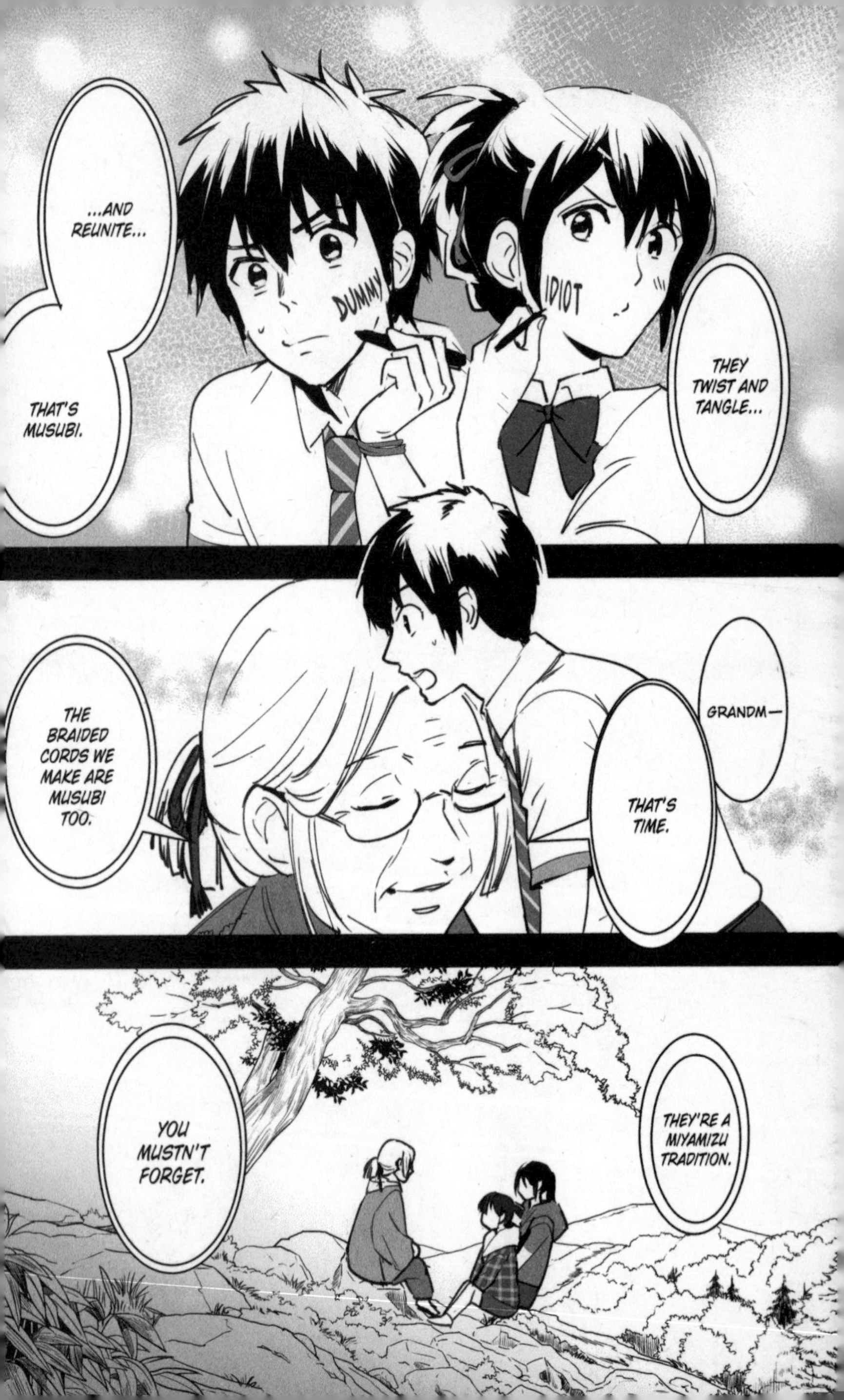
THEY TWIST AND TANGLE...
IDIOT
DUMMY
...AND REUNITE...
THAT'S MUSUBI.
GRANDM—
THAT'S TIME.
THE BRAIDED CORDS WE MAKE ARE MUSUBI TOO.
THEY'RE A MIYAMIZU TRADITION.
YOU MUSTN'T FORGET.

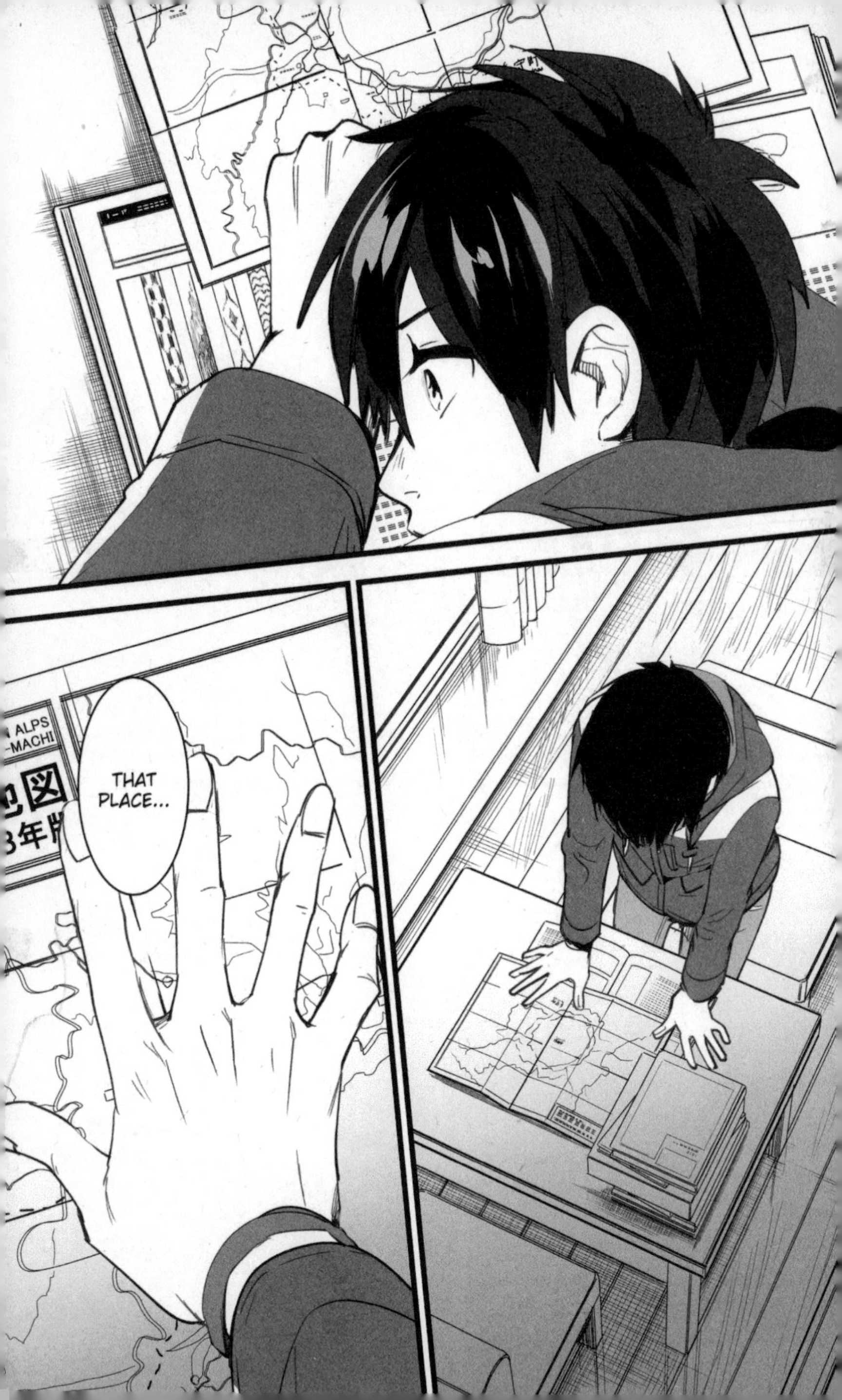
THAT PLACE...

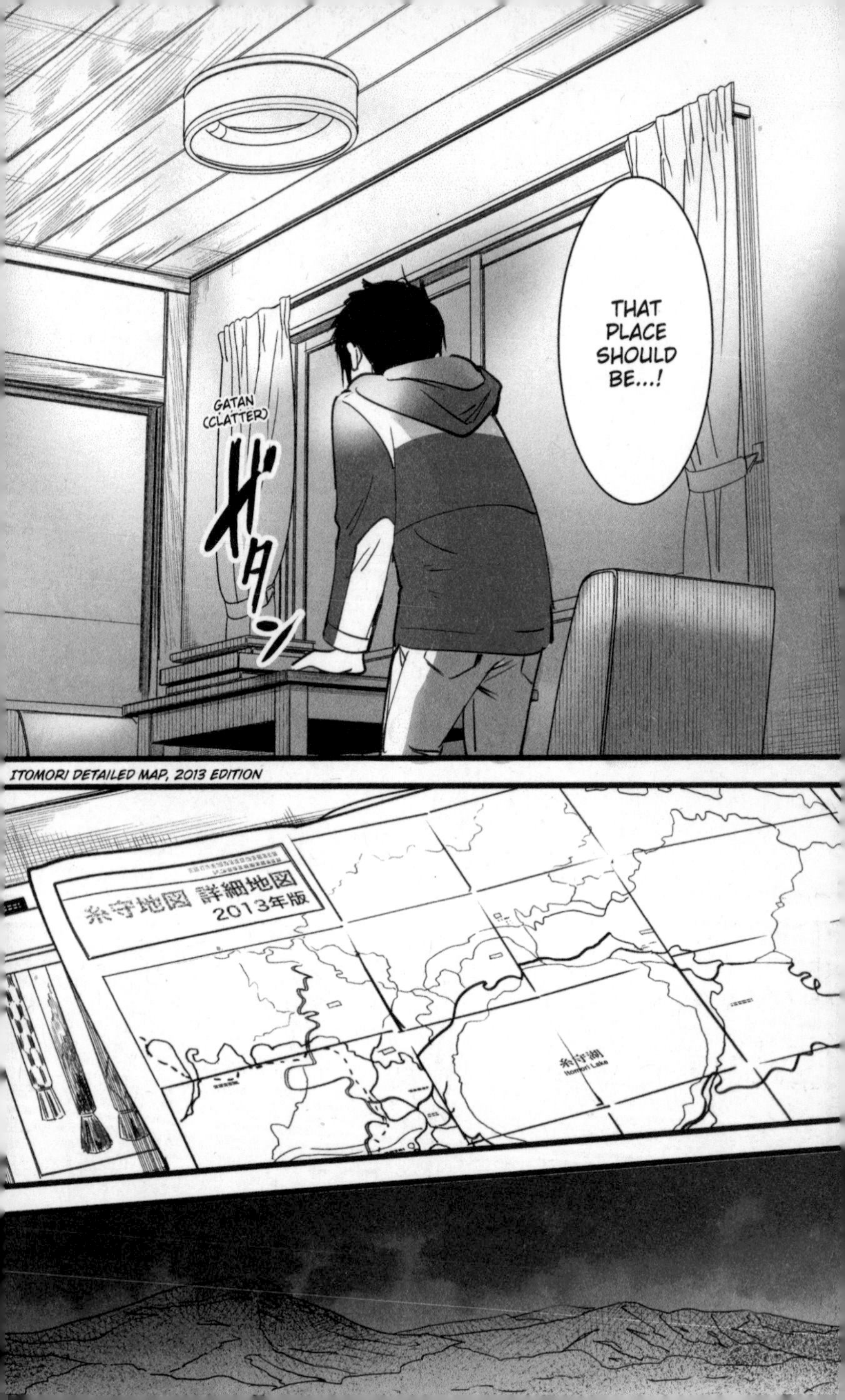
THAT PLACE SHOULD BE...!
GATAN (CLATTER)
ITOMORI DETAILED MAP, 2013 EDITION
糸守地図 詳細地図
2013年版
糸守湖
Itomori Lake

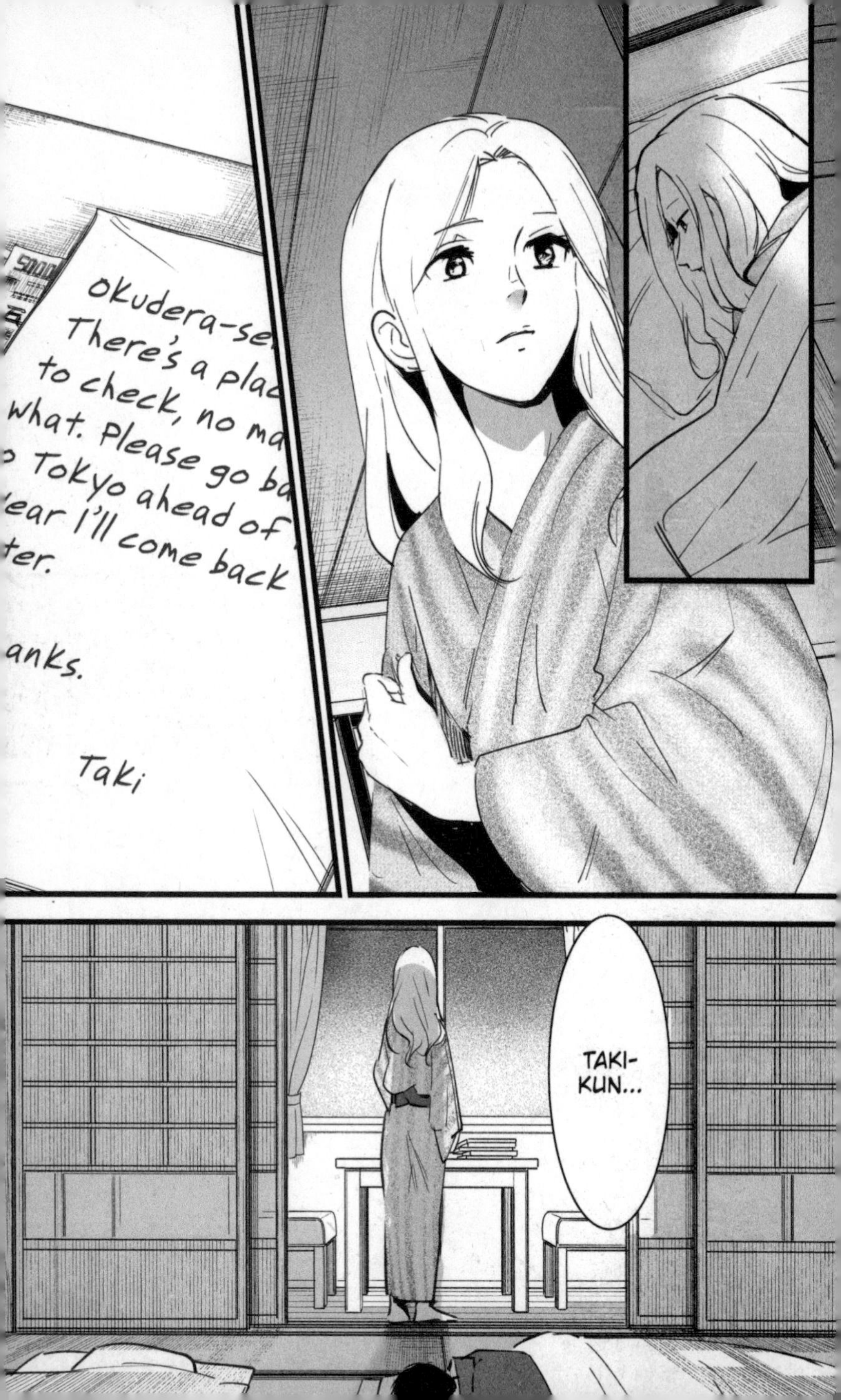
Okudera-se
There's a plac
to check, no ma
what. Please go ba
Tokyo ahead of
ear I'll come back
ter.
anks.
Taki
TAKI-KUN...

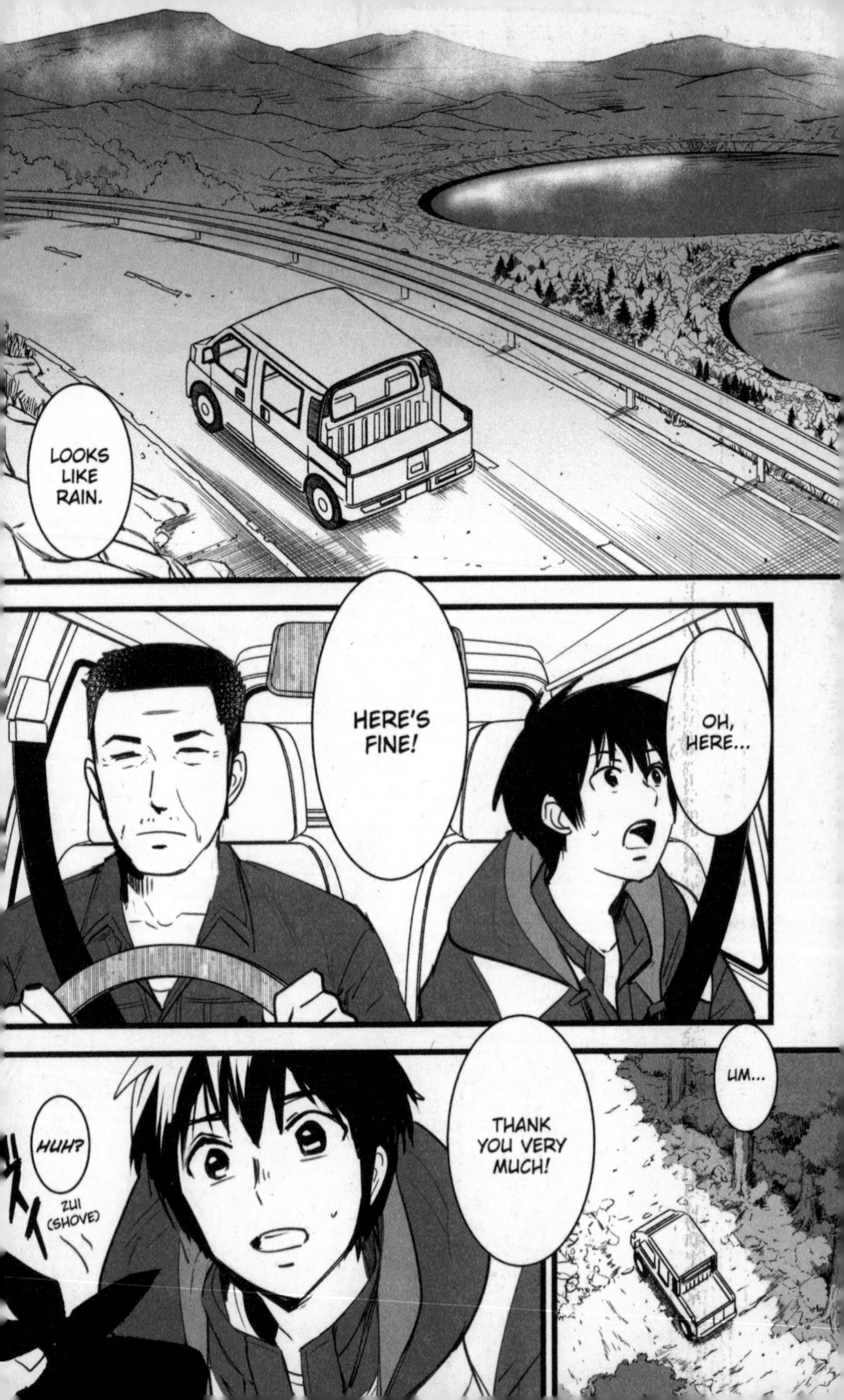
LOOKS LIKE RAIN.
OH, HERE...
HERE'S FINE!
UM...
THANK YOU VERY MUCH!
HUH?
ZUI (SHOVE)

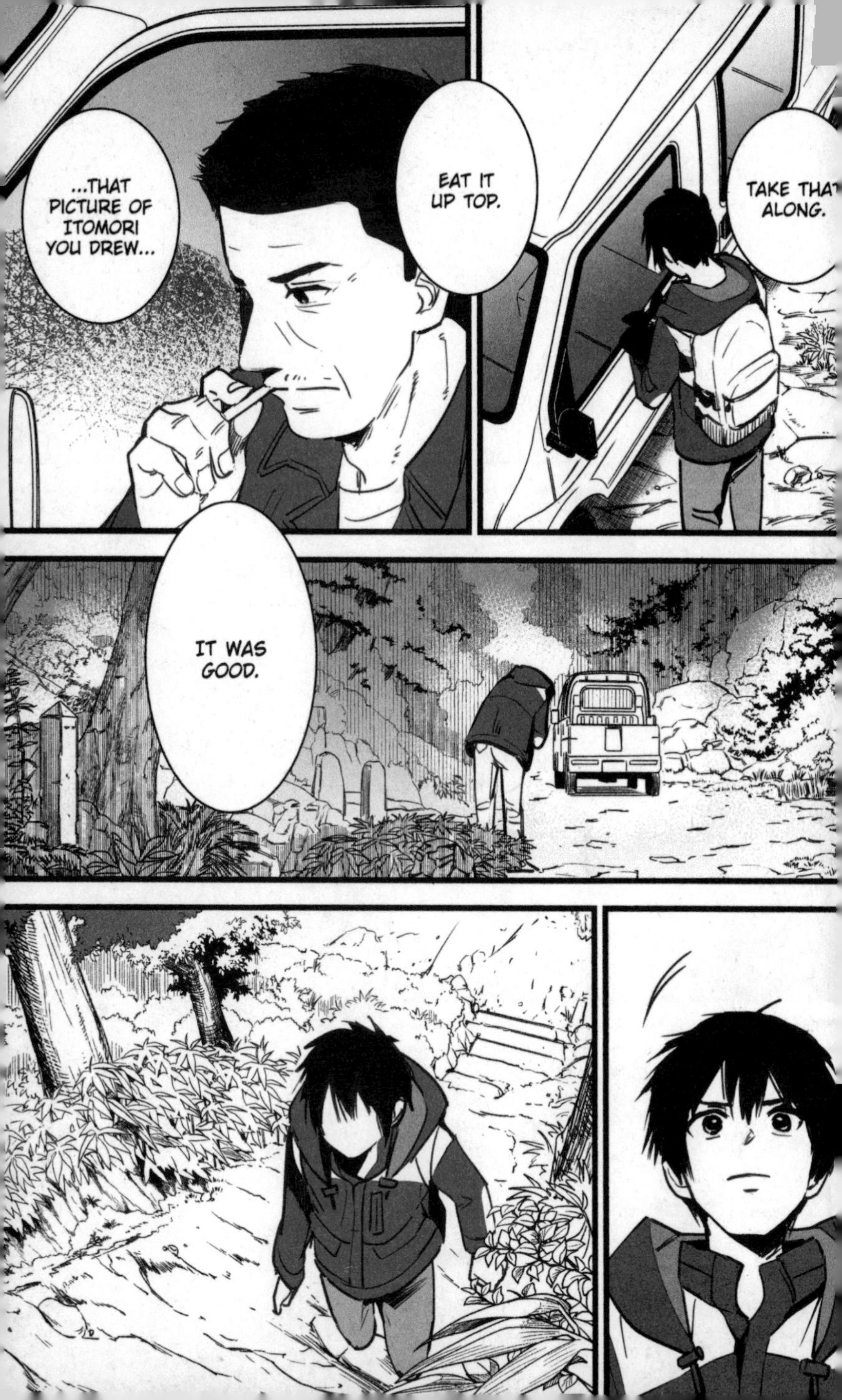
TAKE THAT ALONG.
EAT IT UP TOP.
...THAT PICTURE OF ITOMORI YOU DREW...
IT WAS GOOD.

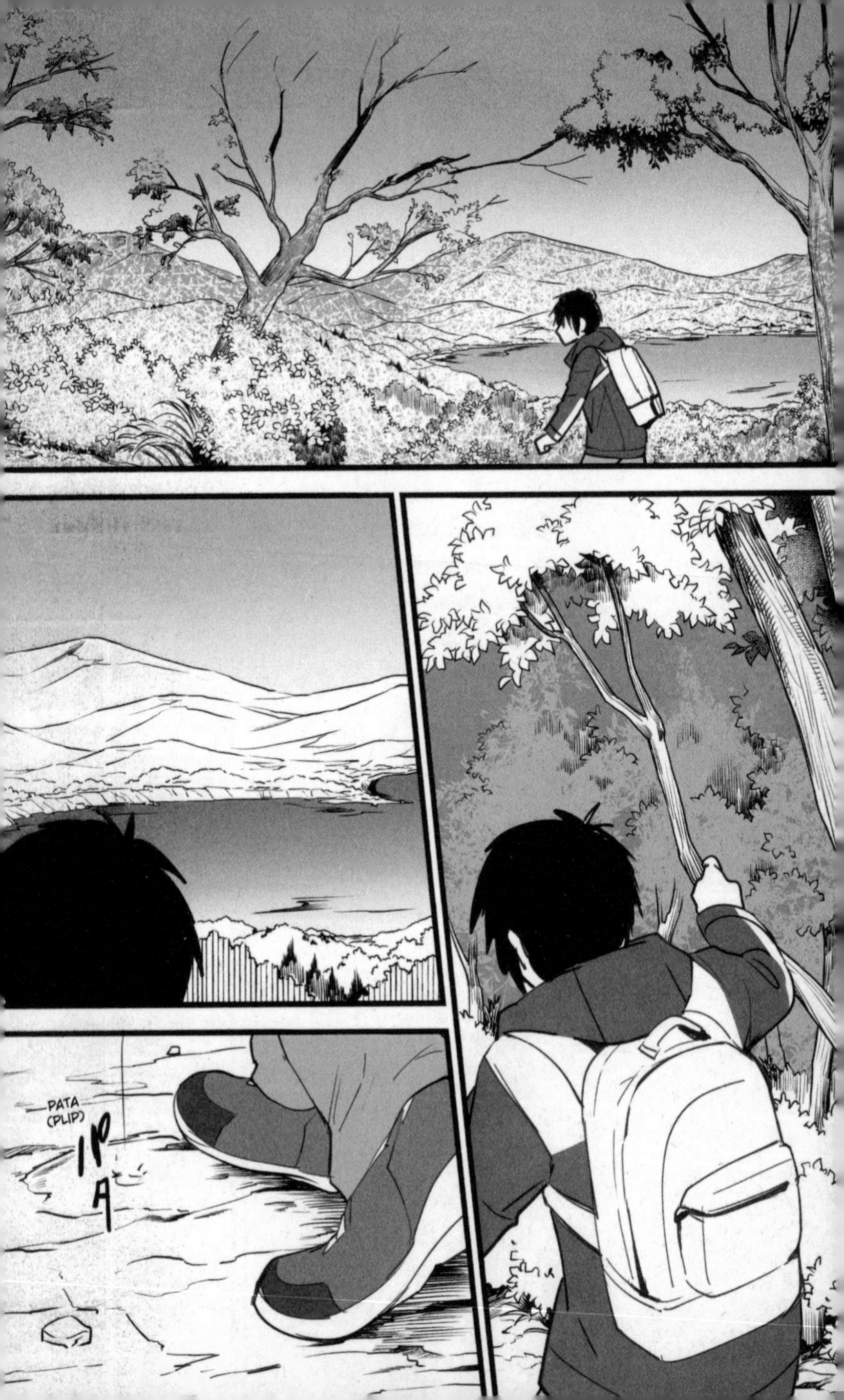
PATA (PLIP)

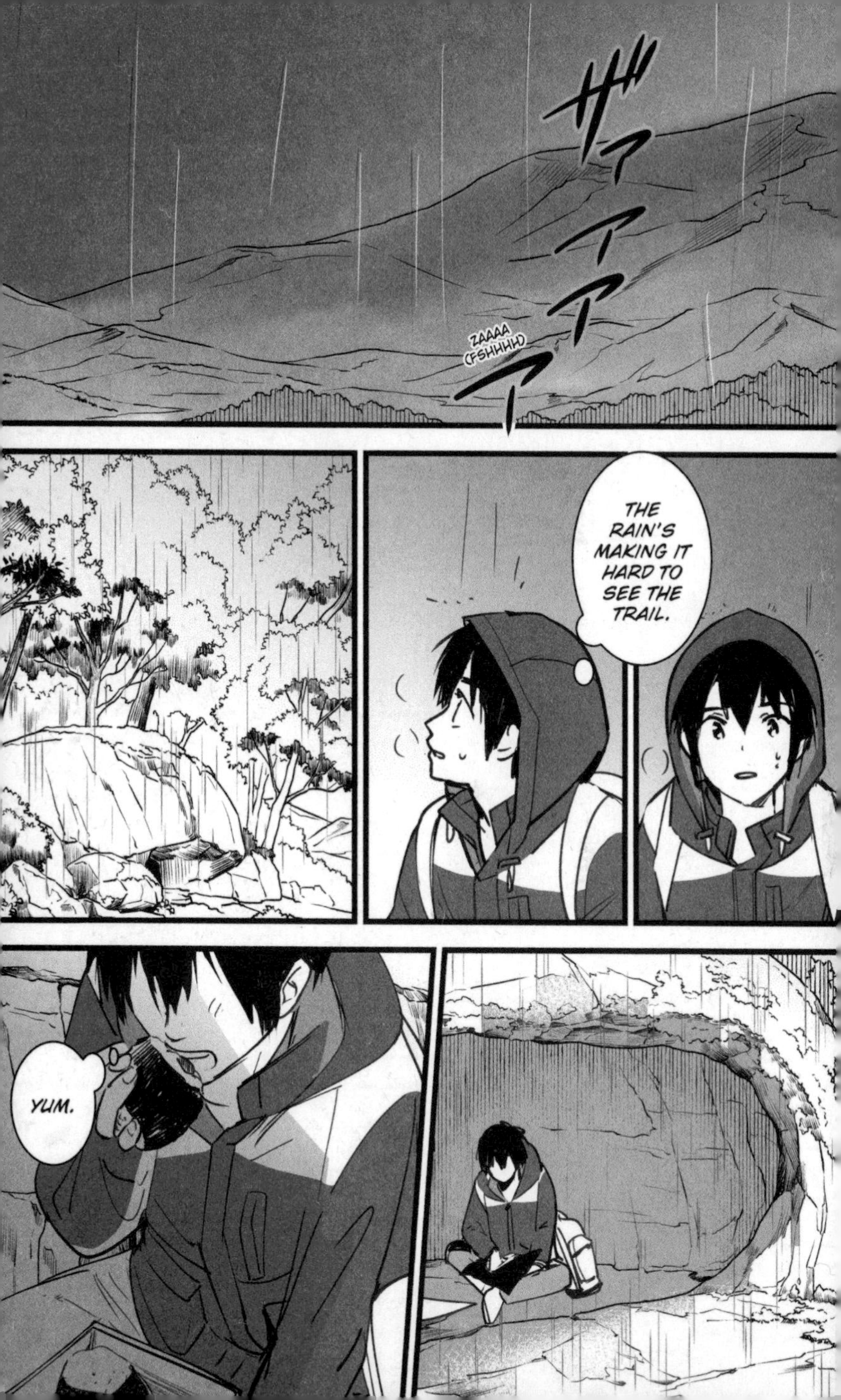
ザァァァァ
ZAAAA (FSHHHH)
THE RAIN'S MAKING IT HARD TO SEE THE TRAIL.
YUM.

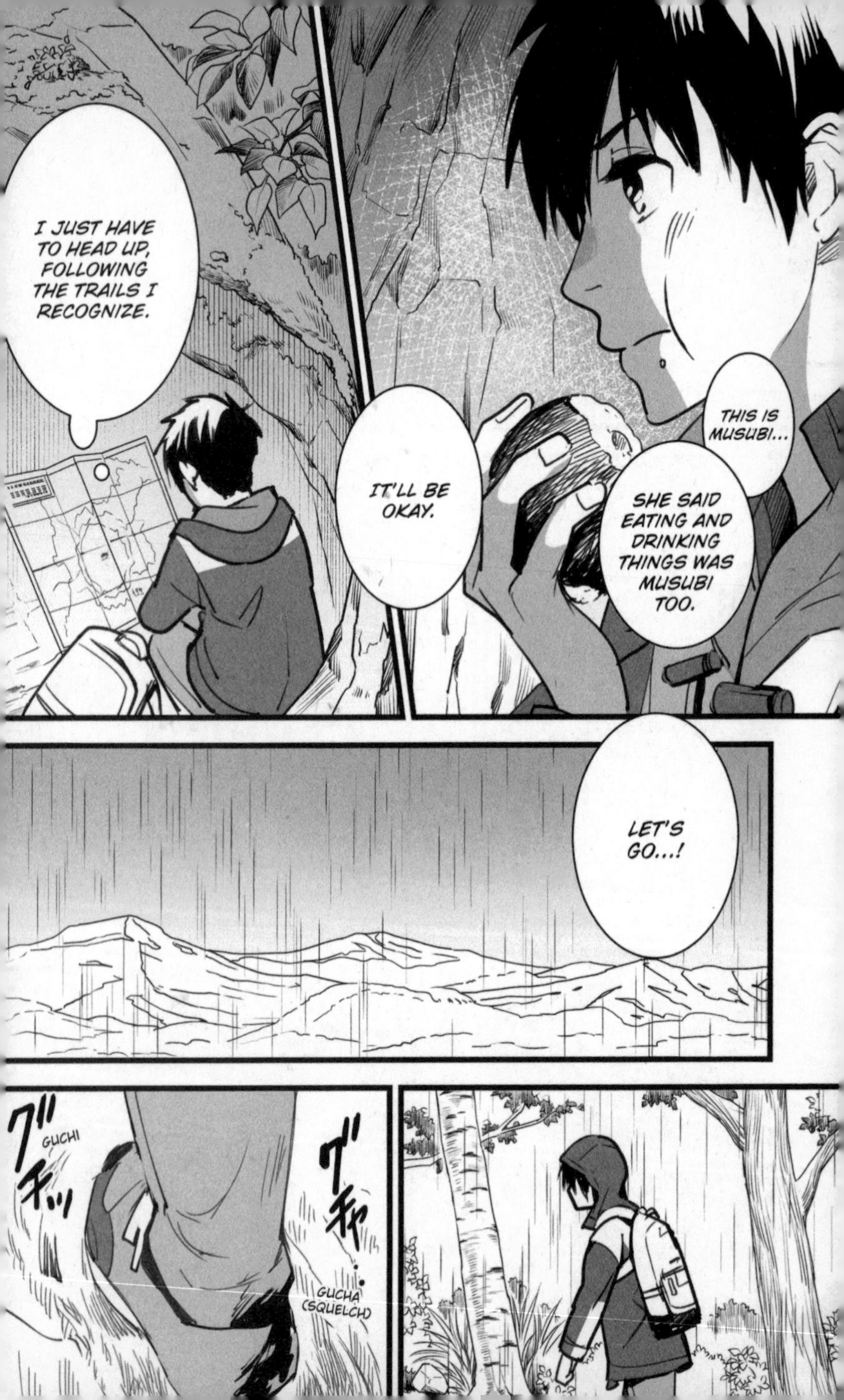
THIS IS MUSUBI...
SHE SAID EATING AND DRINKING THINGS WAS MUSUBI TOO.
IT'LL BE OKAY.
I JUST HAVE TO HEAD UP, FOLLOWING THE TRAILS I RECOGNIZE.
LET'S GO...!
グチャ
GUCHA (SQUELCH)
グチッ
GUCHI

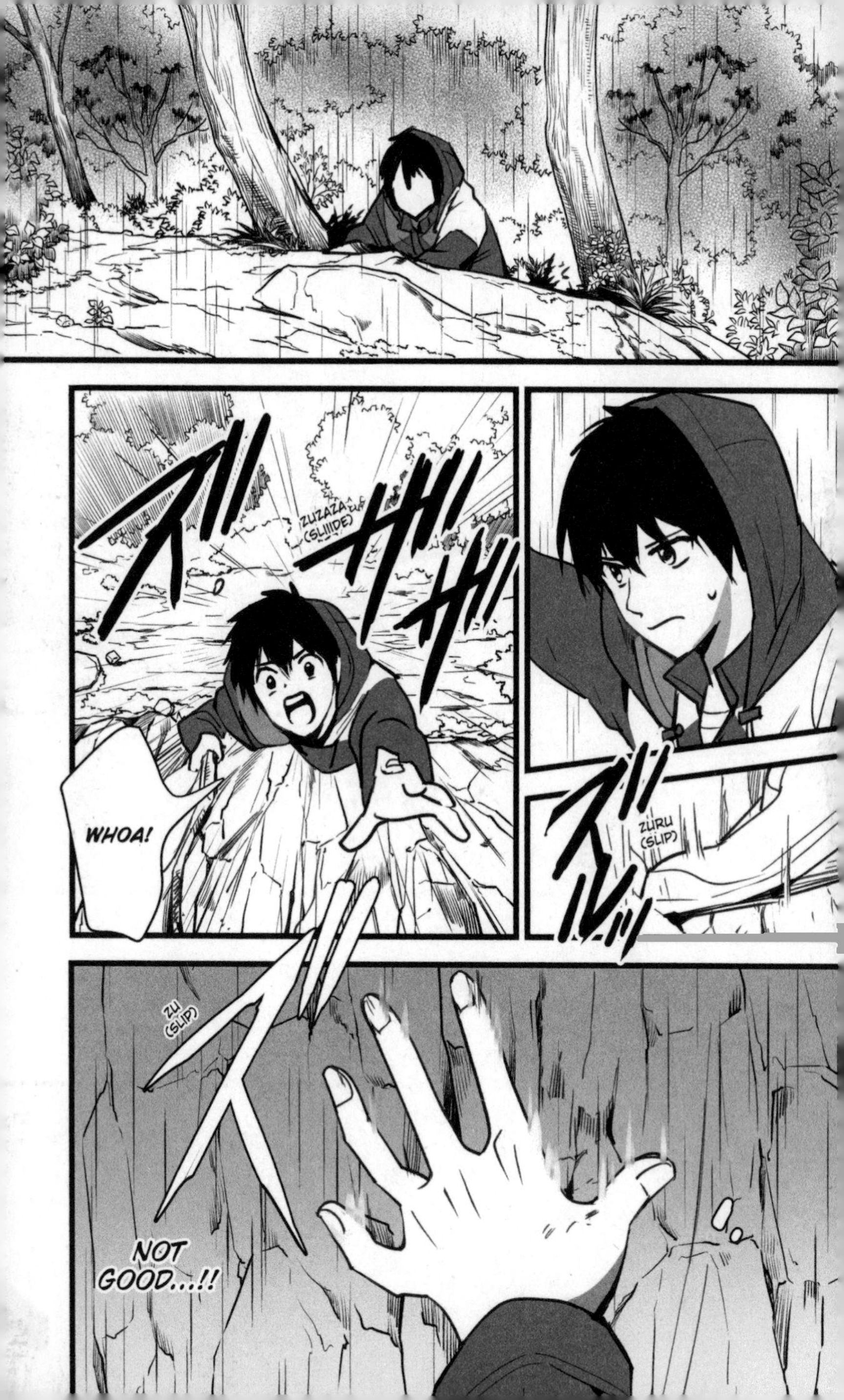
ZURU (SLIP)
ZUZAZA (SLIIIDE)
WHOA!
ZU (SLIP)
NOT GOOD...!!

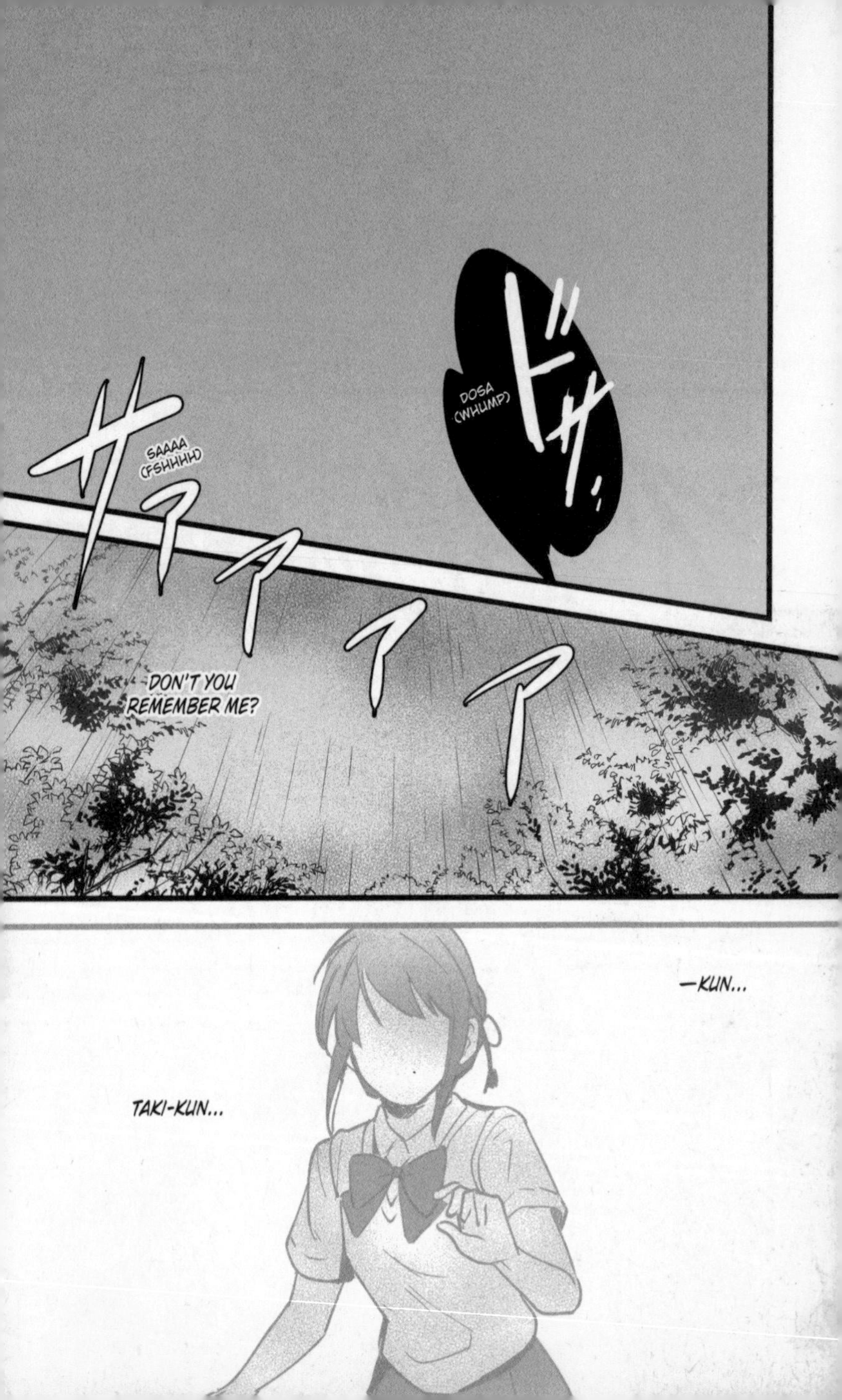
ドサッ
DOSA (WHUMP)
サァァァァ
SAAAA (FSHHHH)
DON'T YOU REMEMBER ME?
—KUN...
TAKI-KUN...

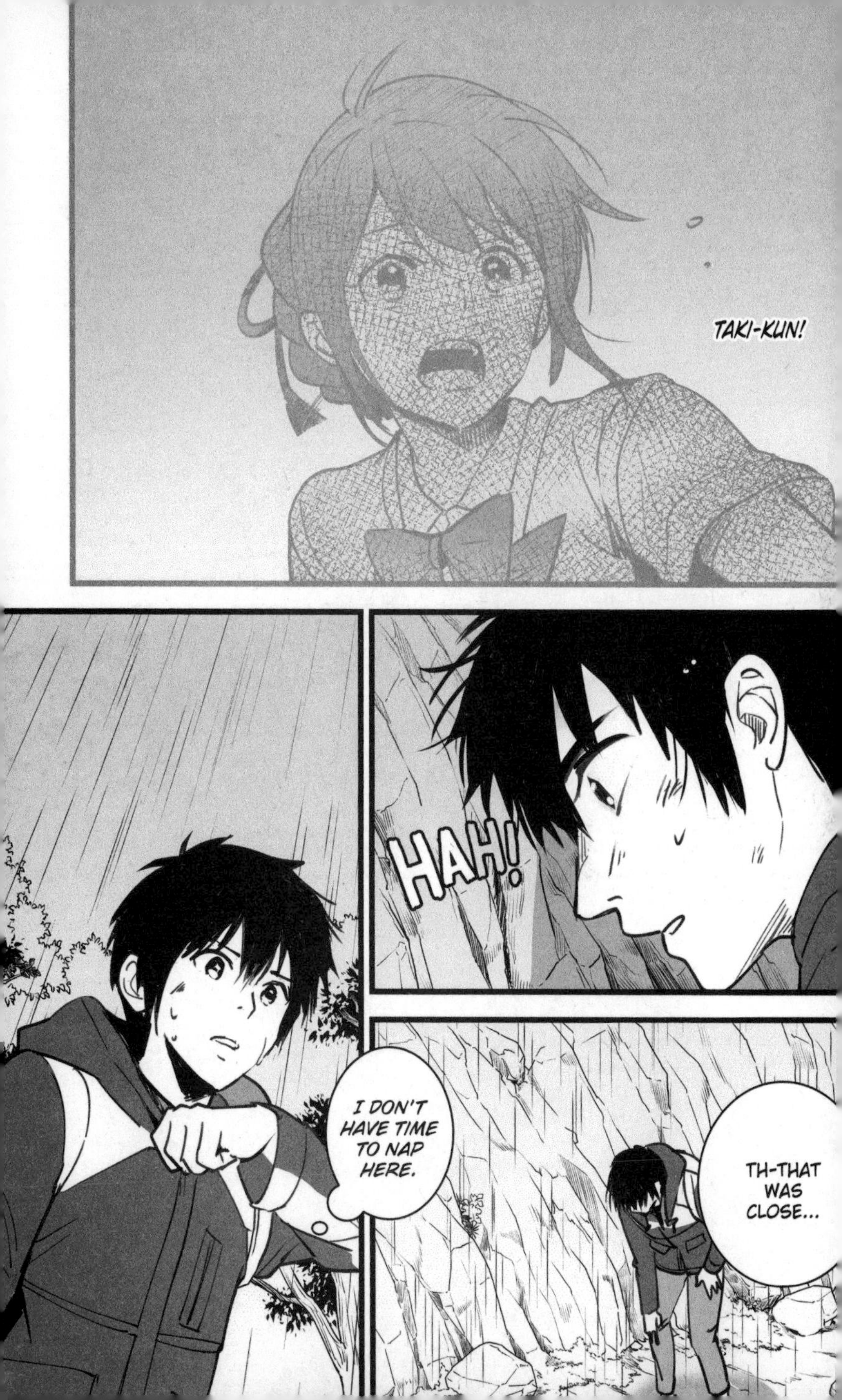
TAKI-KUN!
HAH!
TH-THAT WAS CLOSE...
I DON'T HAVE TIME TO NAP HERE.

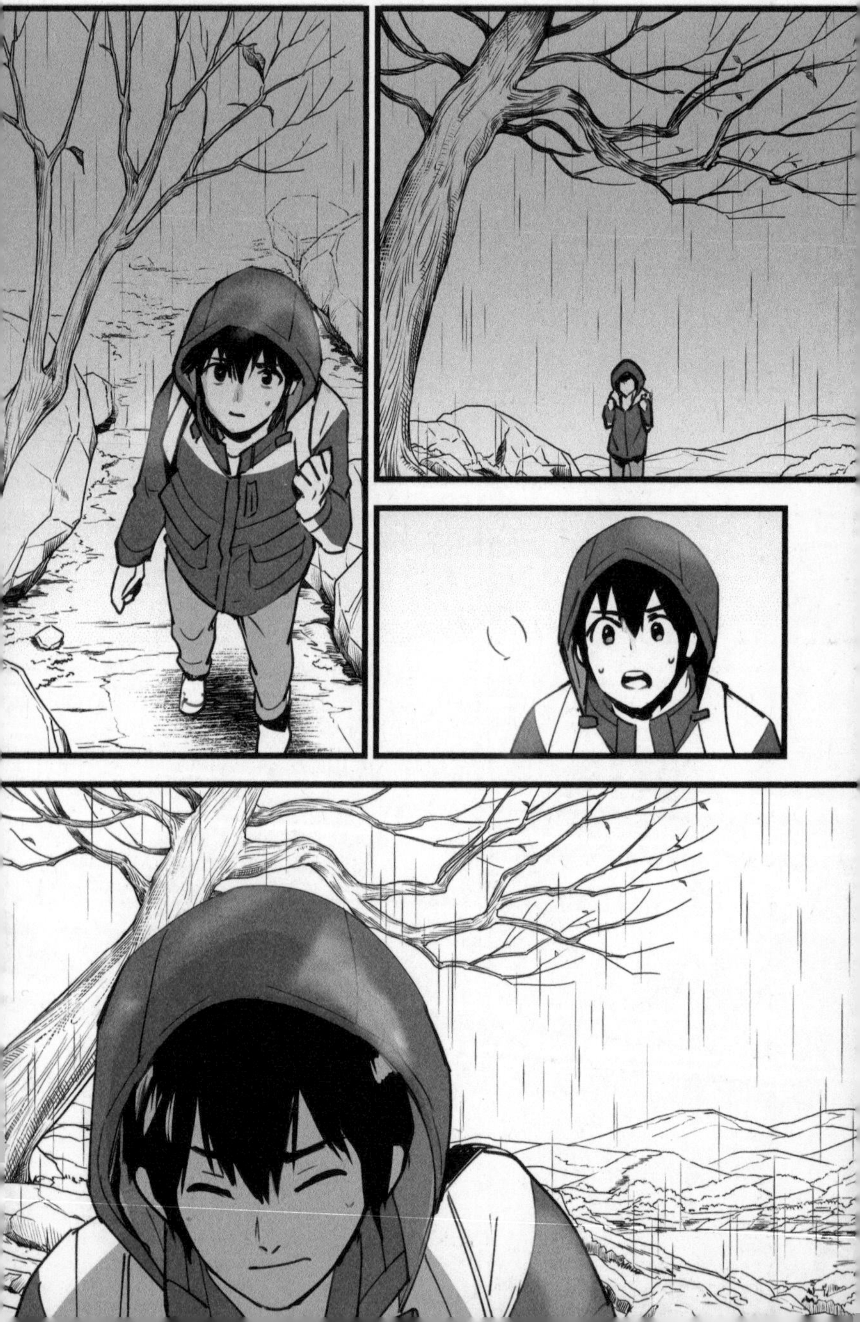

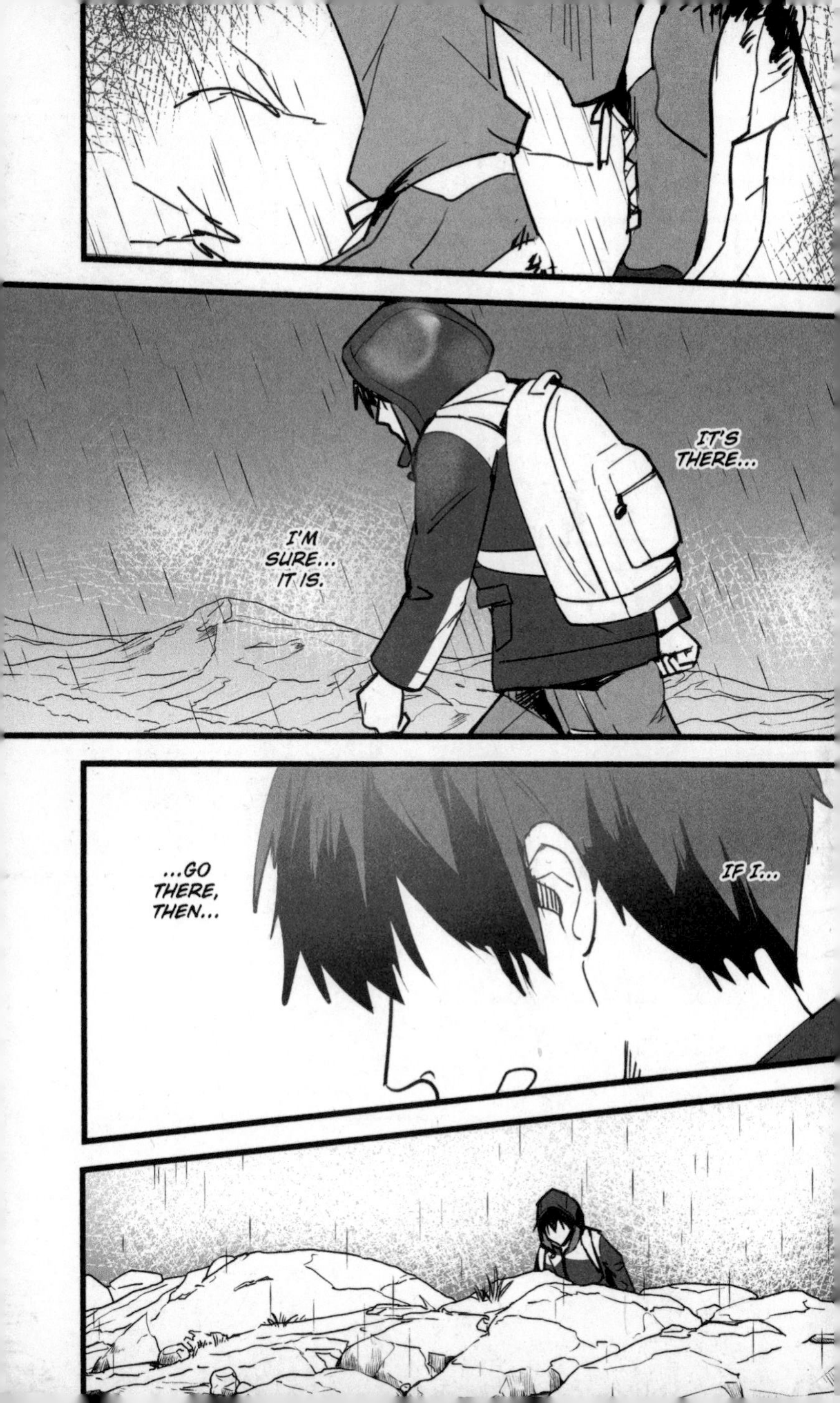
IT'S THERE...
I'M SURE... IT IS.
IF I...
...GO THERE, THEN...

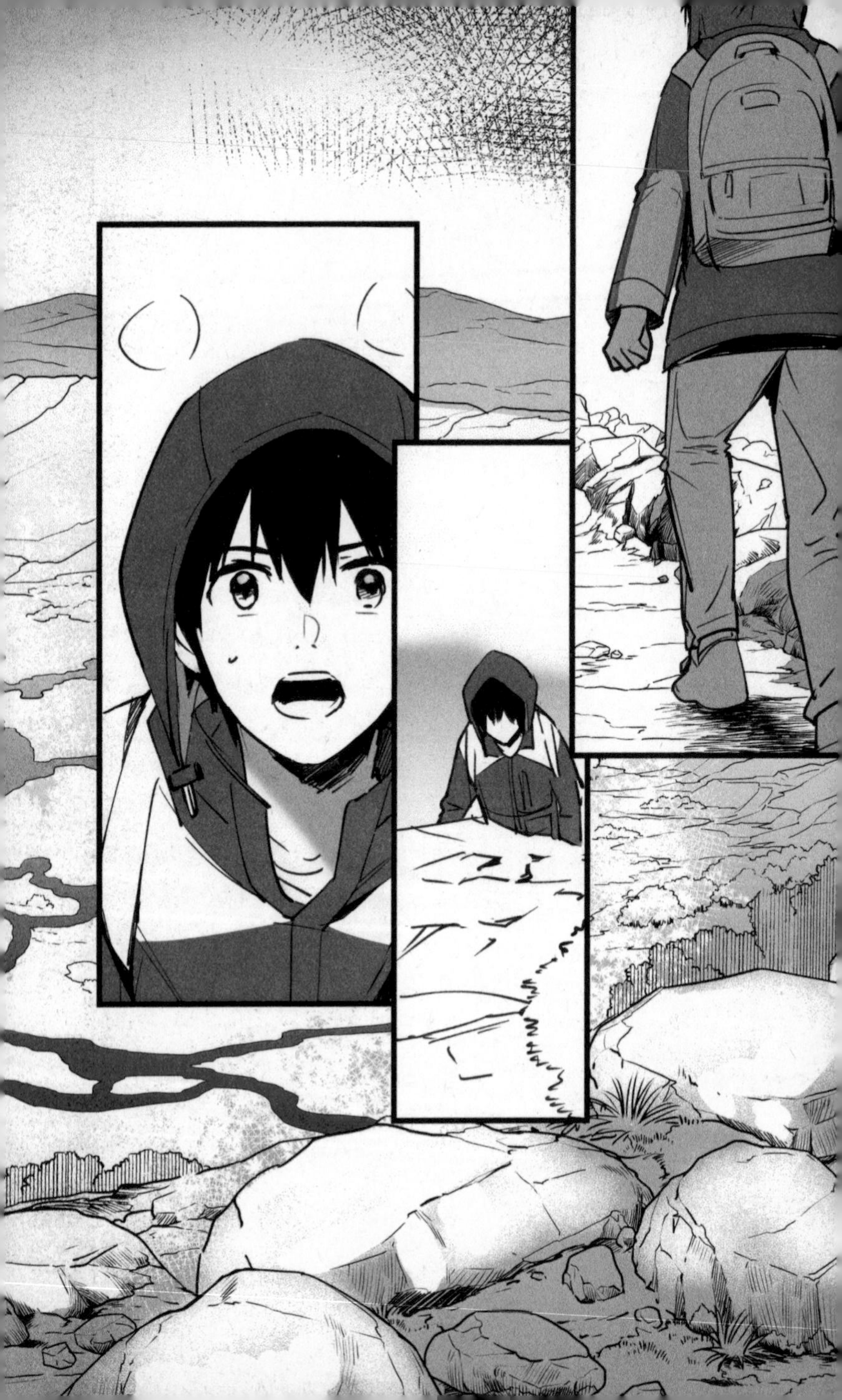

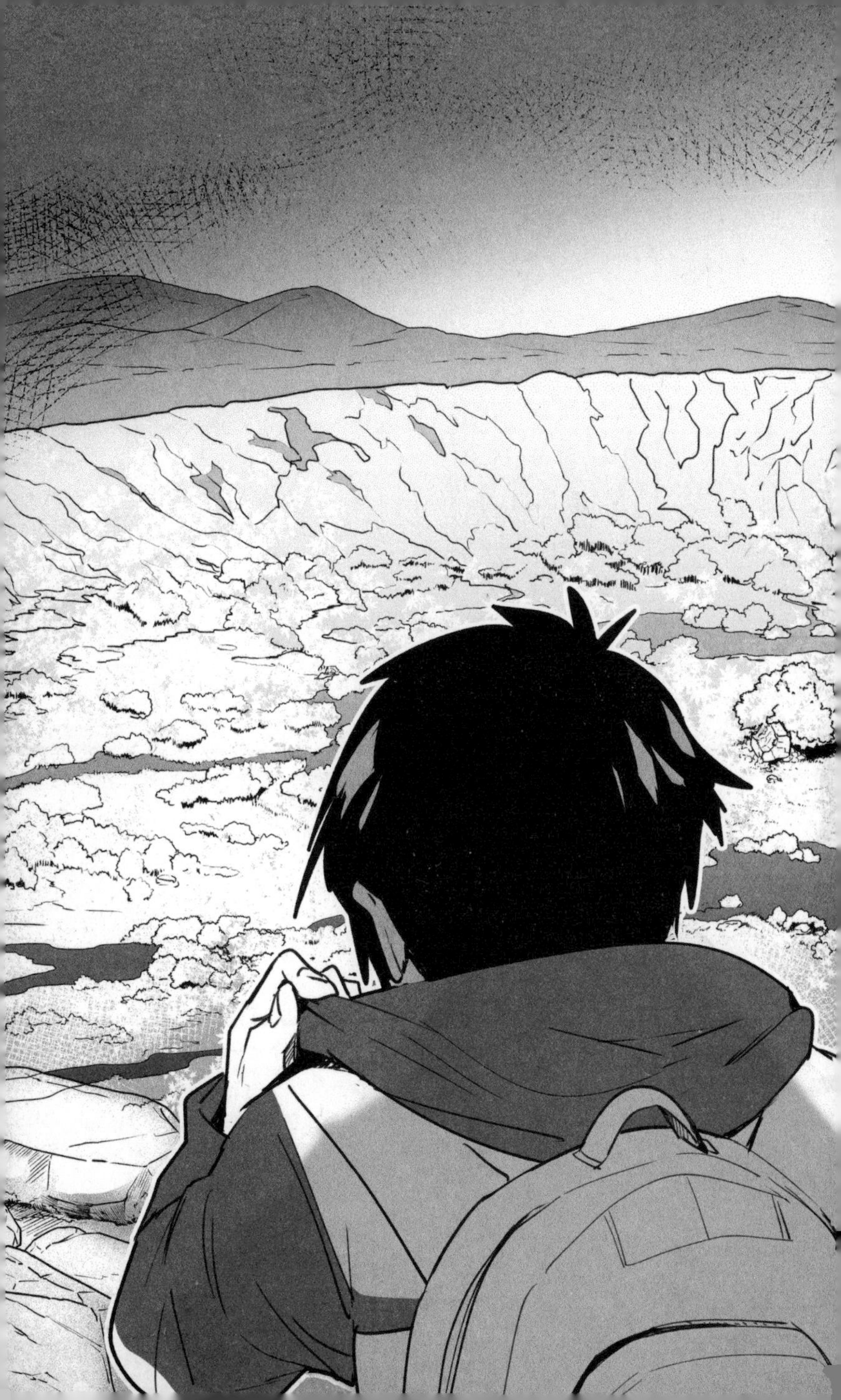

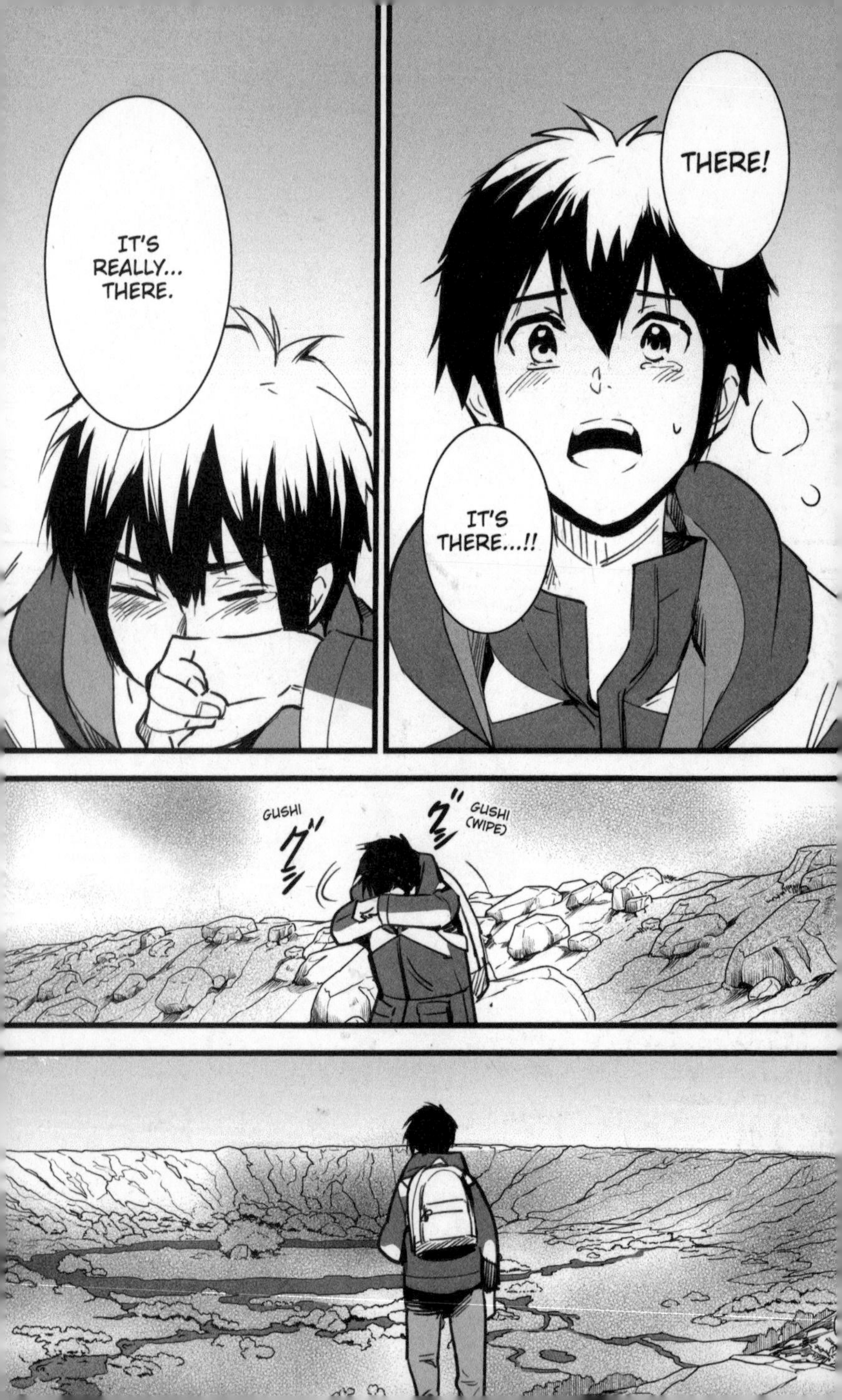
THERE!
IT'S THERE...!!
IT'S REALLY... THERE.
GUSHI (WIPE)
GUSHI

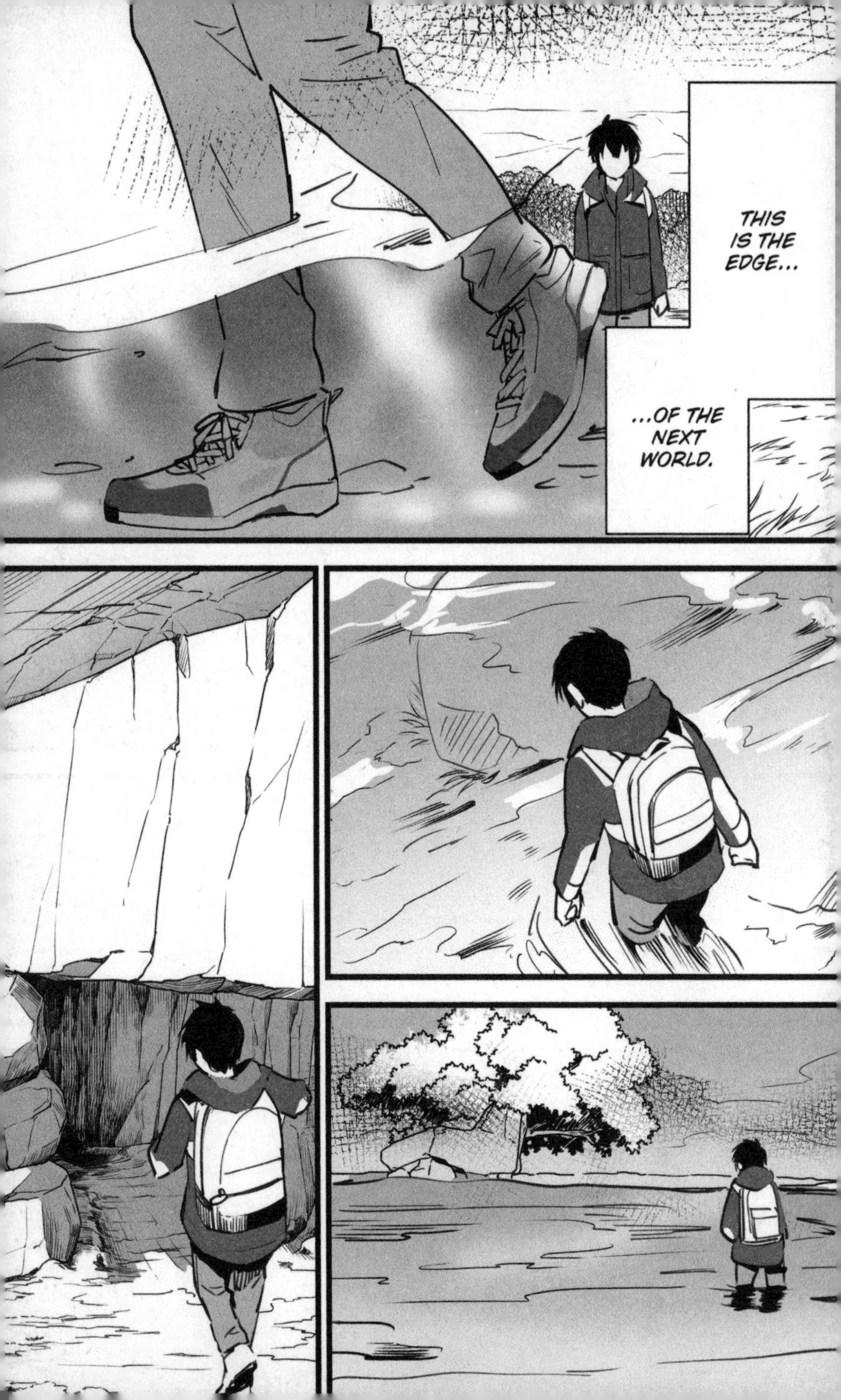
THIS IS THE EDGE...
...OF THE NEXT WORLD.

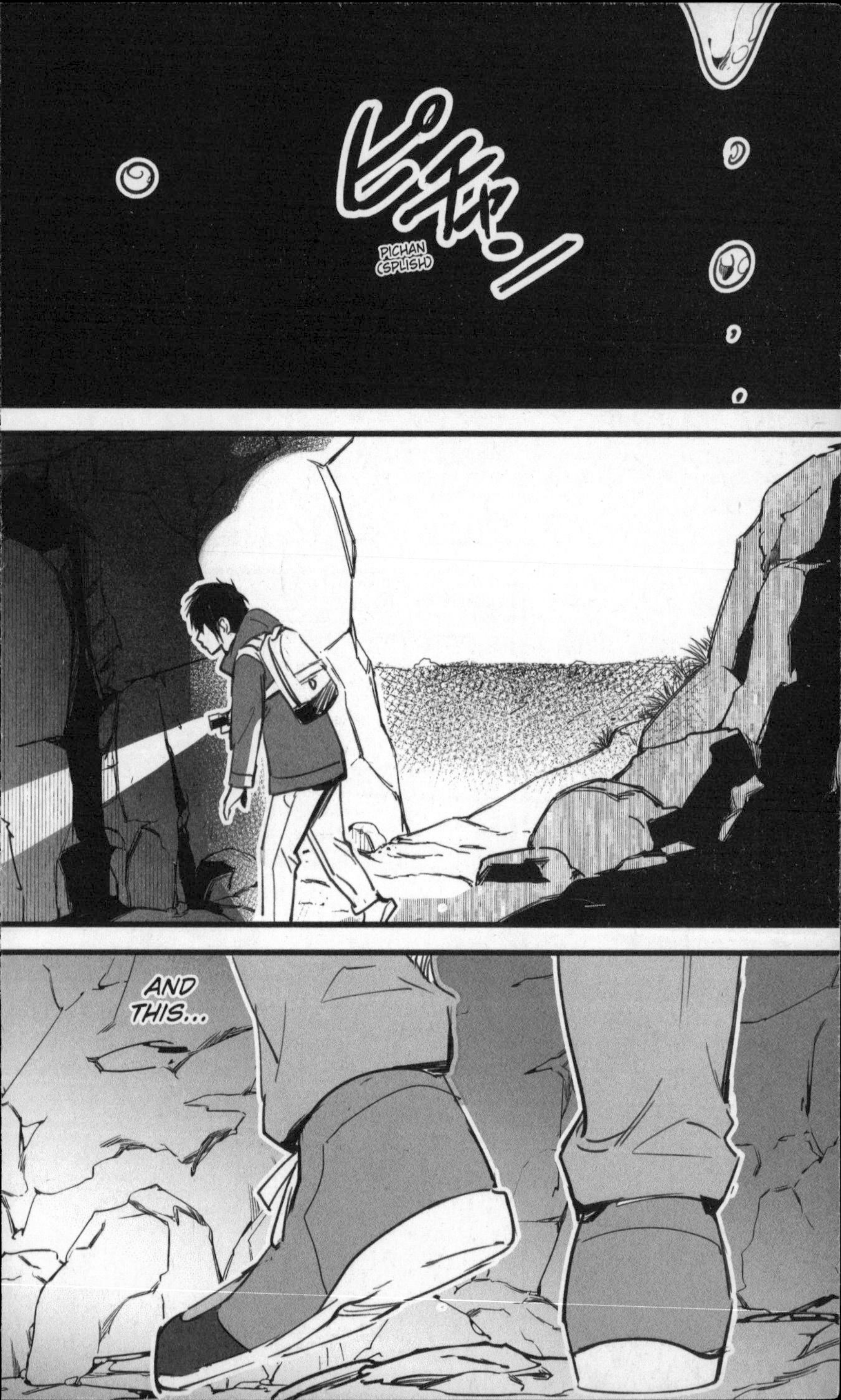
ピチャ
PICHAN (SPLISH)
AND THIS...

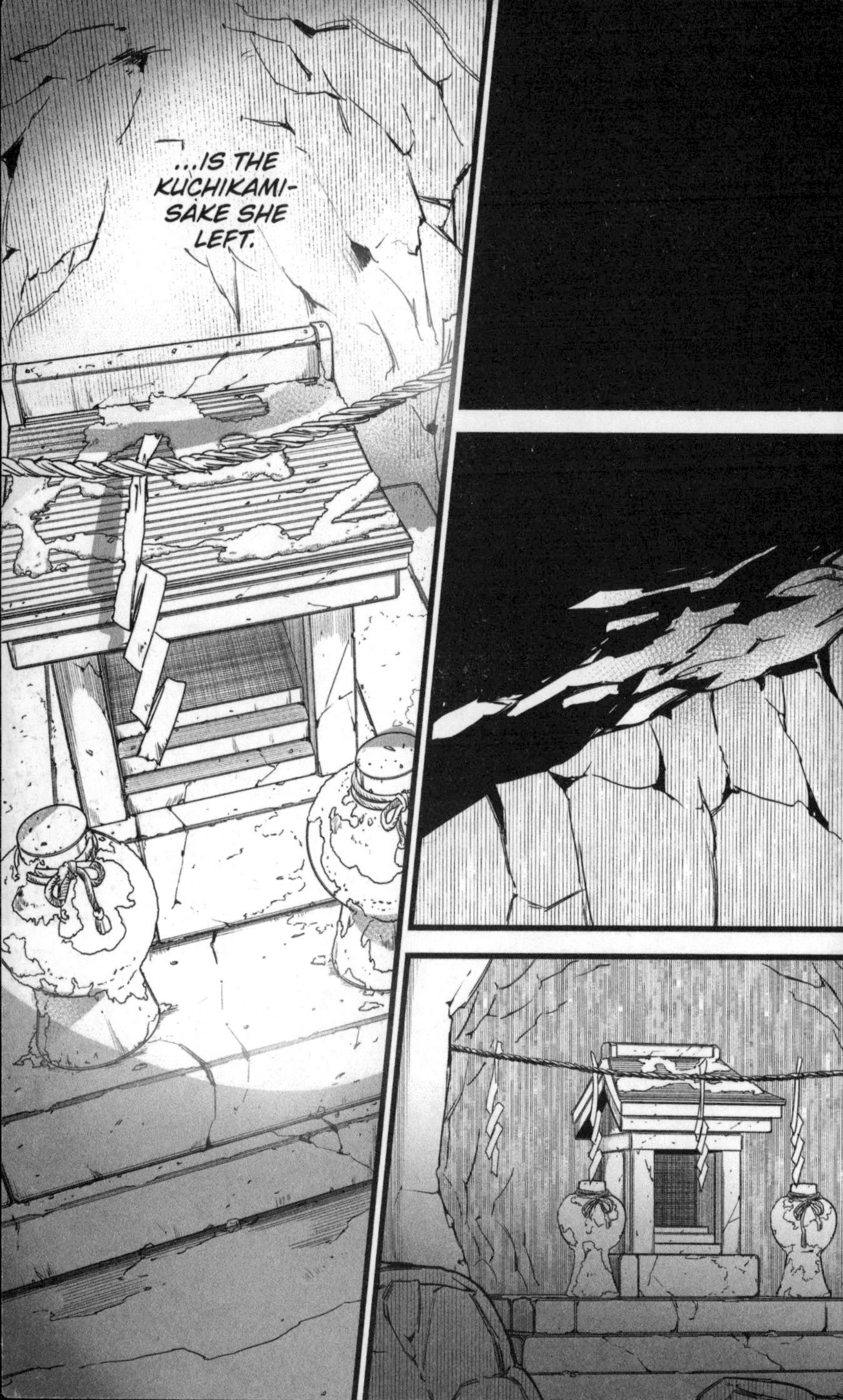
...IS THE KUCHIKAMI-SAKE SHE LEFT.

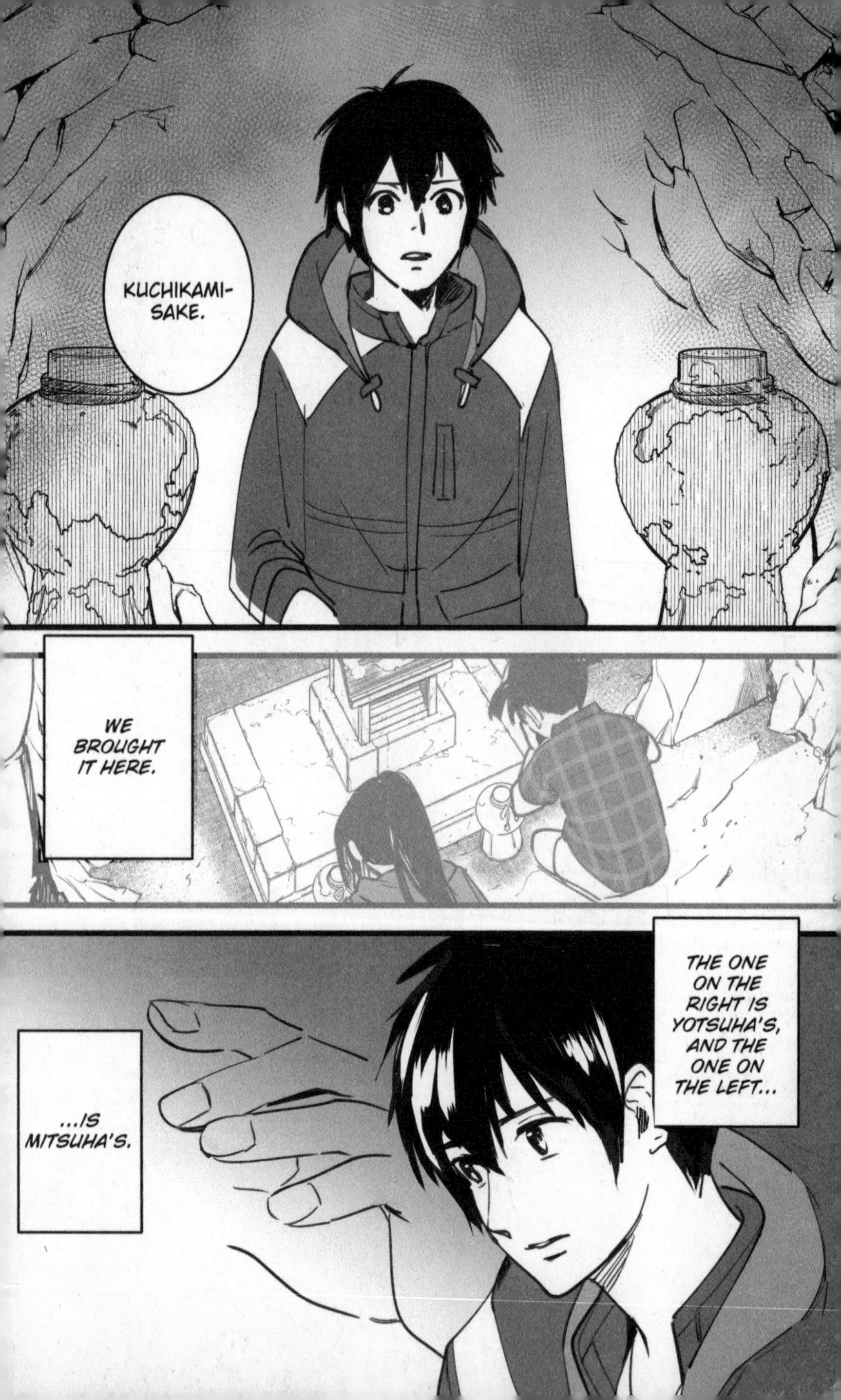
KUCHIKAMI-SAKE.
WE BROUGHT IT HERE.
THE ONE ON THE RIGHT IS YOTSUHA'S, AND THE ONE ON THE LEFT...
...IS MITSUHA'S.

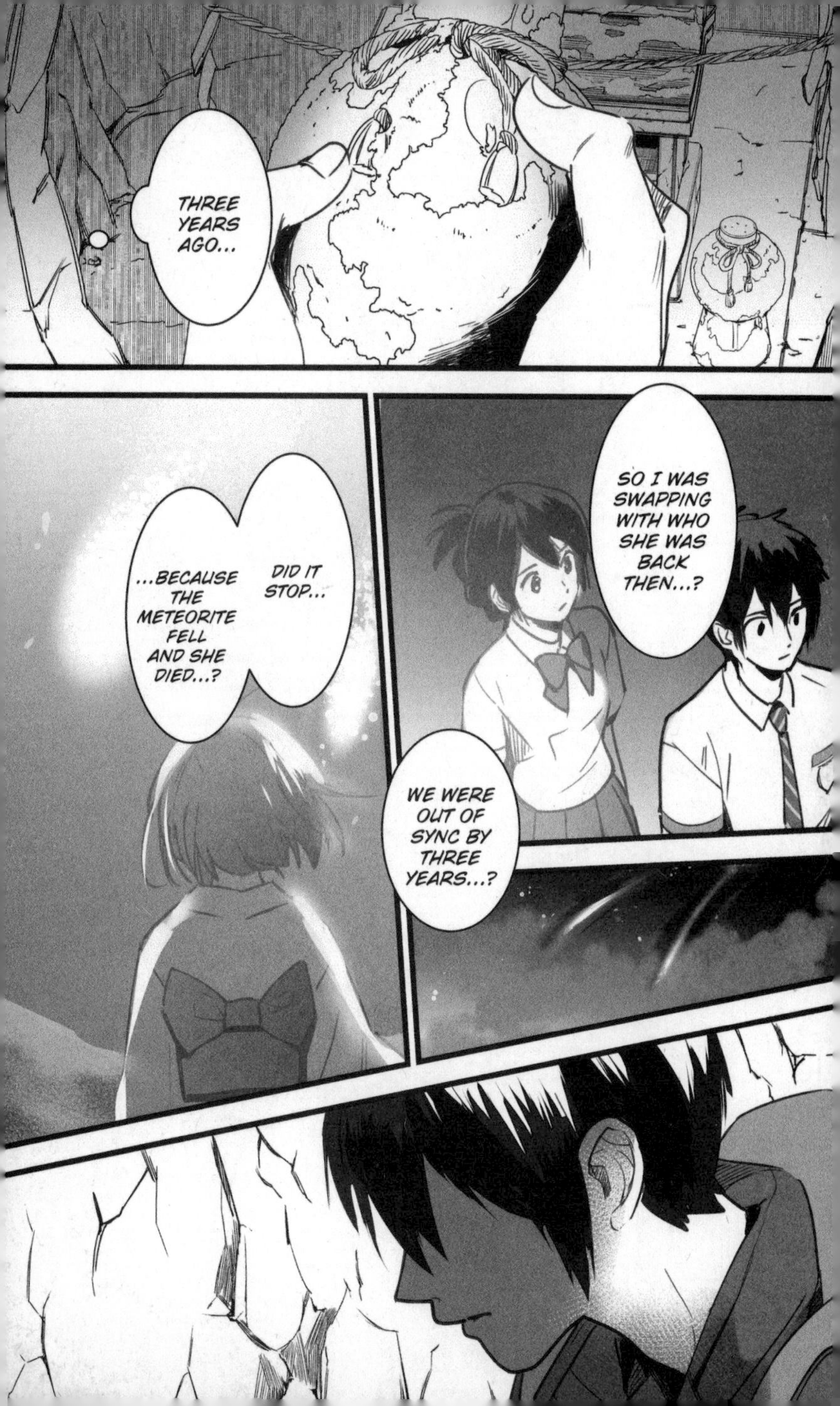
THREE YEARS AGO...
SO I WAS SWAPPING WITH WHO SHE WAS BACK THEN...?
WE WERE OUT OF SYNC BY THREE YEARS...?
DID IT STOP...
...BECAUSE THE METEORITE FELL AND SHE DIED...?

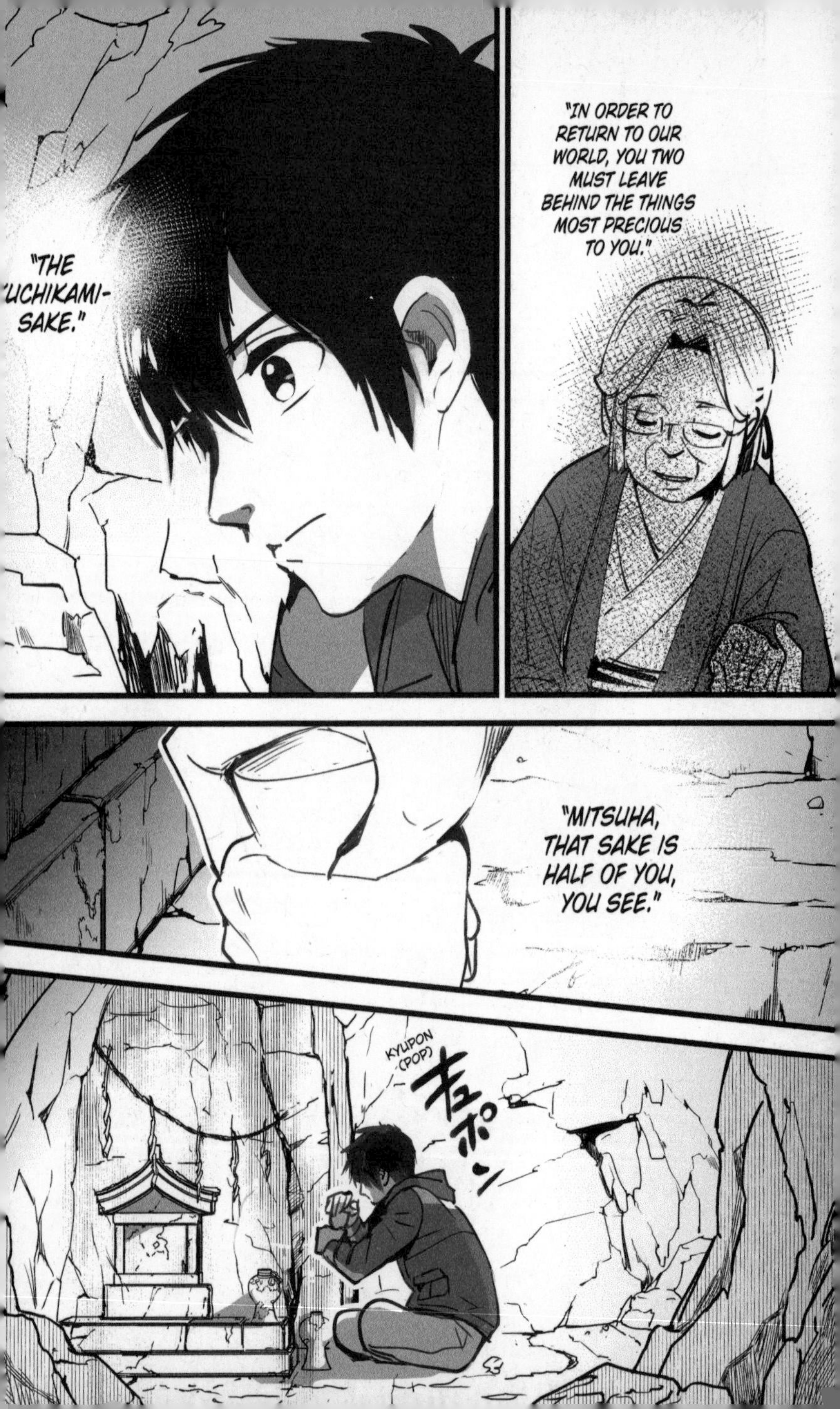
"IN ORDER TO RETURN TO OUR WORLD, YOU TWO MUST LEAVE BEHIND THE THINGS MOST PRECIOUS TO YOU."
"THE UCHIKAMI-SAKE."
"MITSUHA, THAT SAKE IS HALF OF YOU, YOU SEE."
KYUPON (POP)
キュポン

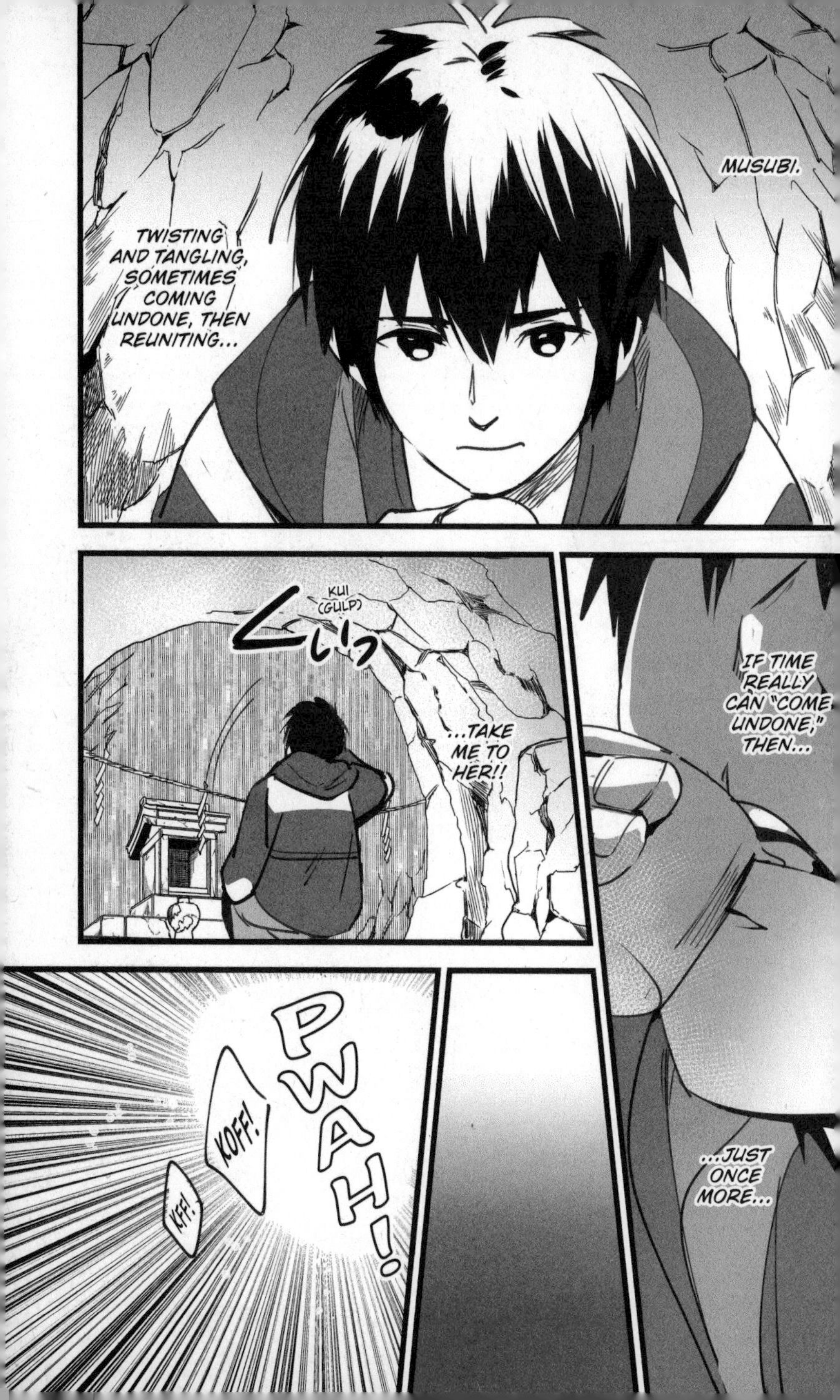
MUSUBI.
TWISTING AND TANGLING, SOMETIMES COMING UNDONE, THEN REUNITING...
IF TIME REALLY CAN "COME UNDONE," THEN...
...JUST ONCE MORE...
KUI (GULP)
...TAKE ME TO HER!!
PWAH!
KOFF!
KFF!

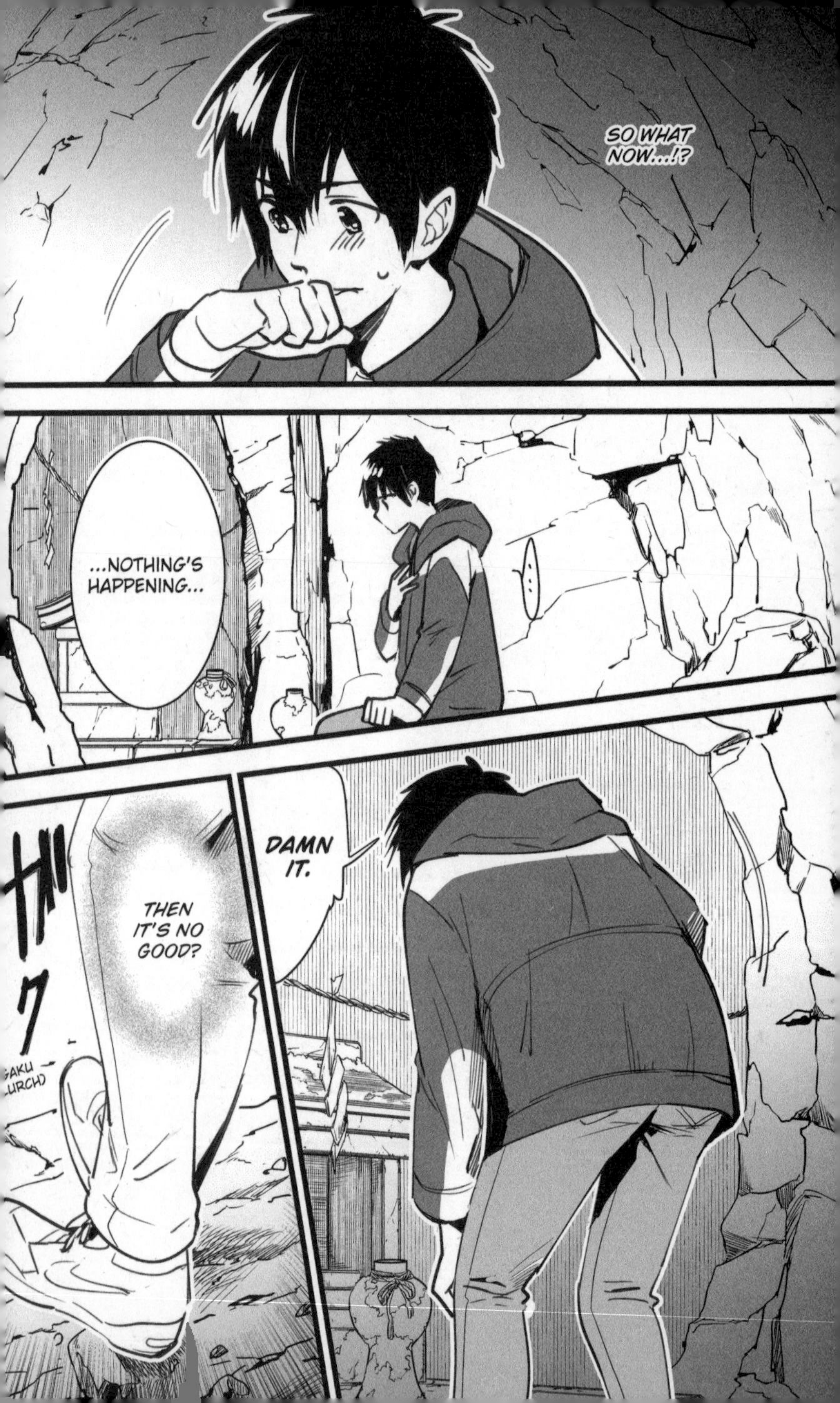
SO WHAT NOW...!?
...
...NOTHING'S HAPPENING...
DAMN IT.
THEN IT'S NO GOOD?

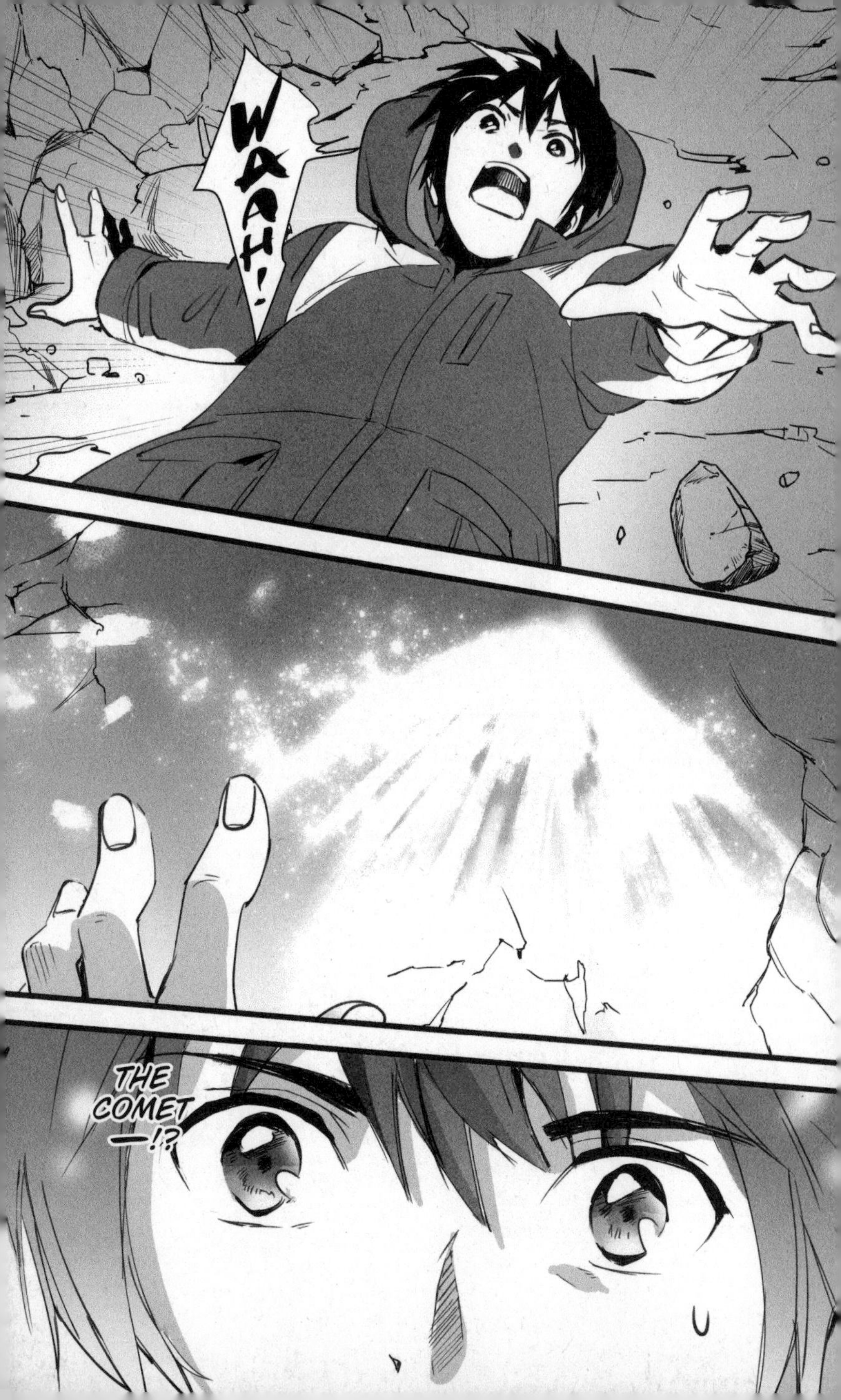
WAAH!
THE COMET —!?

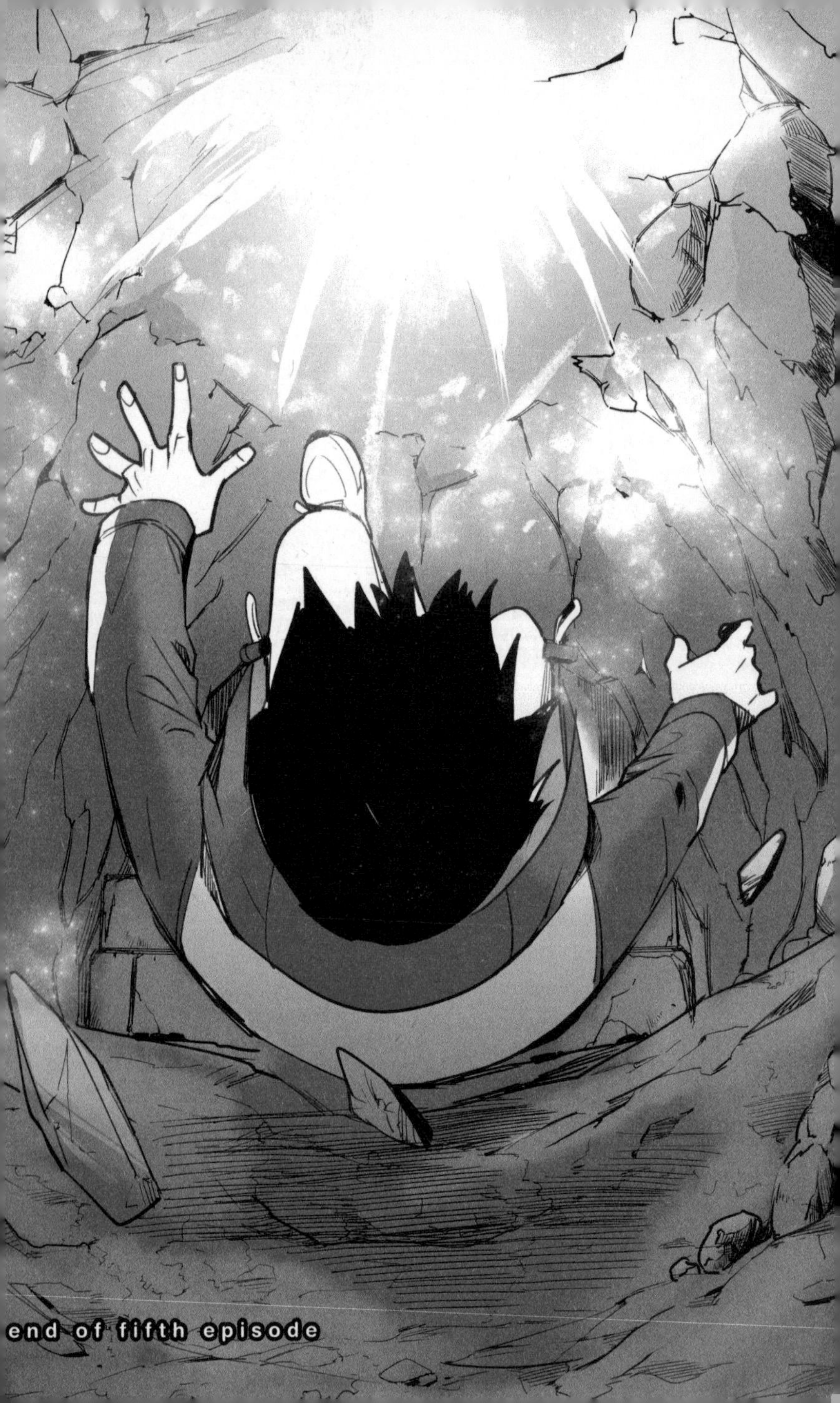
end of fifth episode

your name.

your name.

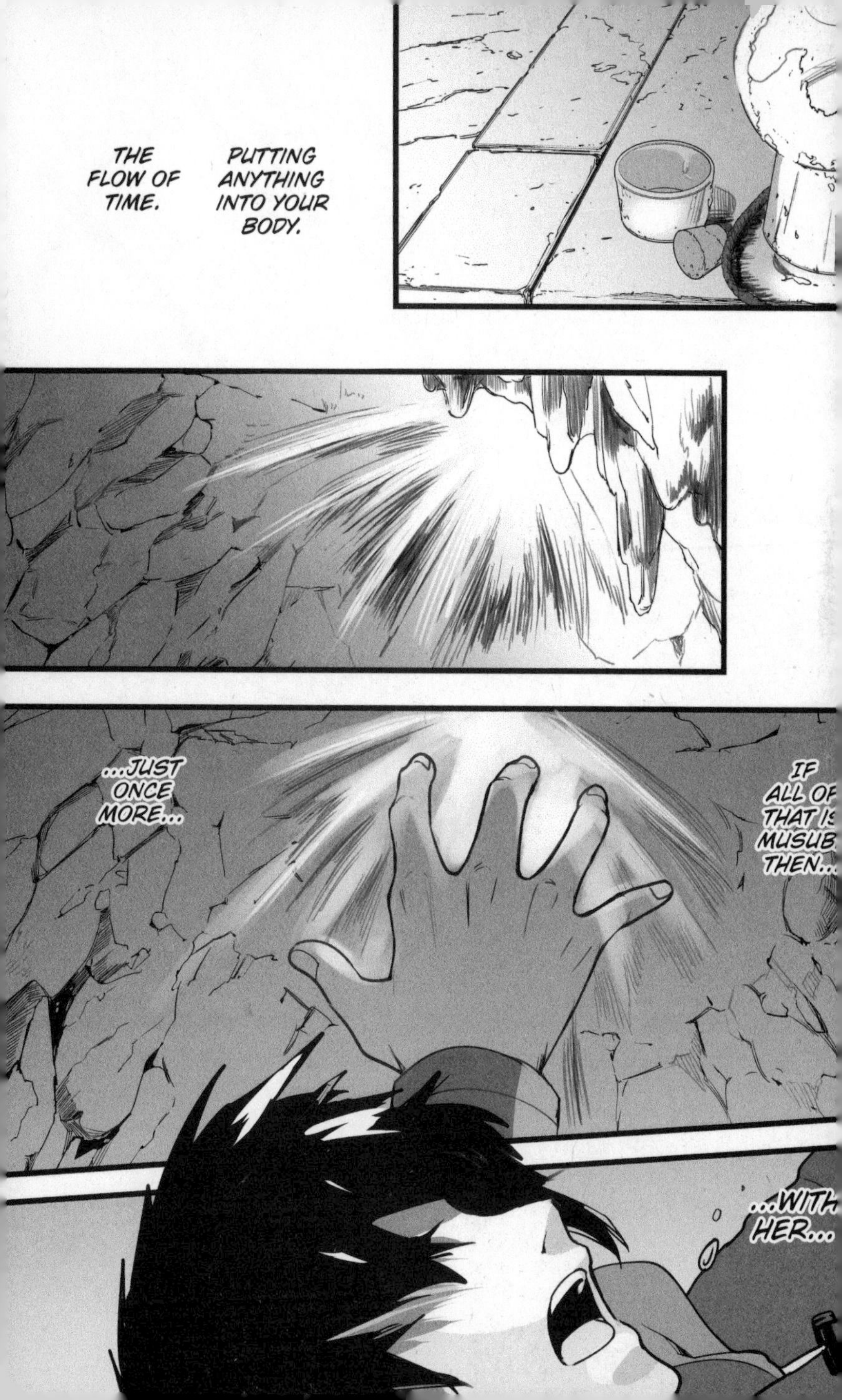
PUTTING ANYTHING INTO YOUR BODY.
THE FLOW OF TIME.
IF ALL OF THAT IS MUSUB THEN...
...JUST ONCE MORE...
...WITH HER...

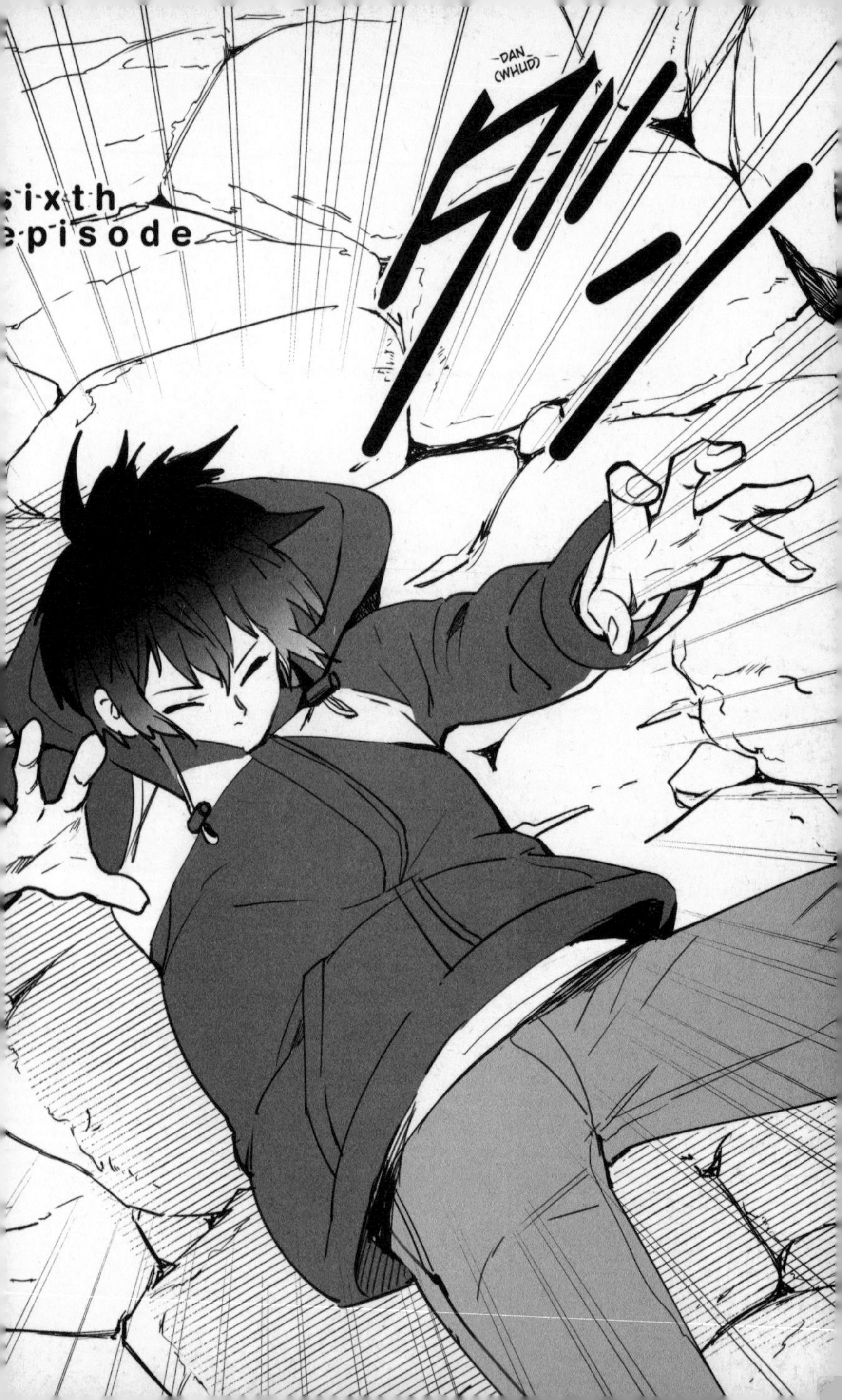
sixth
episode
DAN
(WHUD)
ダン

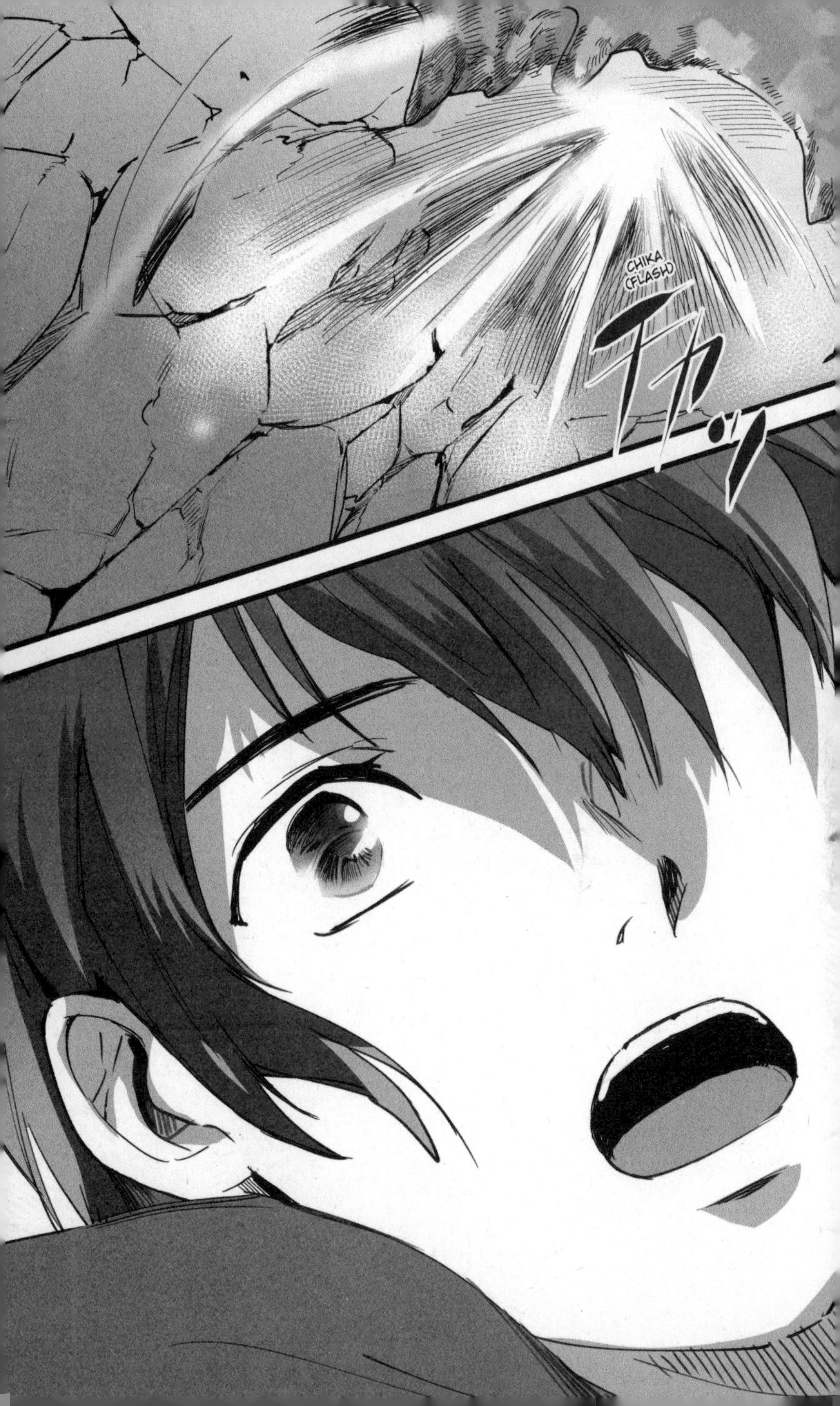
CHIKA
(FLASH)
チカッ

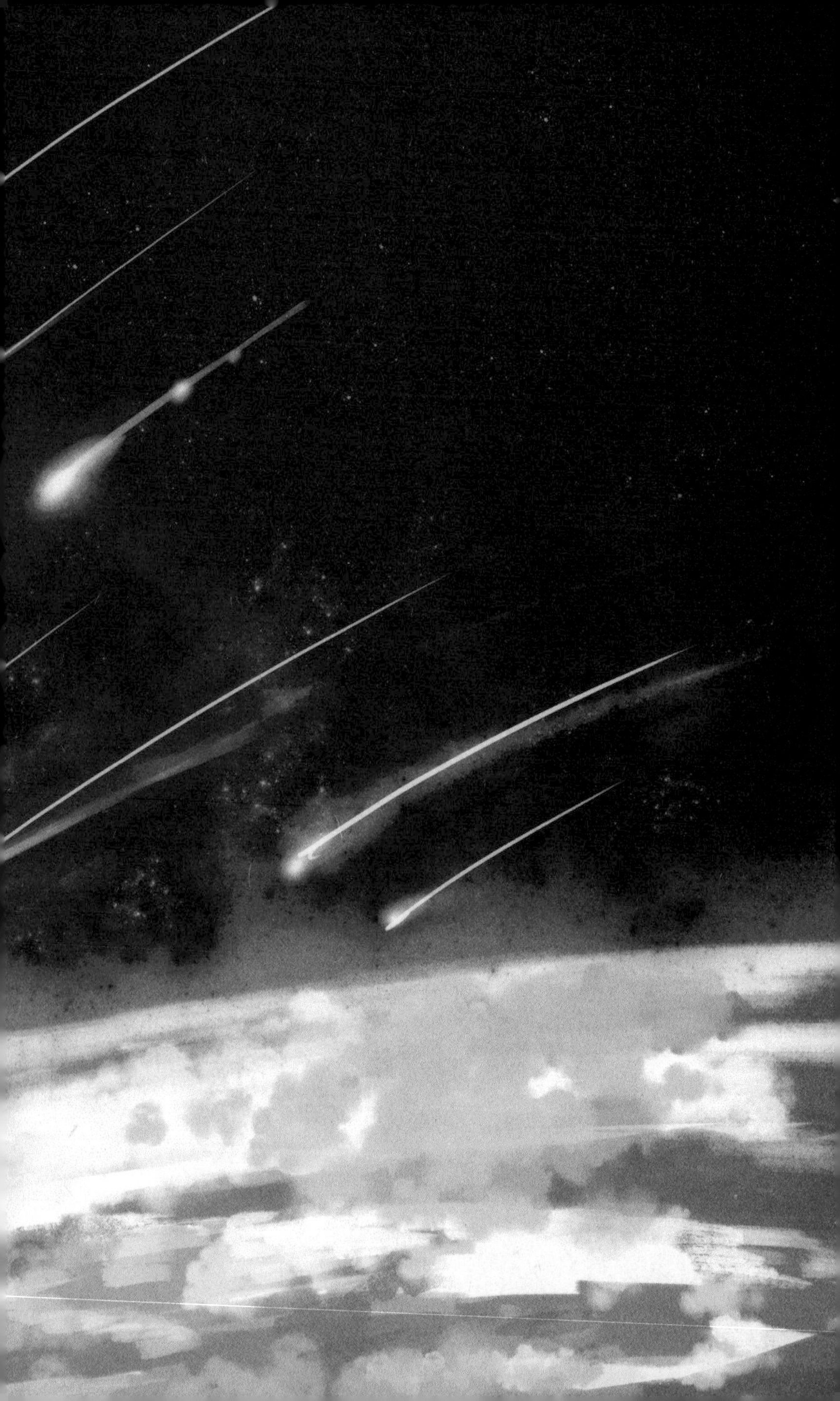

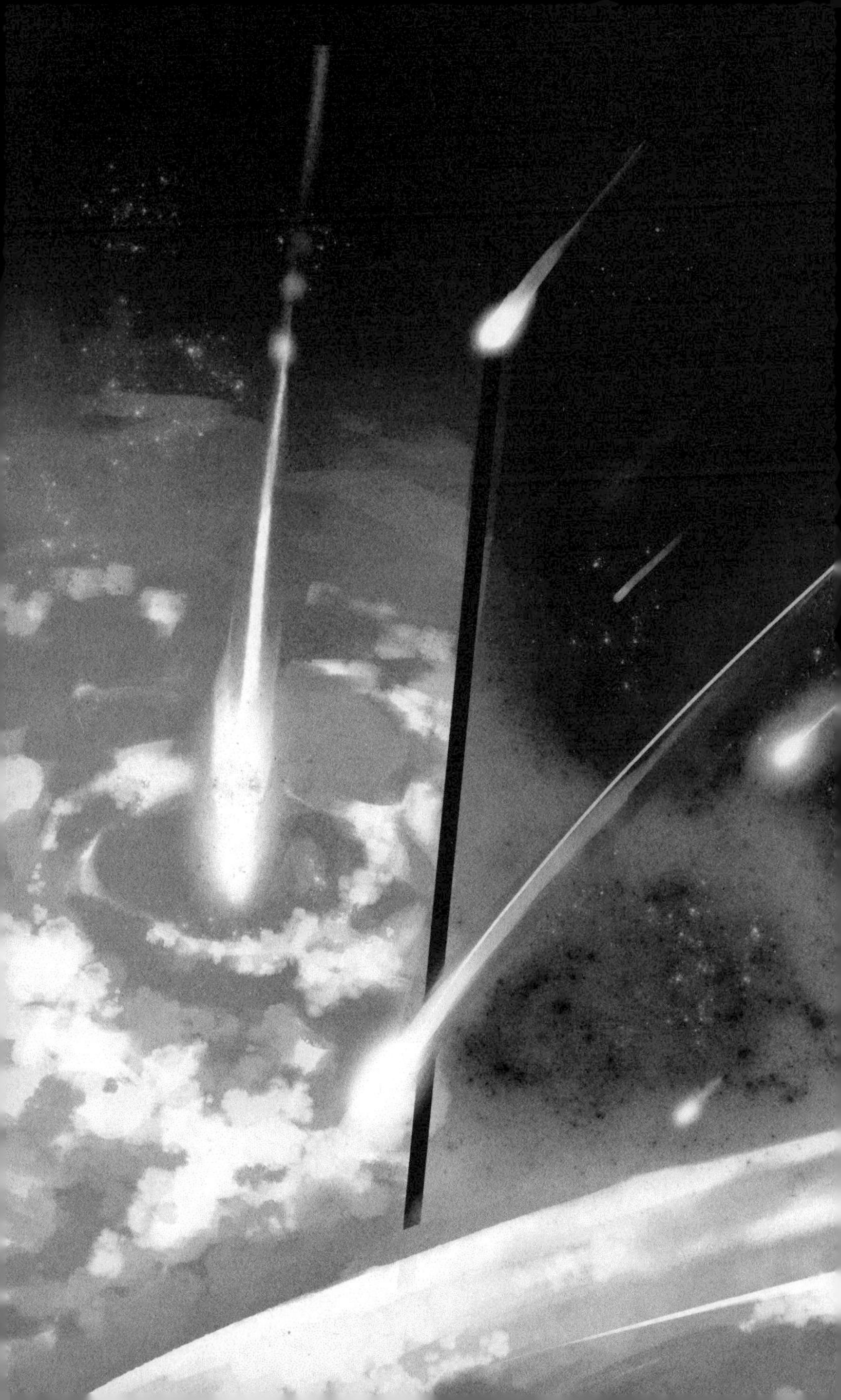

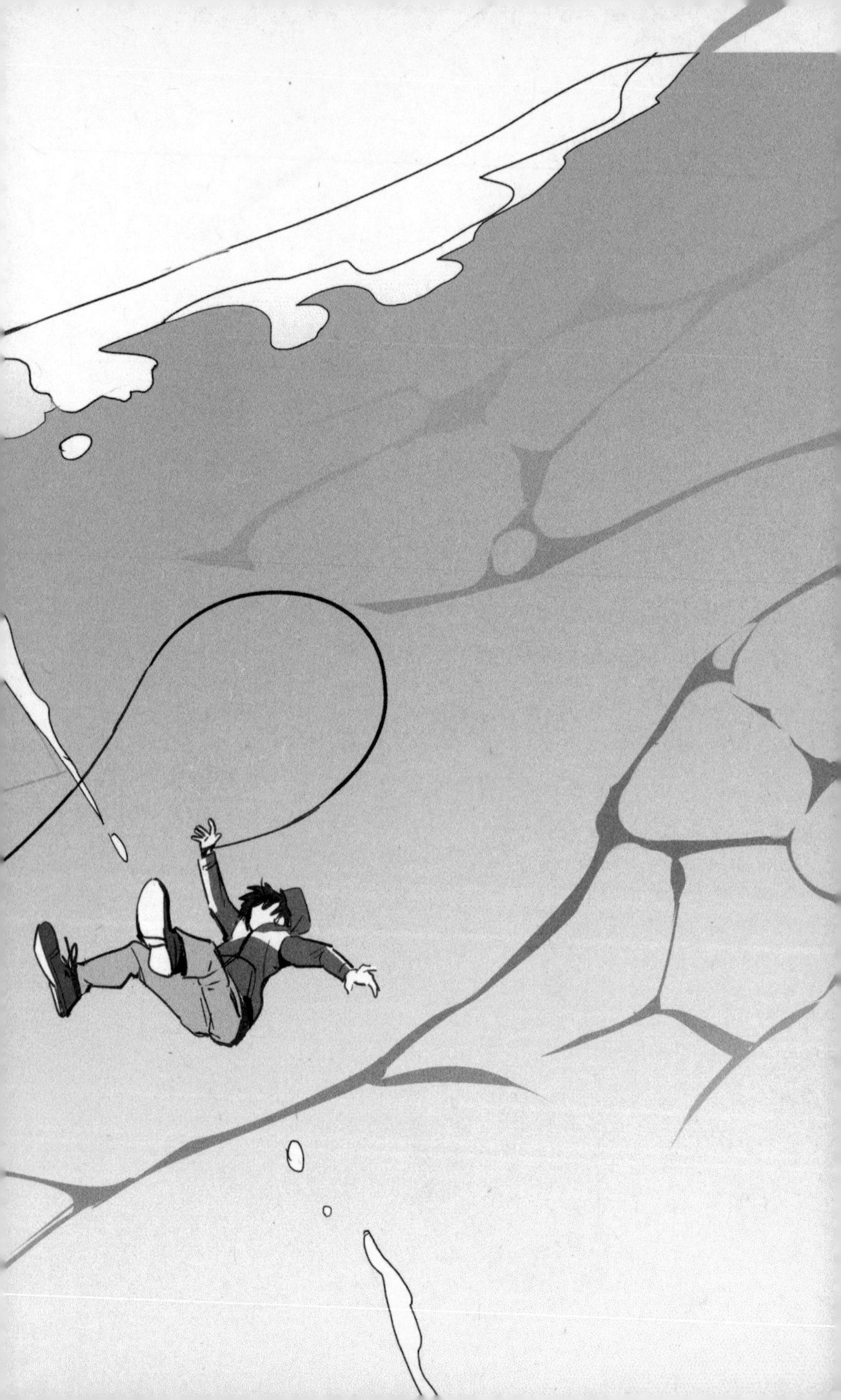

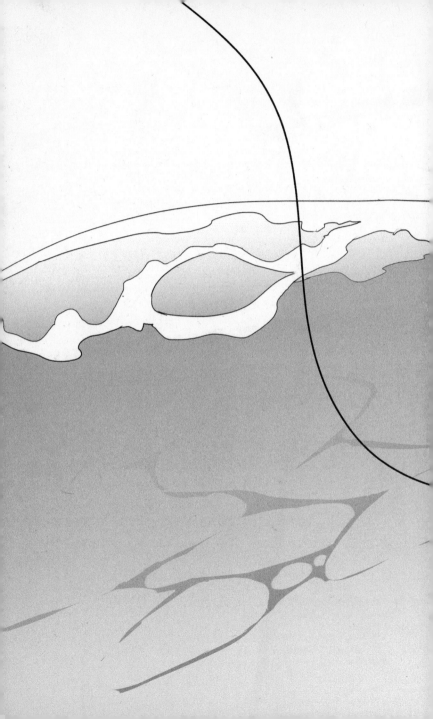

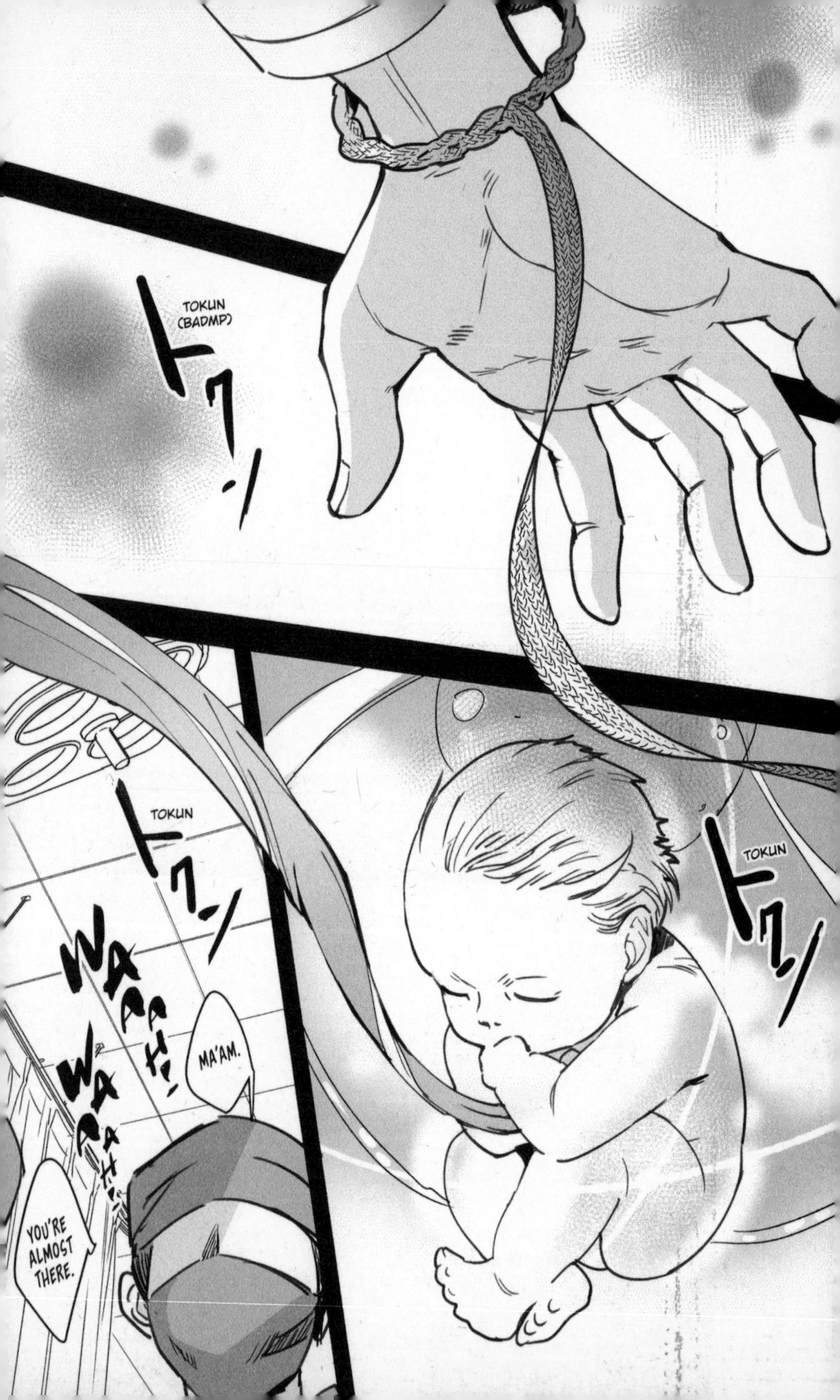

TOKUN (BADMP)
TOKUN
TOKUN
MA'AM.
WAAAH! WAAAH!
YOU'RE ALMOST THERE.

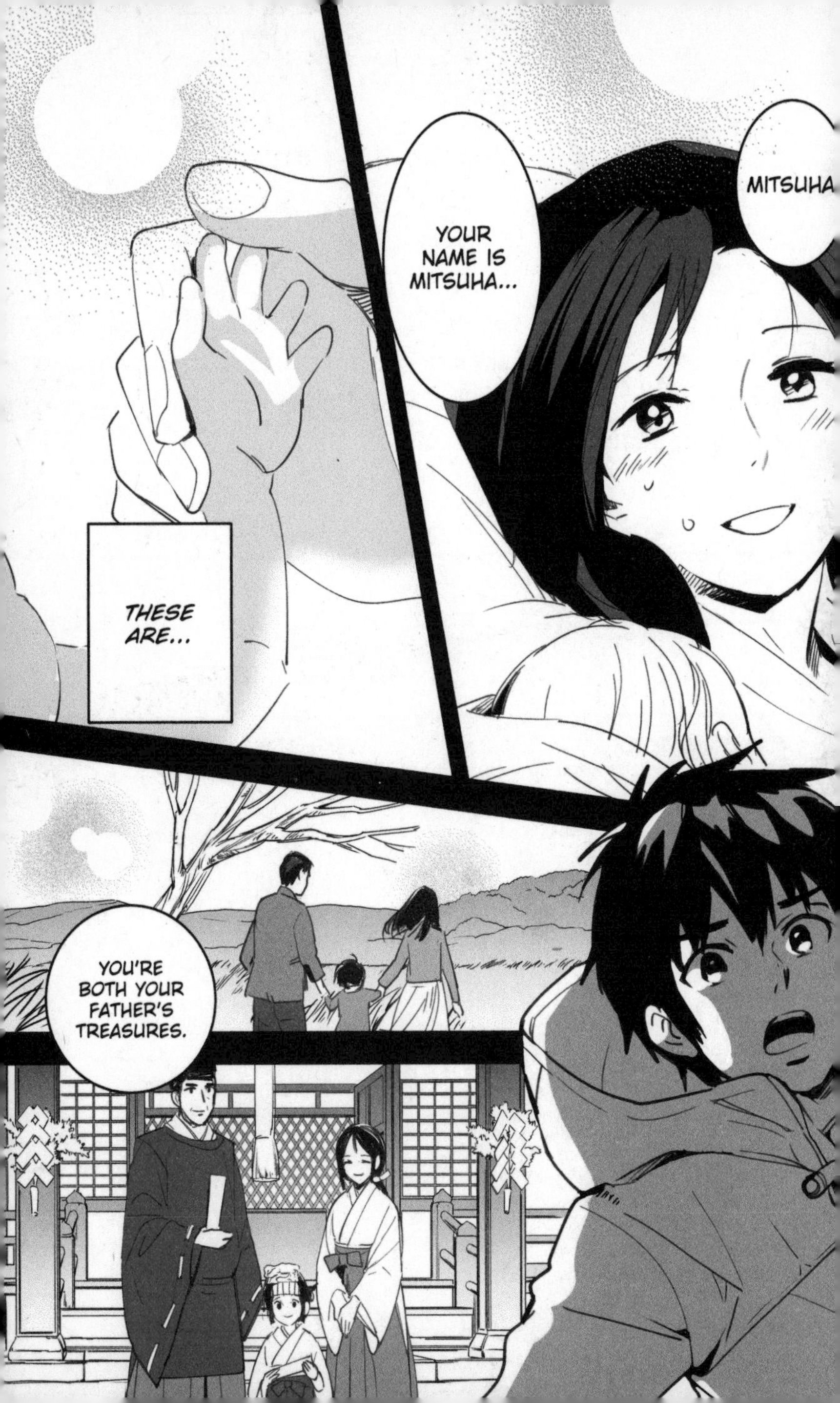
MITSUHA
YOUR NAME IS MITSUHA...
THESE ARE...
YOU'RE BOTH YOUR FATHER'S TREASURES.

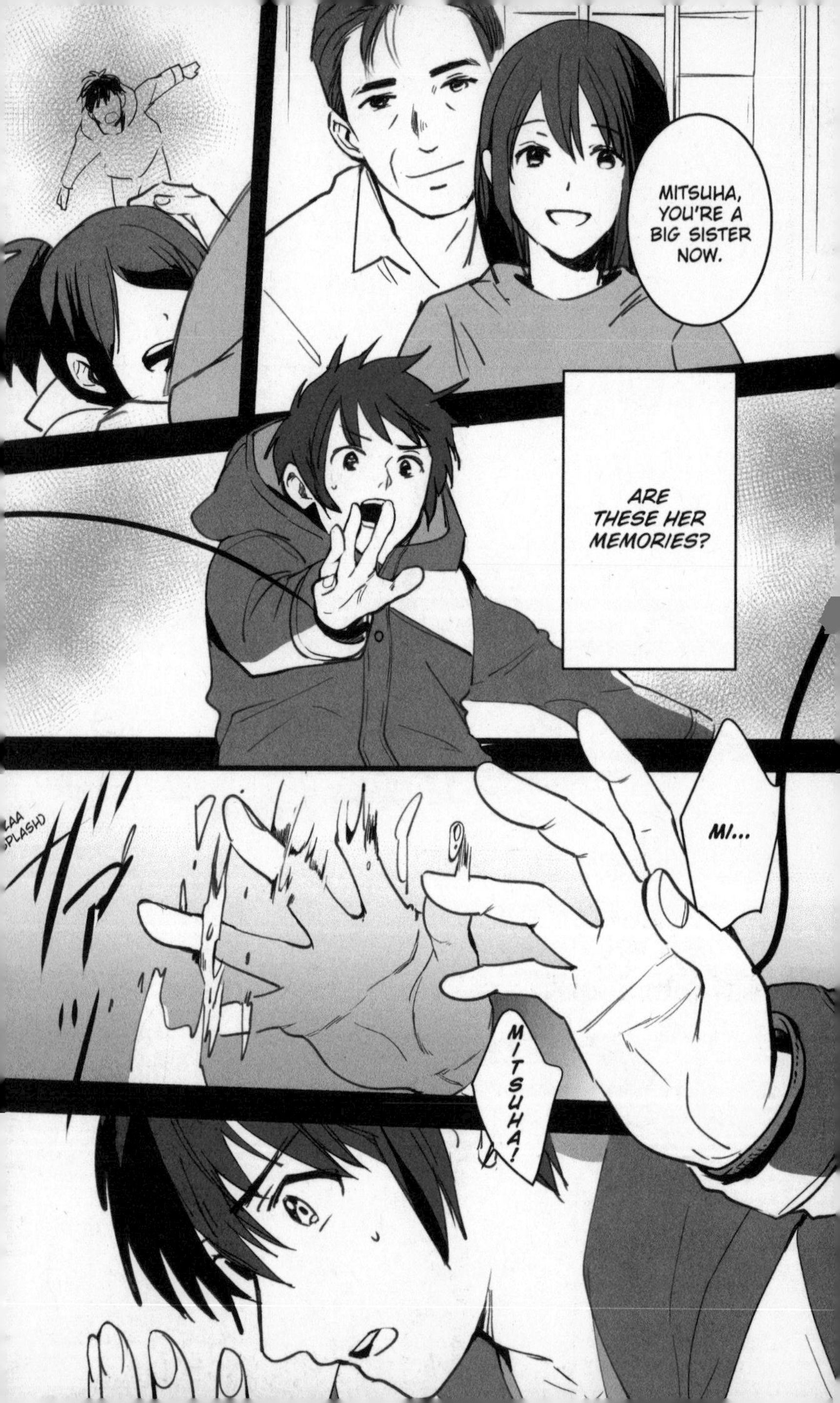
MITSUHA, YOU'RE A BIG SISTER NOW.
ARE THESE HER MEMORIES?
MI...
LAA
SPLASH)
MITSUHA!

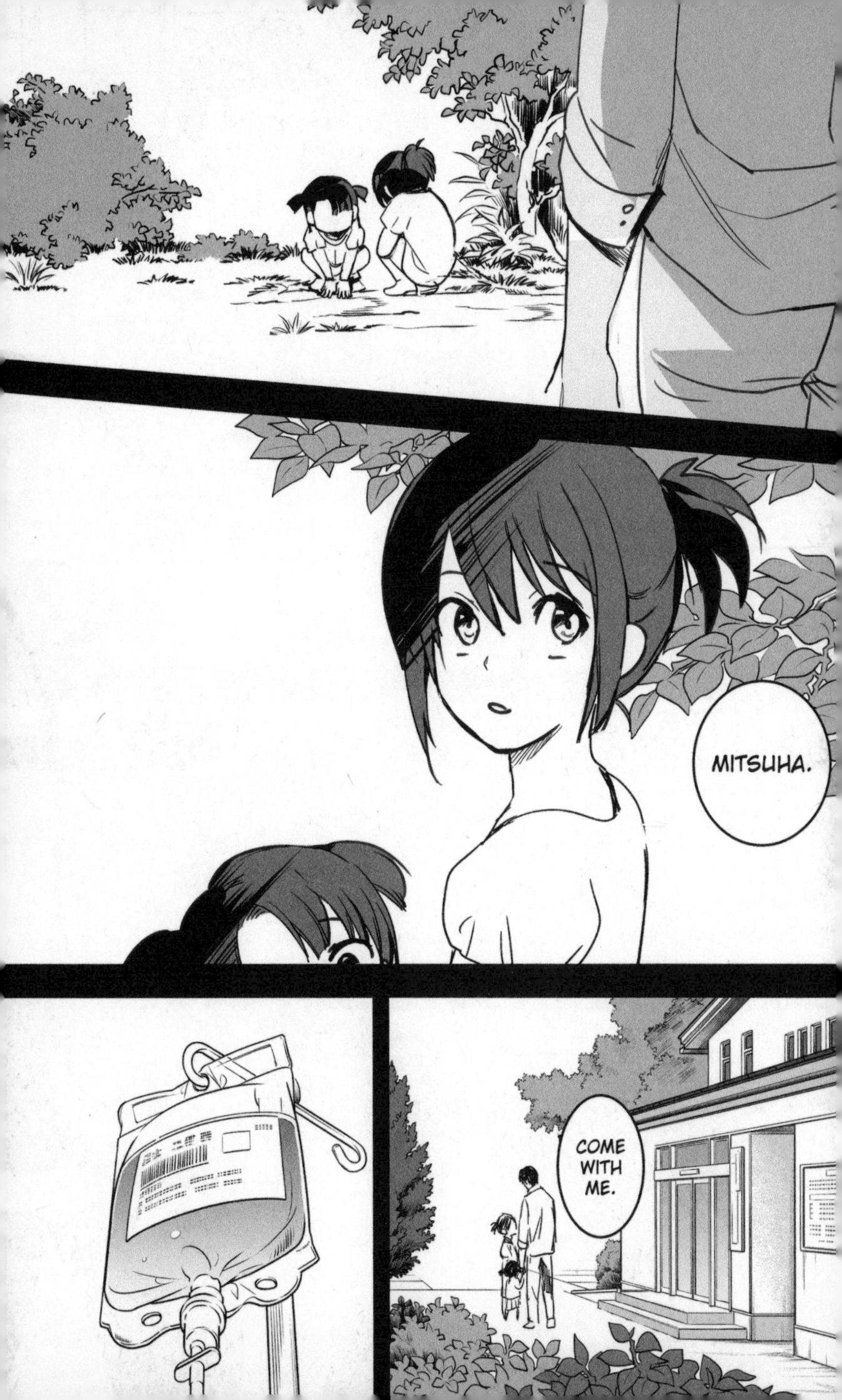
MITSUHA.
COME WITH ME.

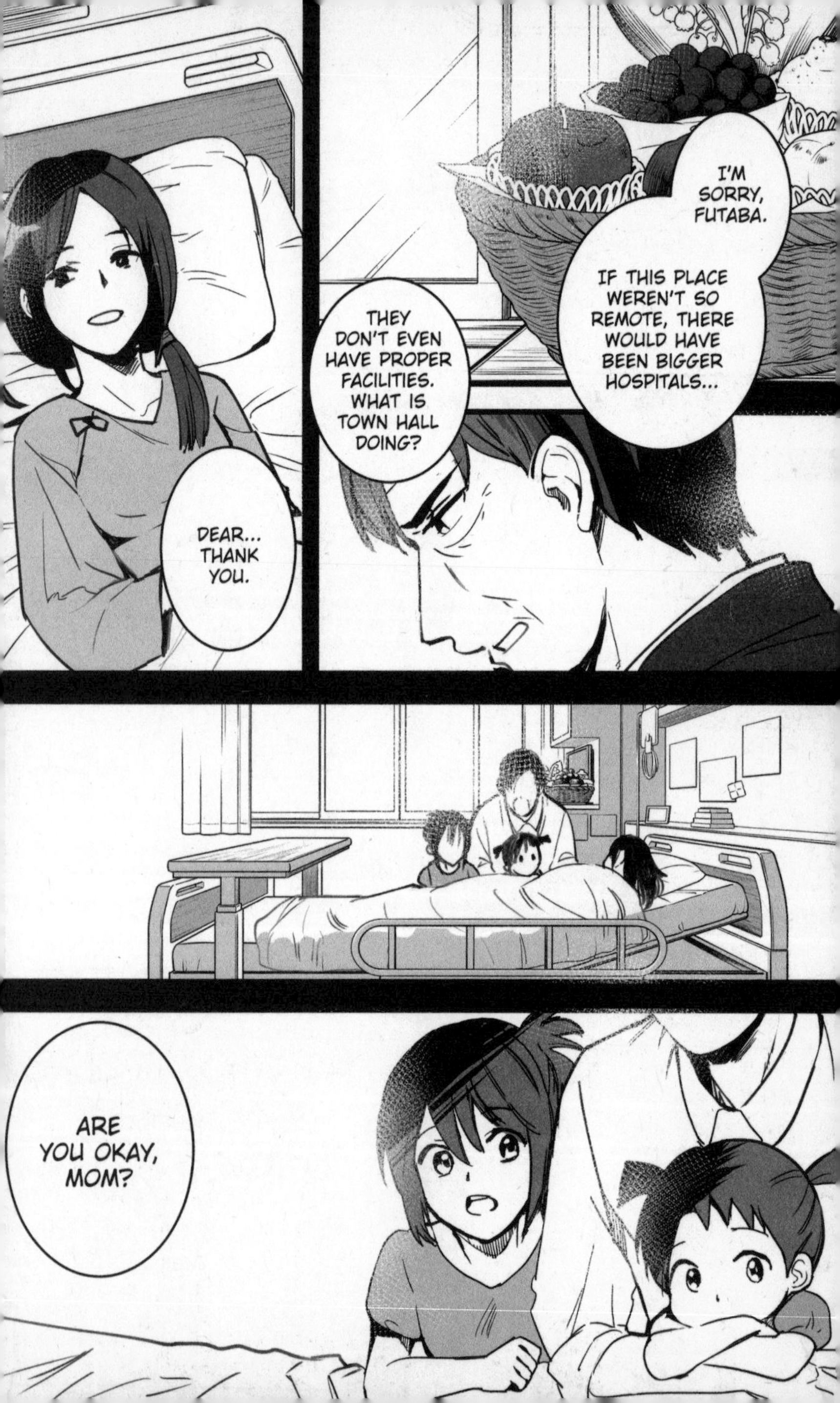
I'M SORRY, FUTABA.
IF THIS PLACE WEREN'T SO REMOTE, THERE WOULD HAVE BEEN BIGGER HOSPITALS...
THEY DON'T EVEN HAVE PROPER FACILITIES. WHAT IS TOWN HALL DOING?
DEAR... THANK YOU.
ARE YOU OKAY, MOM?

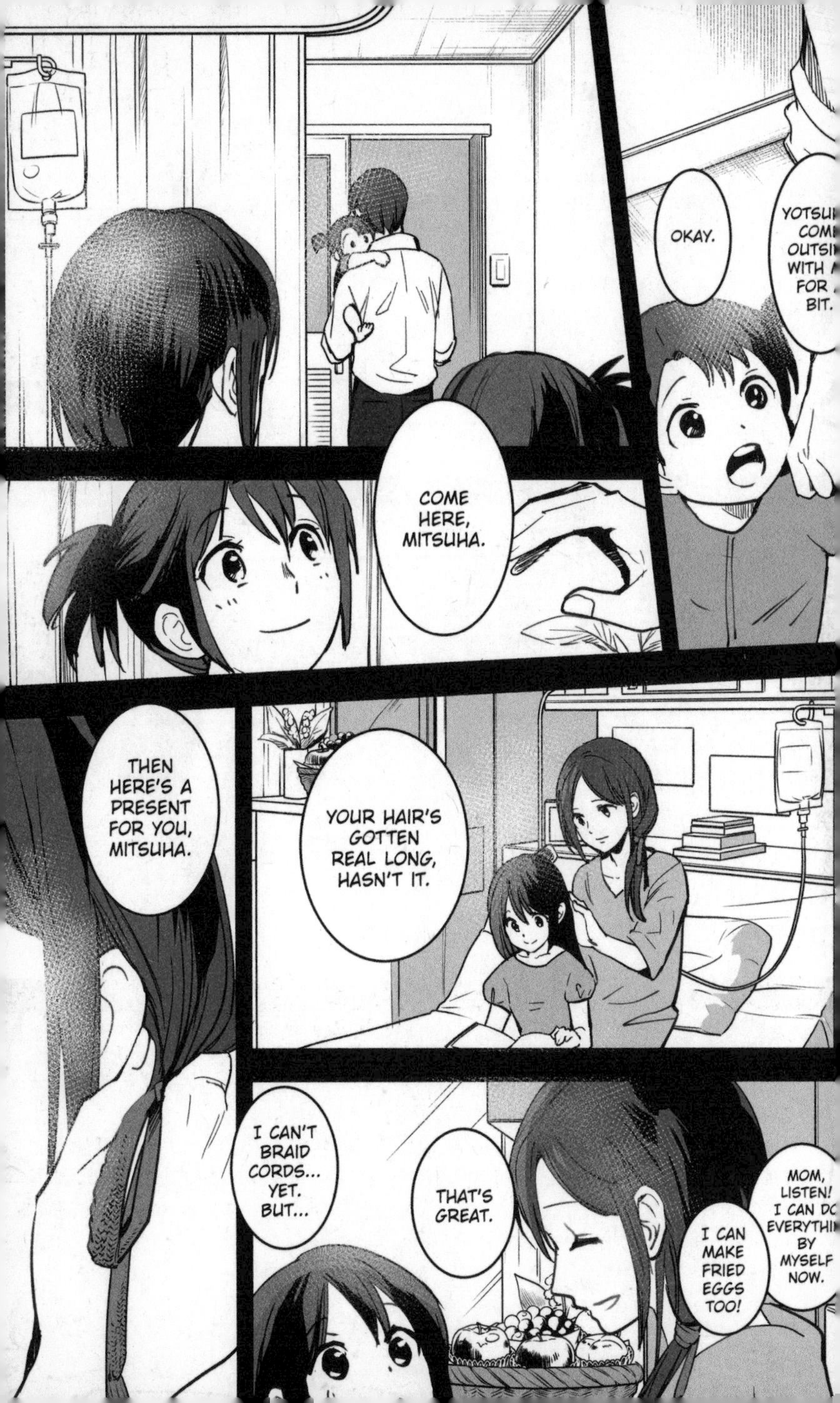
YOTSU COM OUTSI WITH FOR BIT.
OKAY.
COME HERE, MITSUHA.
YOUR HAIR'S GOTTEN REAL LONG, HASN'T IT.
MOM, LISTEN! I CAN DO EVERYTHI BY MYSELF NOW.
I CAN MAKE FRIED EGGS TOO!
THAT'S GREAT.
I CAN'T BRAID CORDS... YET. BUT...
THEN HERE'S A PRESENT FOR YOU, MITSUHA.

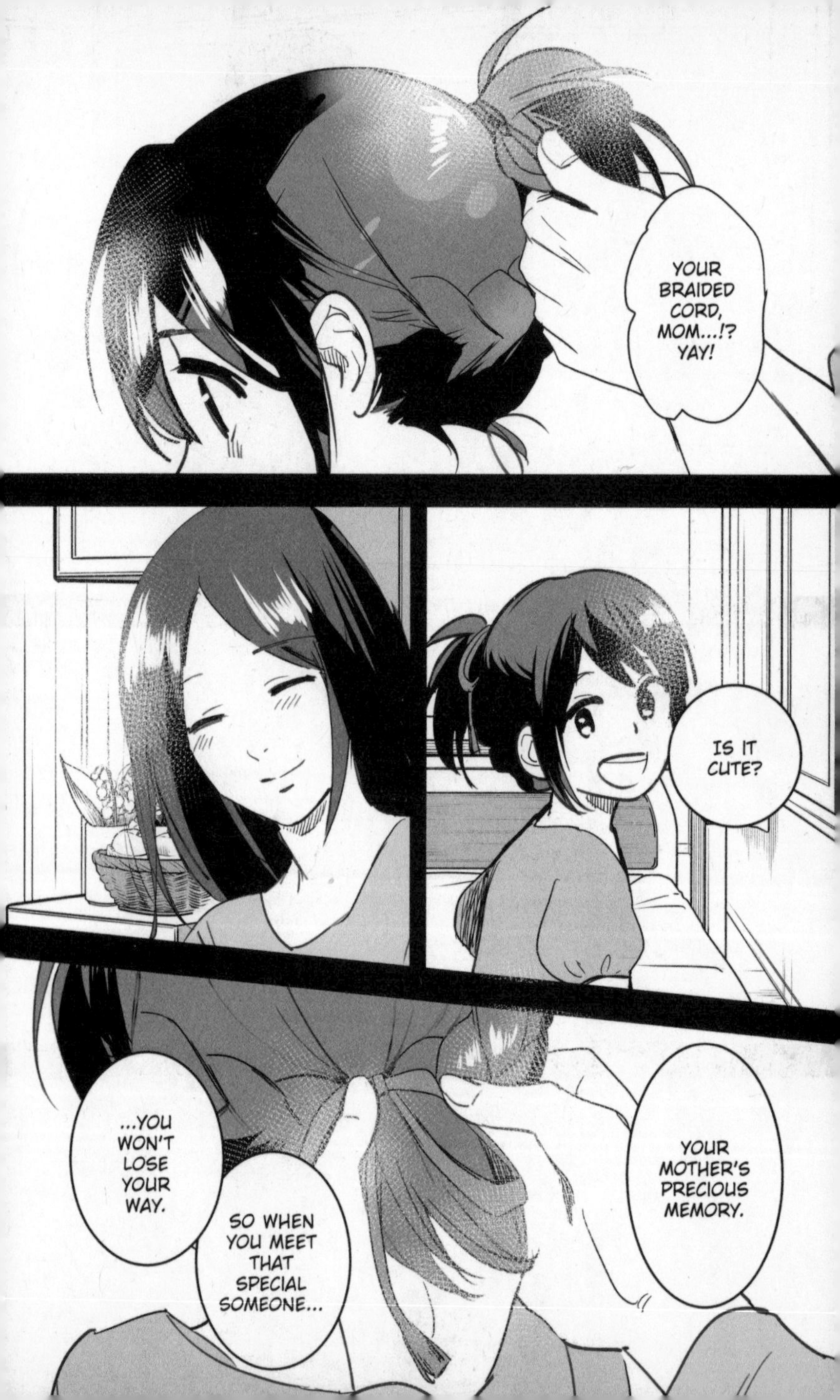
YOUR BRAIDED CORD, MOM...!? YAY!
IS IT CUTE?
YOUR MOTHER'S PRECIOUS MEMORY.
SO WHEN YOU MEET THAT SPECIAL SOMEONE...
...YOU WON'T LOSE YOUR WAY.

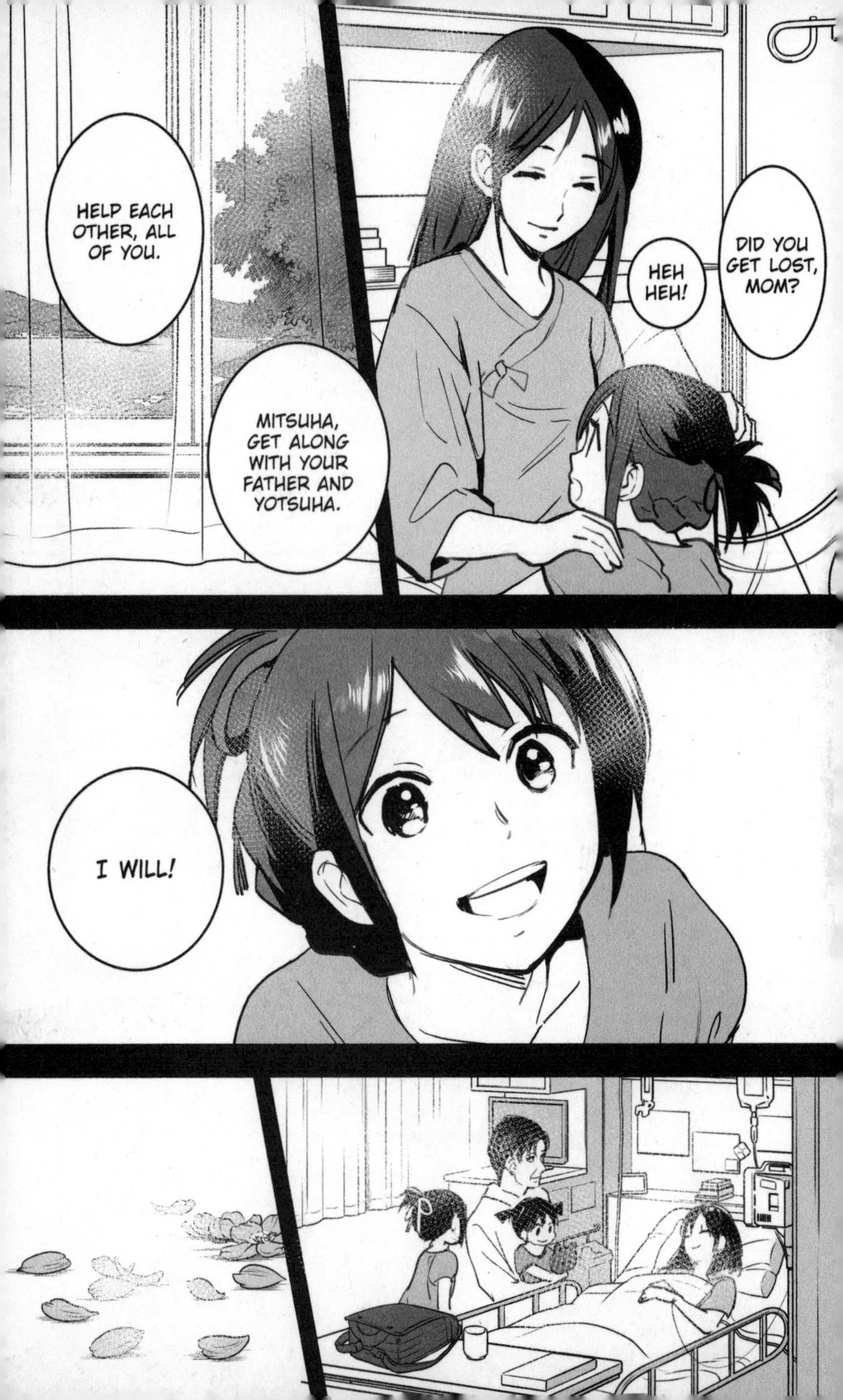
DID YOU GET LOST, MOM?
HEH HEH!
MITSUHA, GET ALONG WITH YOUR FATHER AND YOTSUHA.
HELP EACH OTHER, ALL OF YOU.
I WILL!

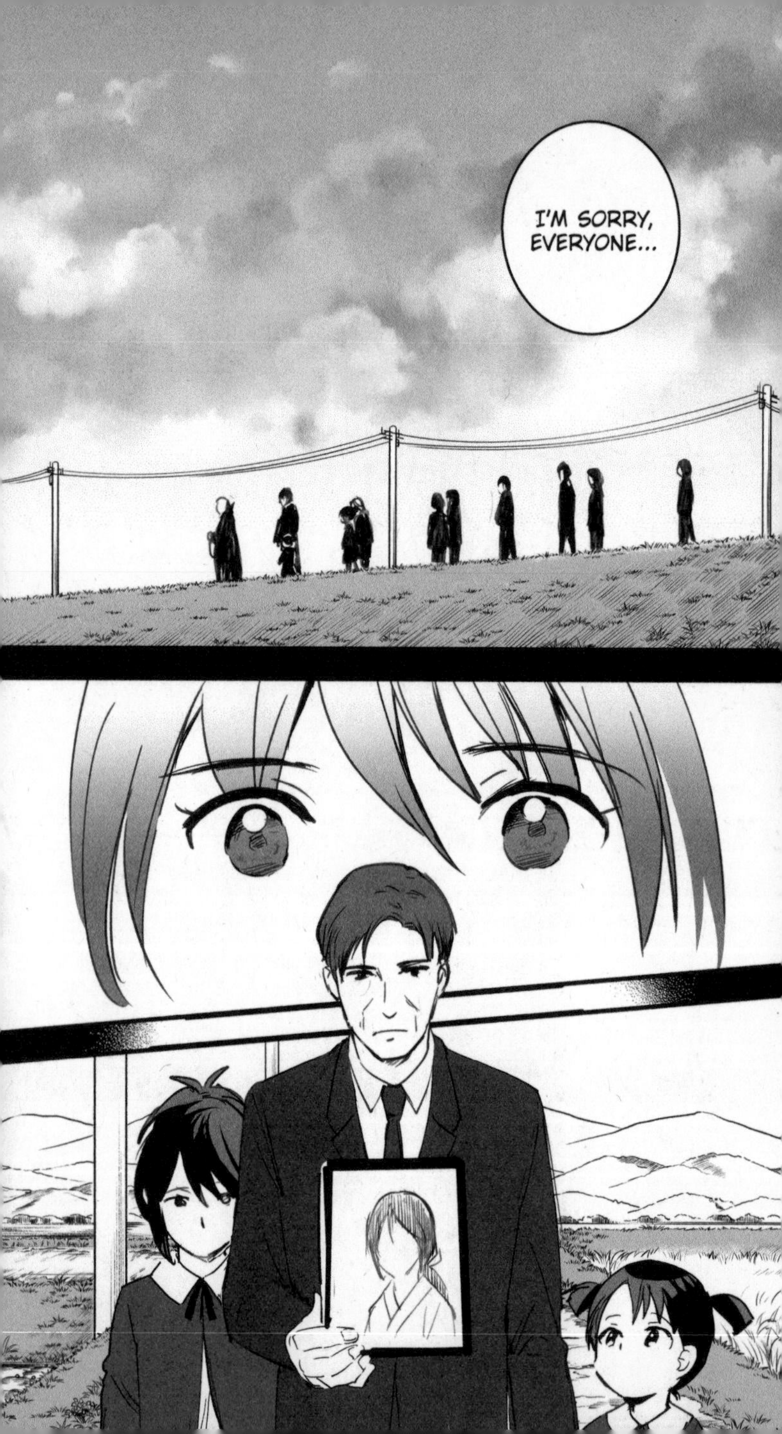
I'M SORRY,
EVERYONE...

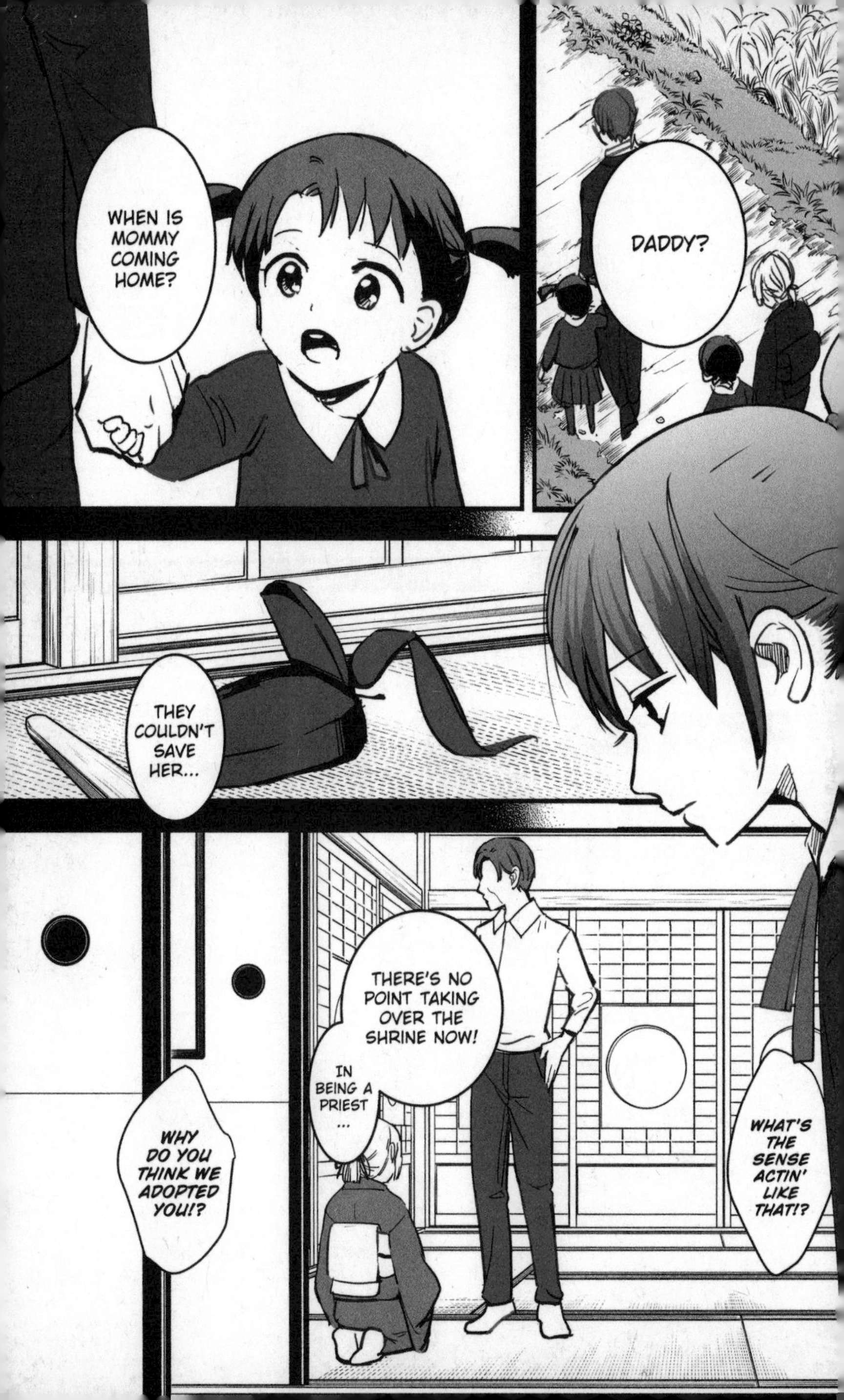
DADDY?
WHEN IS MOMMY COMING HOME?
THEY COULDN'T SAVE HER...
WHAT'S THE SENSE ACTIN' LIKE THAT!?
THERE'S NO POINT TAKING OVER THE SHRINE NOW!
IN BEING A PRIEST ...
WHY DO YOU THINK WE ADOPTED YOU!?

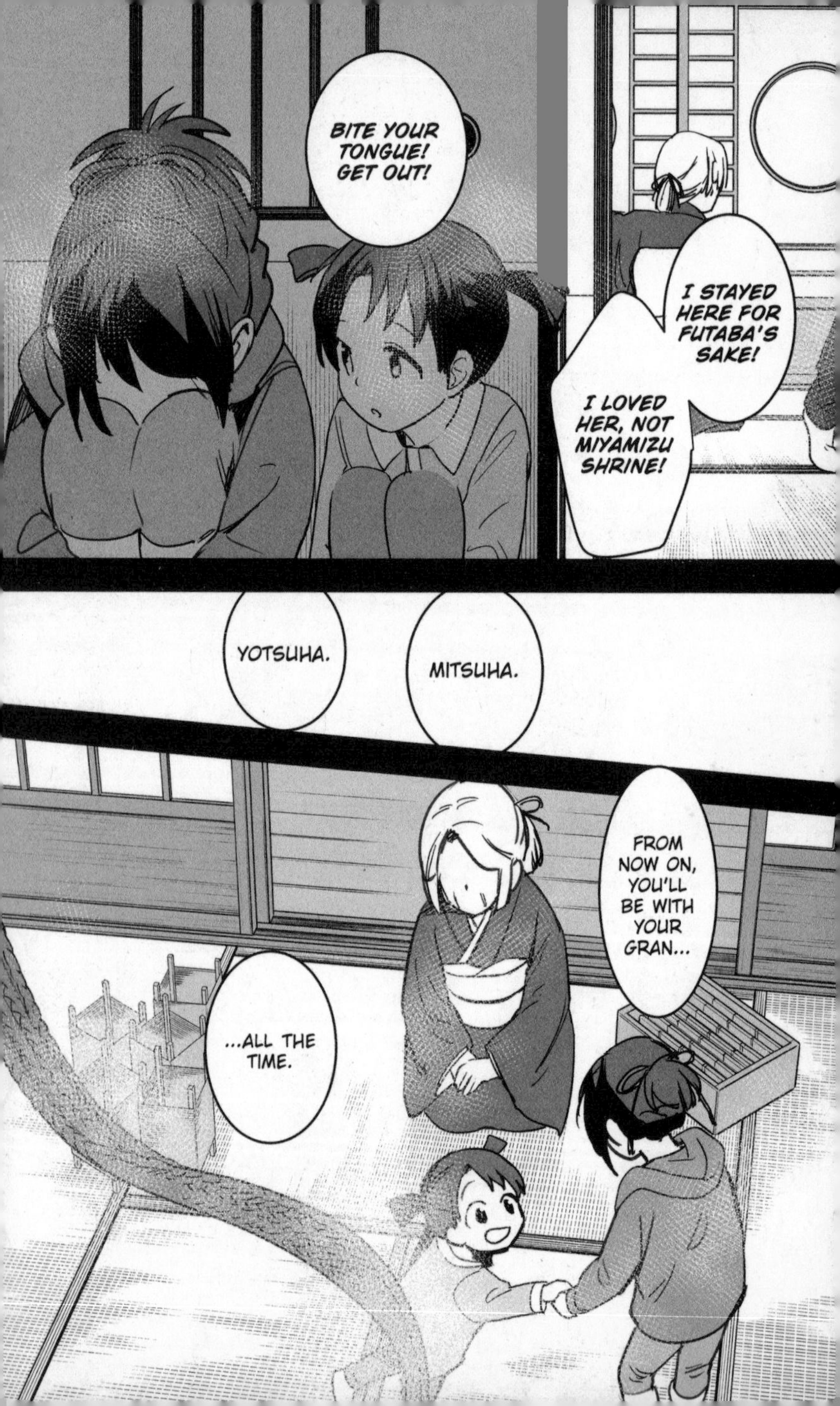
I STAYED HERE FOR FUTABA'S SAKE!
I LOVED HER, NOT MIYAMIZU SHRINE!
BITE YOUR TONGUE! GET OUT!
MITSUHA.
YOTSUHA.
FROM NOW ON, YOU'LL BE WITH YOUR GRAN...
...ALL THE TIME.

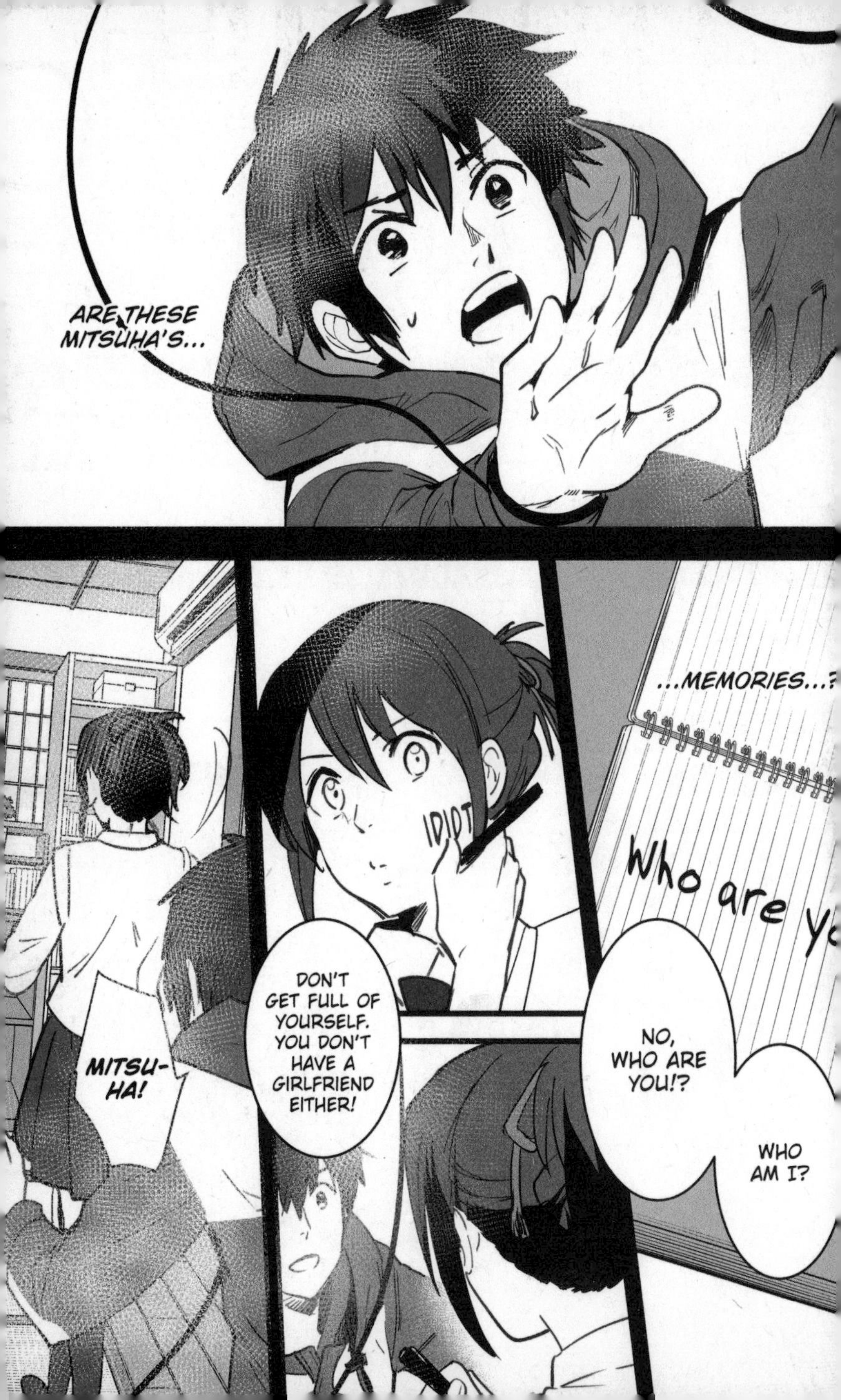
ARE THESE MITSUHA'S...
...MEMORIES...?
Who are y
NO, WHO ARE YOU!?
WHO AM I?
IDIOT
DON'T GET FULL OF YOURSELF. YOU DON'T HAVE A GIRLFRIEND EITHER!
MITSU-HA!

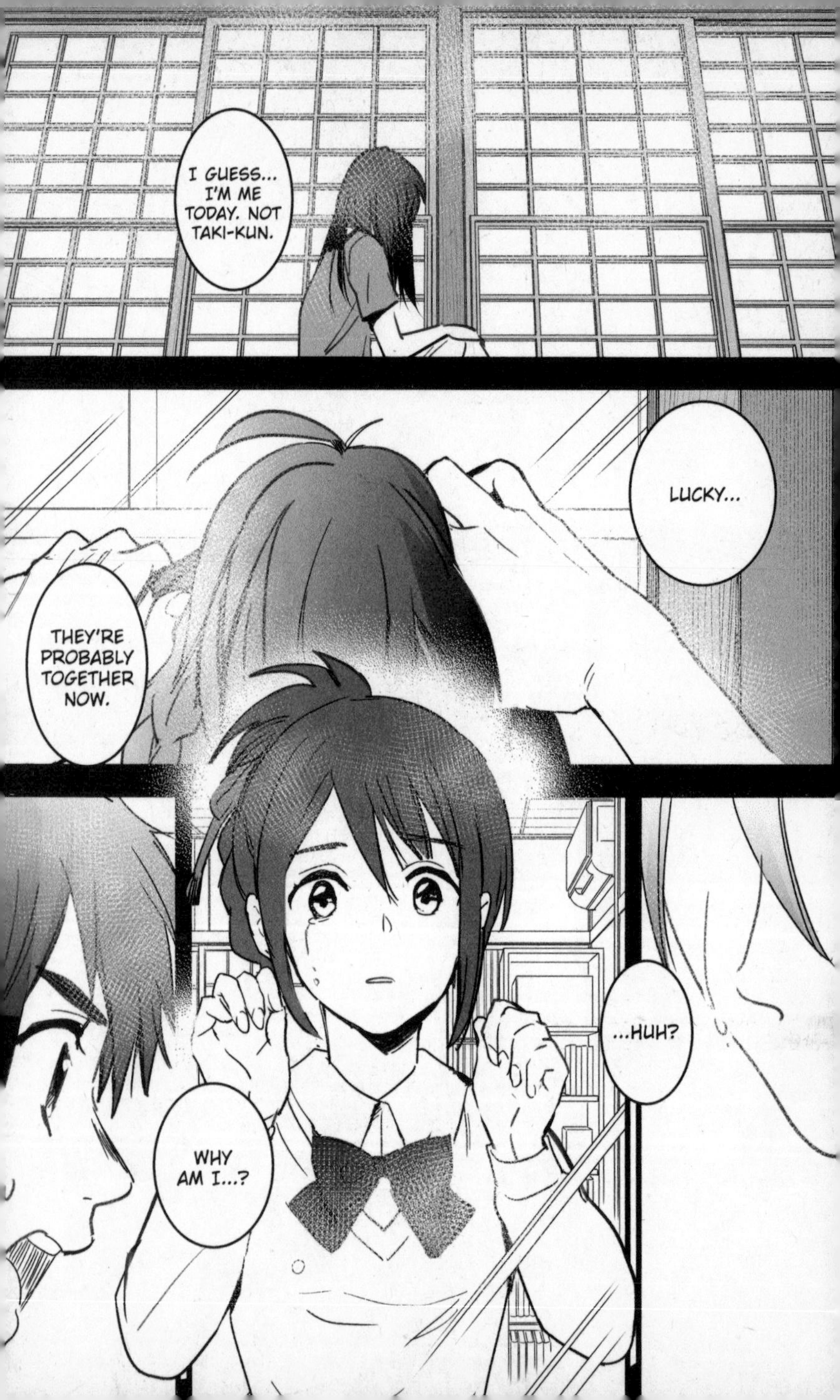
I GUESS... I'M ME TODAY. NOT TAKI-KUN.
LUCKY...
THEY'RE PROBABLY TOGETHER NOW.
...HUH?
WHY AM I...?

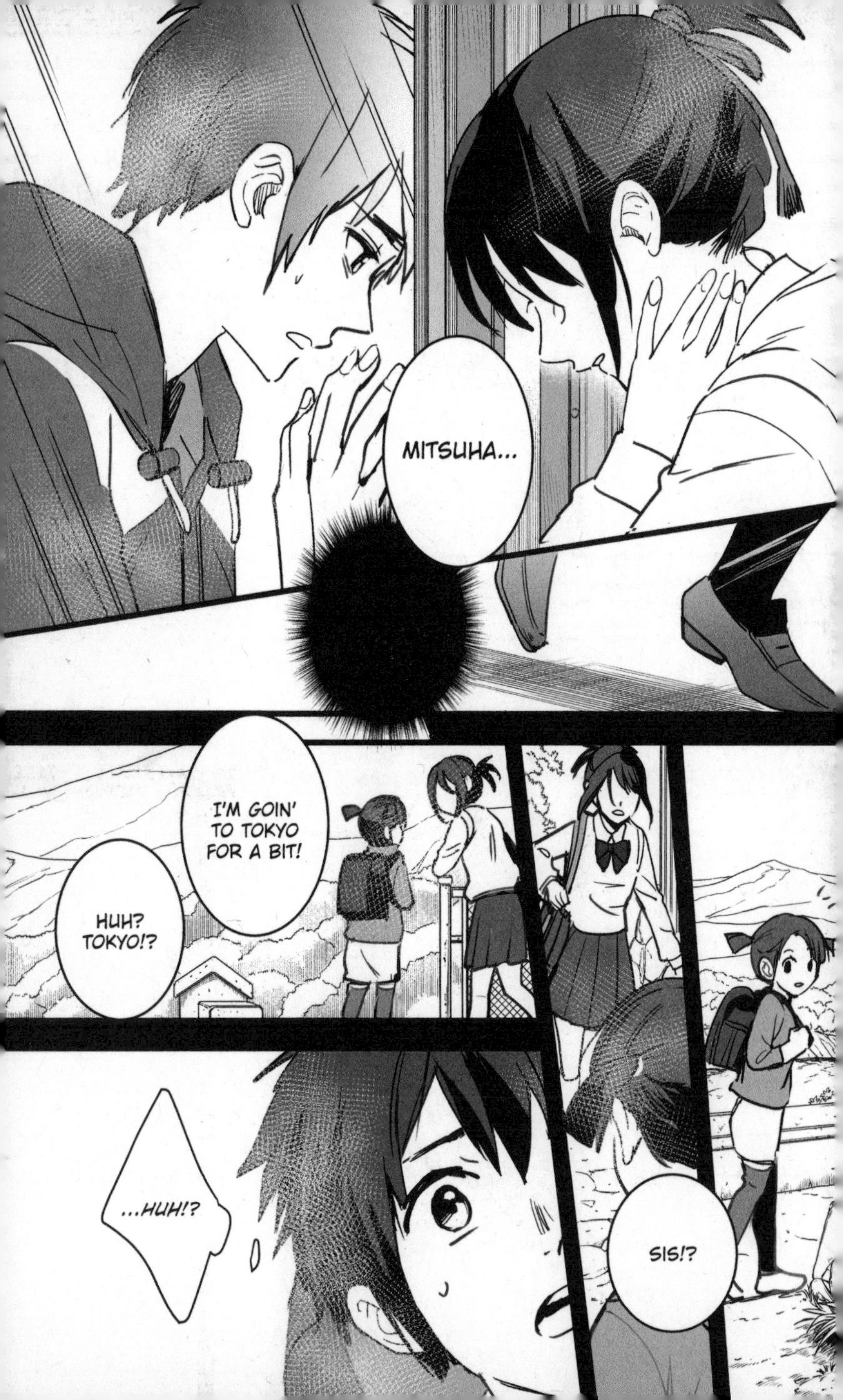
MITSUHA...
SIS!?
I'M GOIN' TO TOKYO FOR A BIT!
HUH? TOKYO!?
...HUH!?

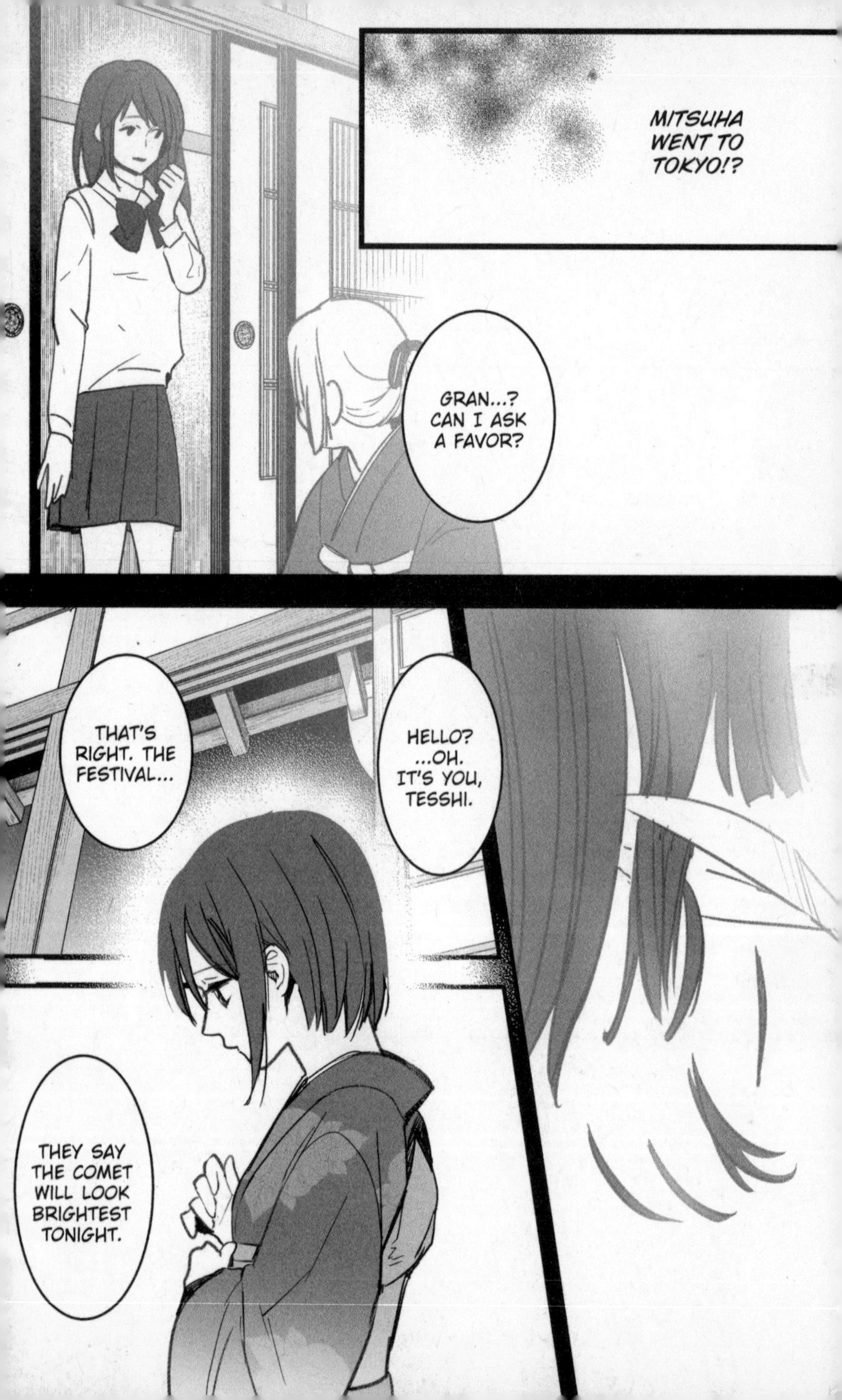
MITSUHA WENT TO TOKYO!?
GRAN...? CAN I ASK A FAVOR?
HELLO? ...OH. IT'S YOU, TESSHI.
THAT'S RIGHT. THE FESTIVAL...
THEY SAY THE COMET WILL LOOK BRIGHTEST TONIGHT.

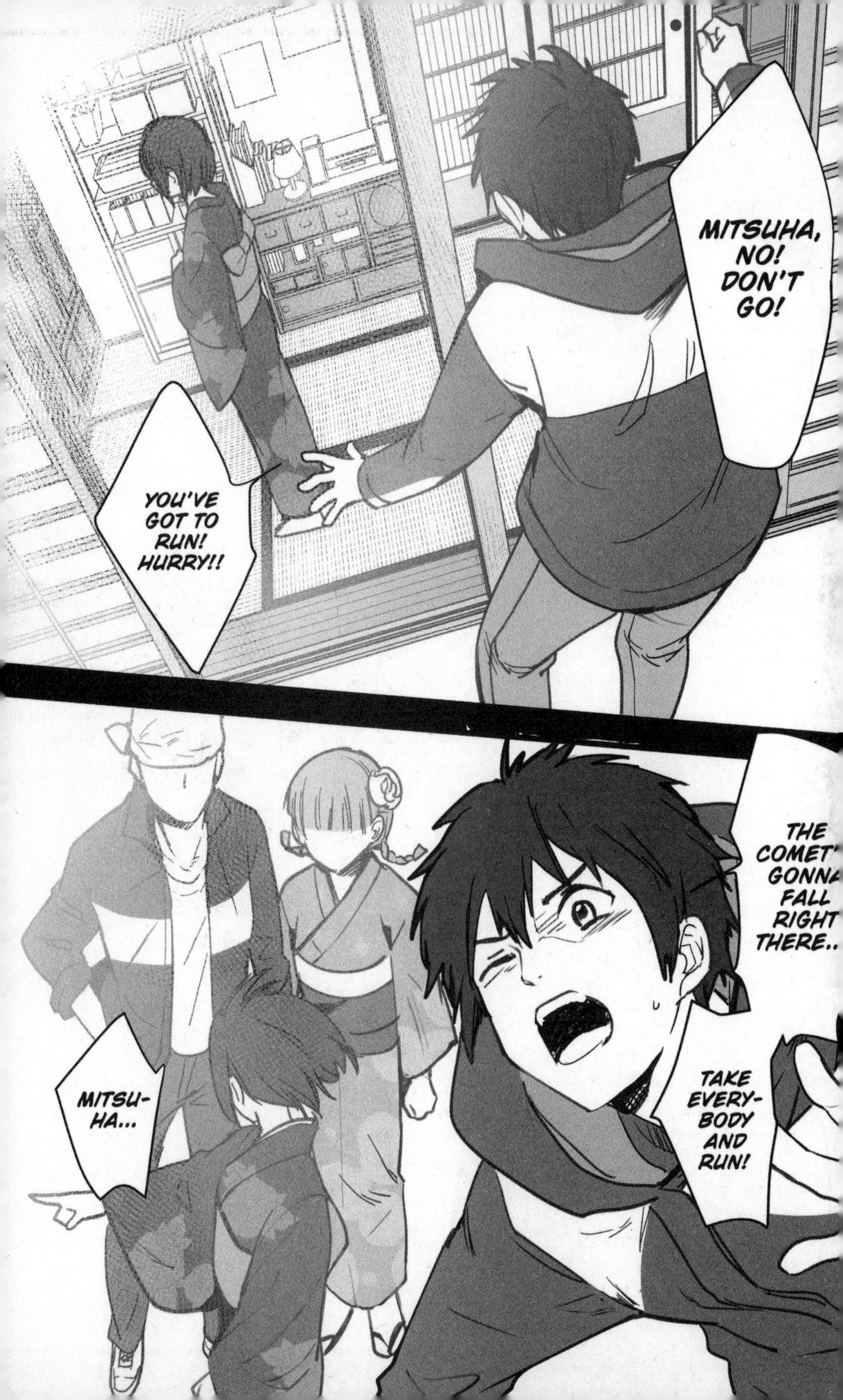
MITSUHA, NO! DON'T GO!
YOU'VE GOT TO RUN! HURRY!!
THE COMET' GONN FALL RIGHT THERE..
TAKE EVERY-BODY AND RUN!
MITSU-HA...

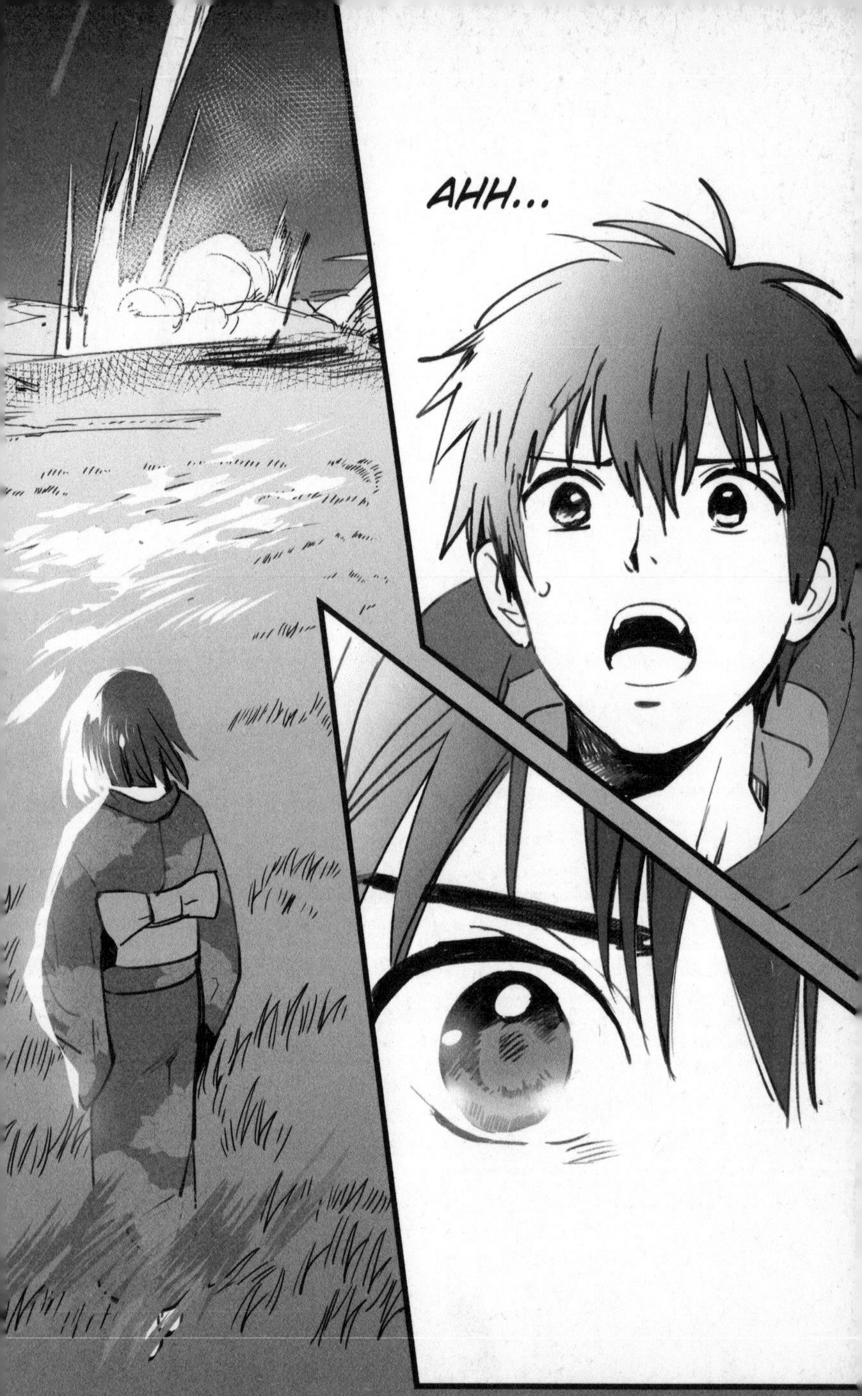
AHH...

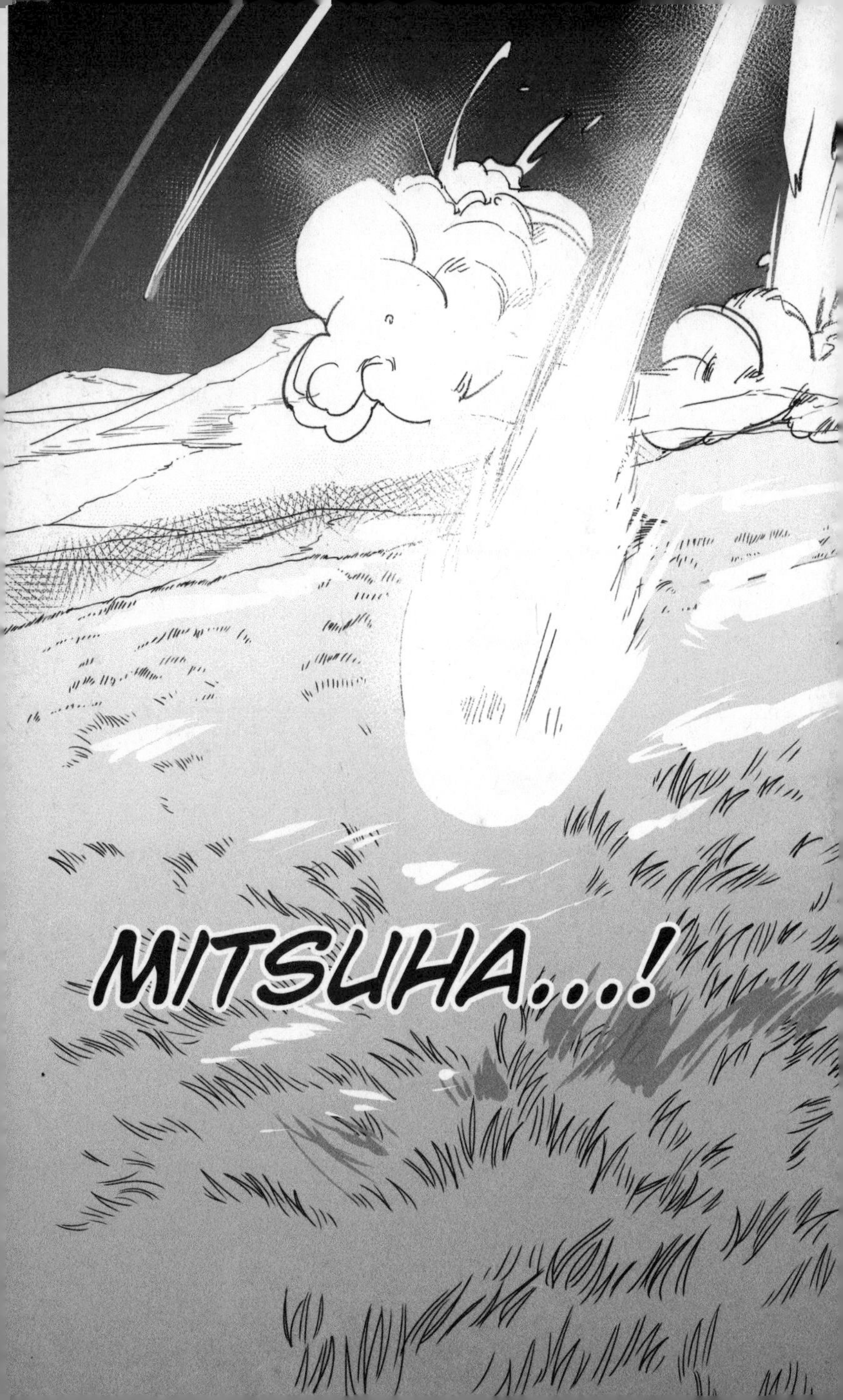
MITSUHA...!

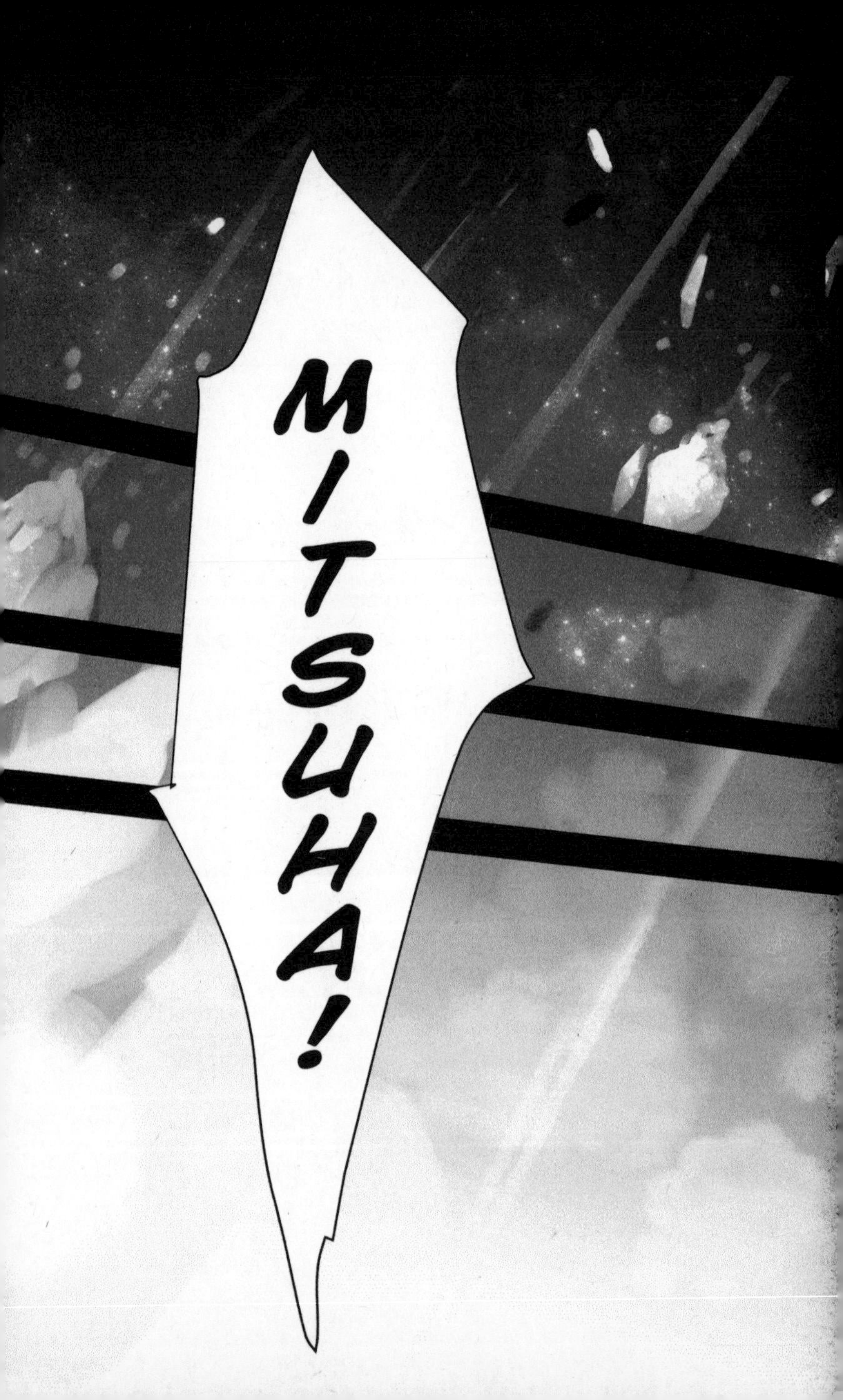
MITSUHA!

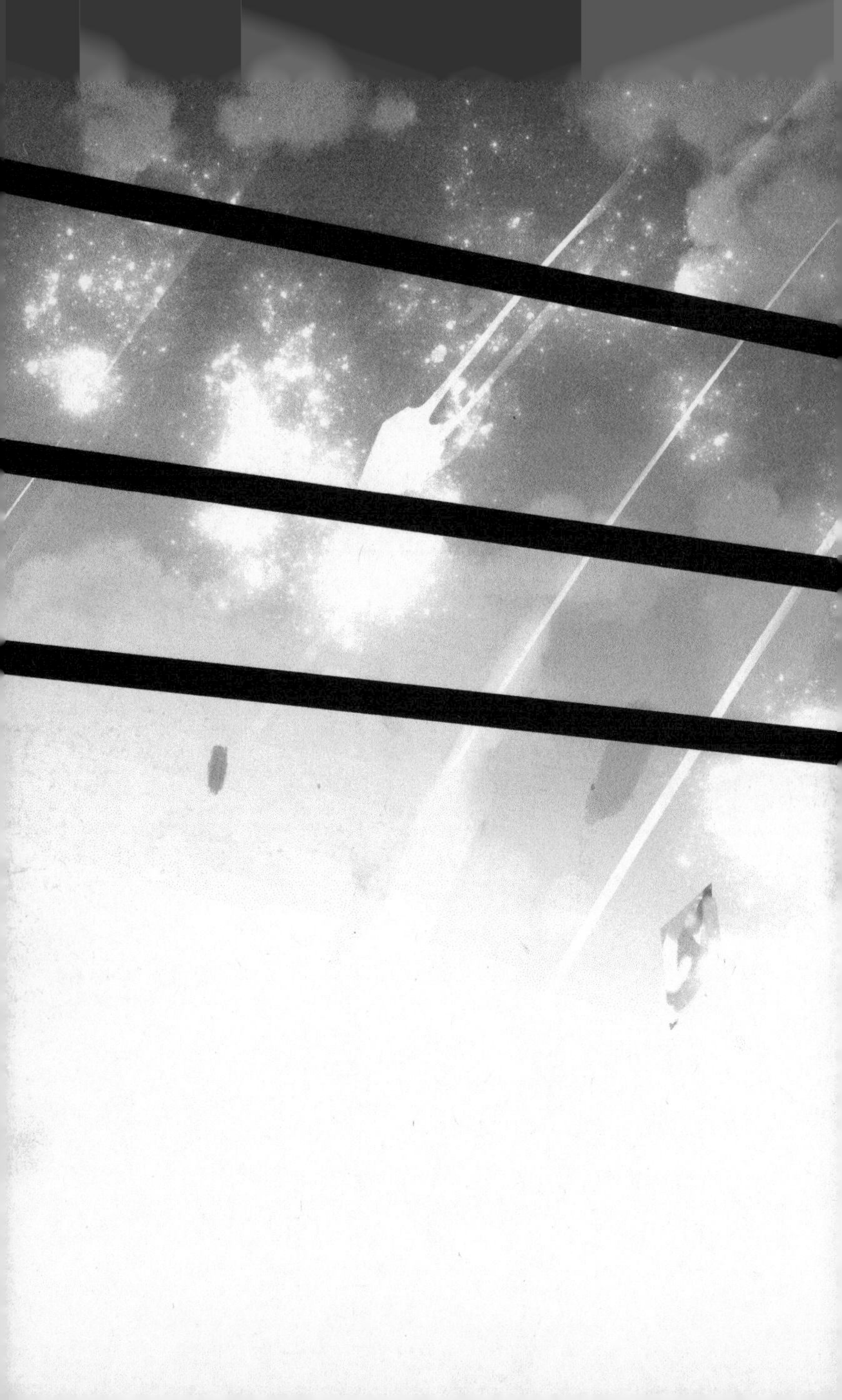

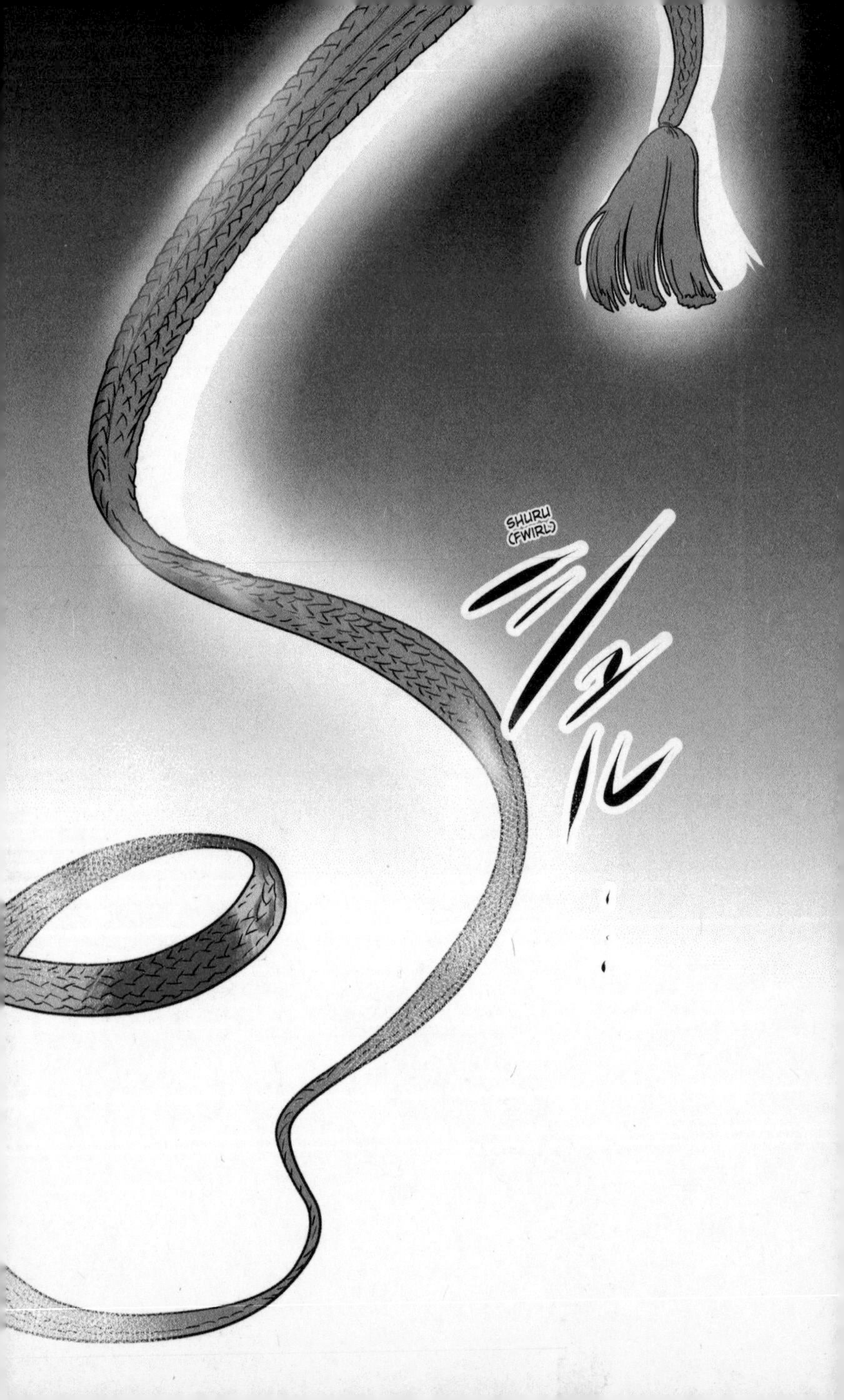
SHURU
(FWIRL)
シュル

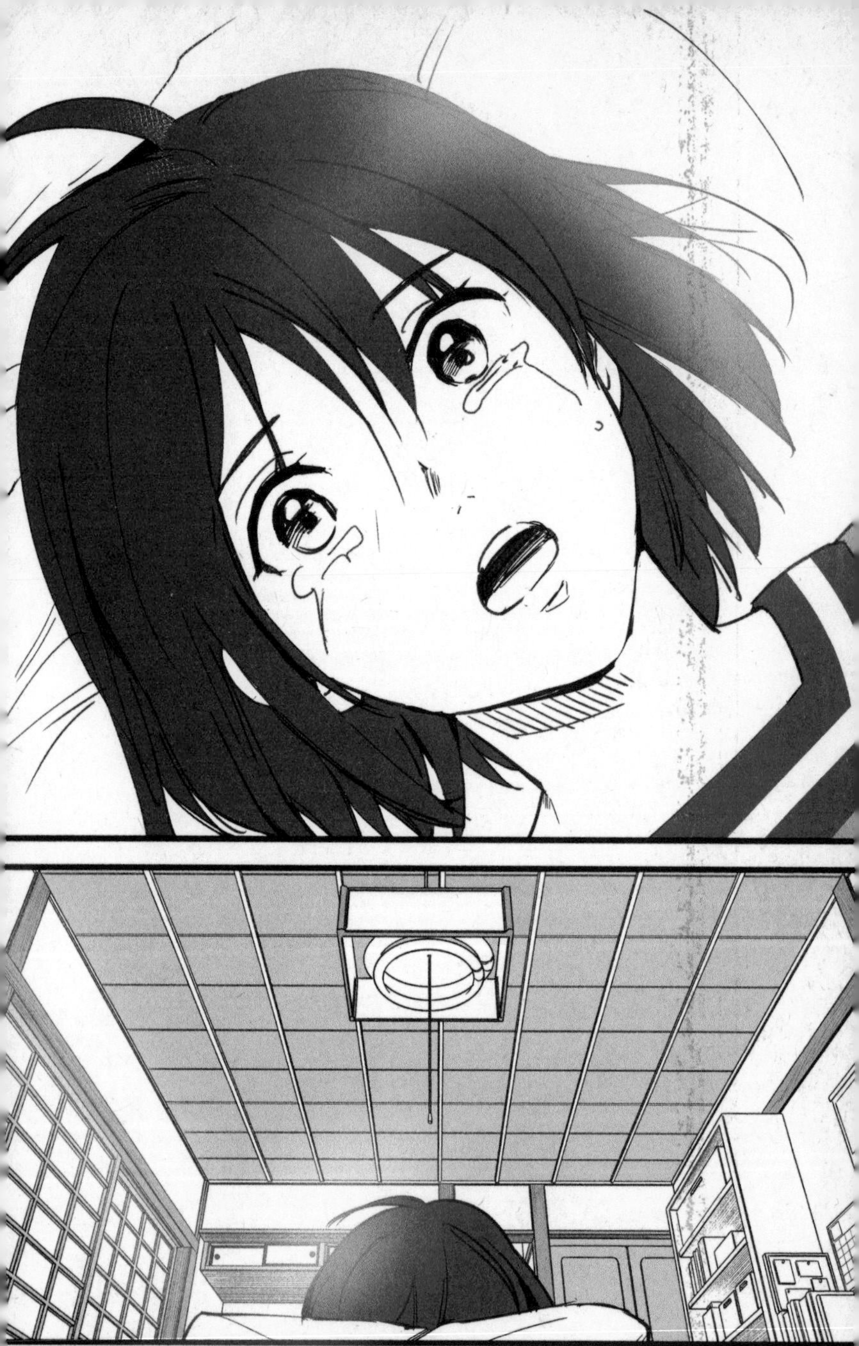

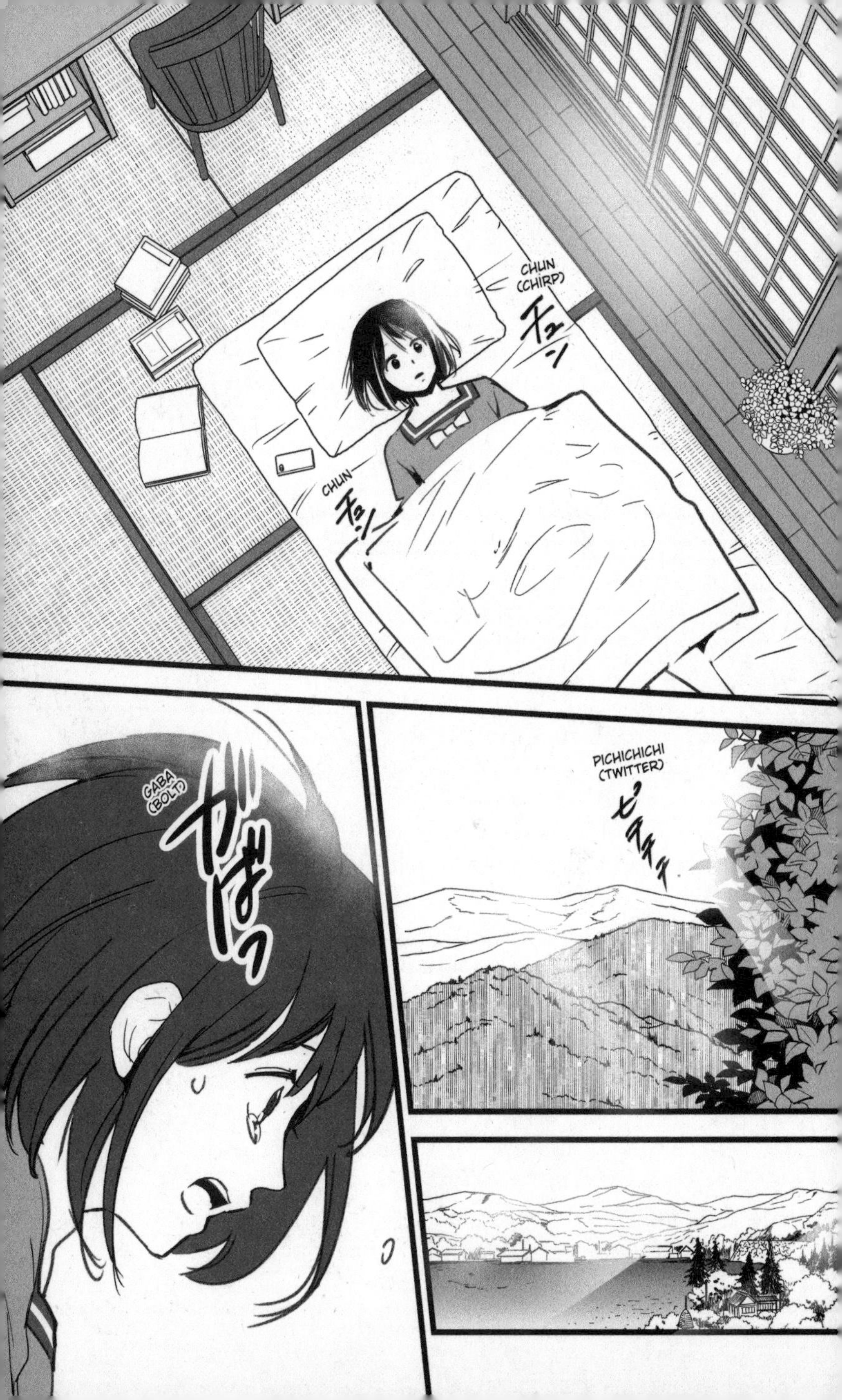
CHUN (CHIRP)
チュン
CHUN
チュン
PICHICHICHI (TWITTER)
ピチチチ
GABA (BOLT)
がばっ

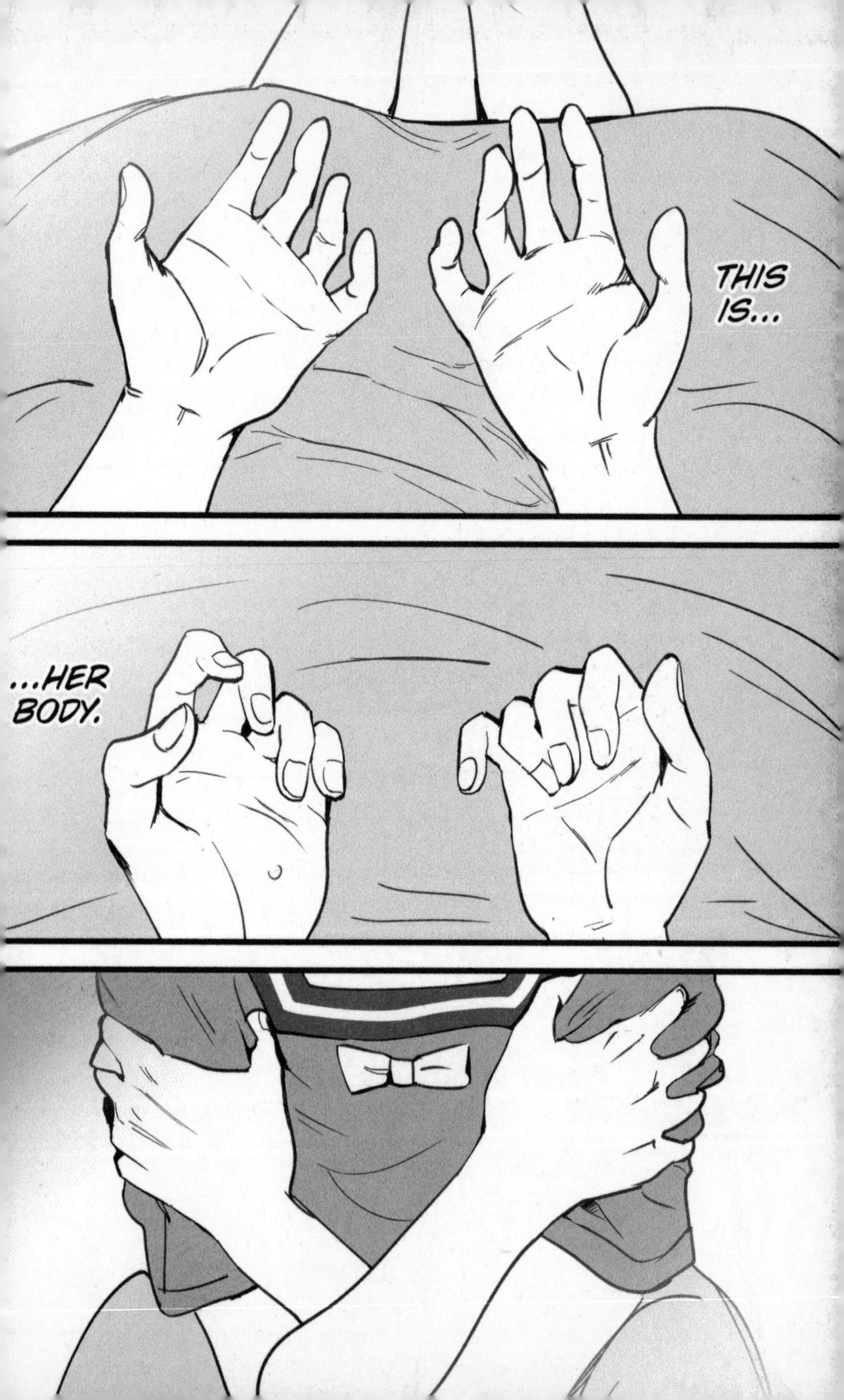
THIS IS...
...HER BODY.

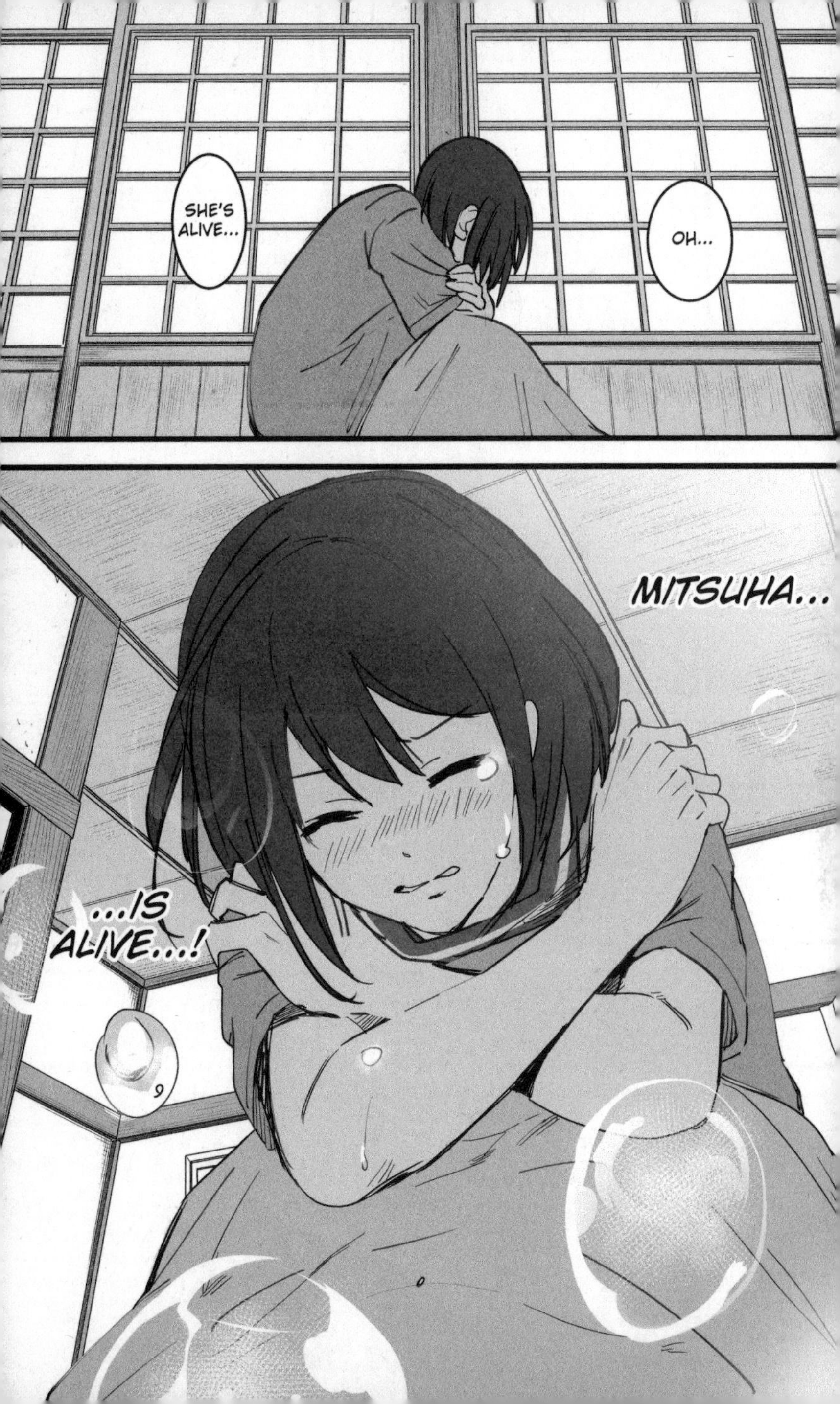
OH...
SHE'S ALIVE...
MITSUHA...
...IS ALIVE...!

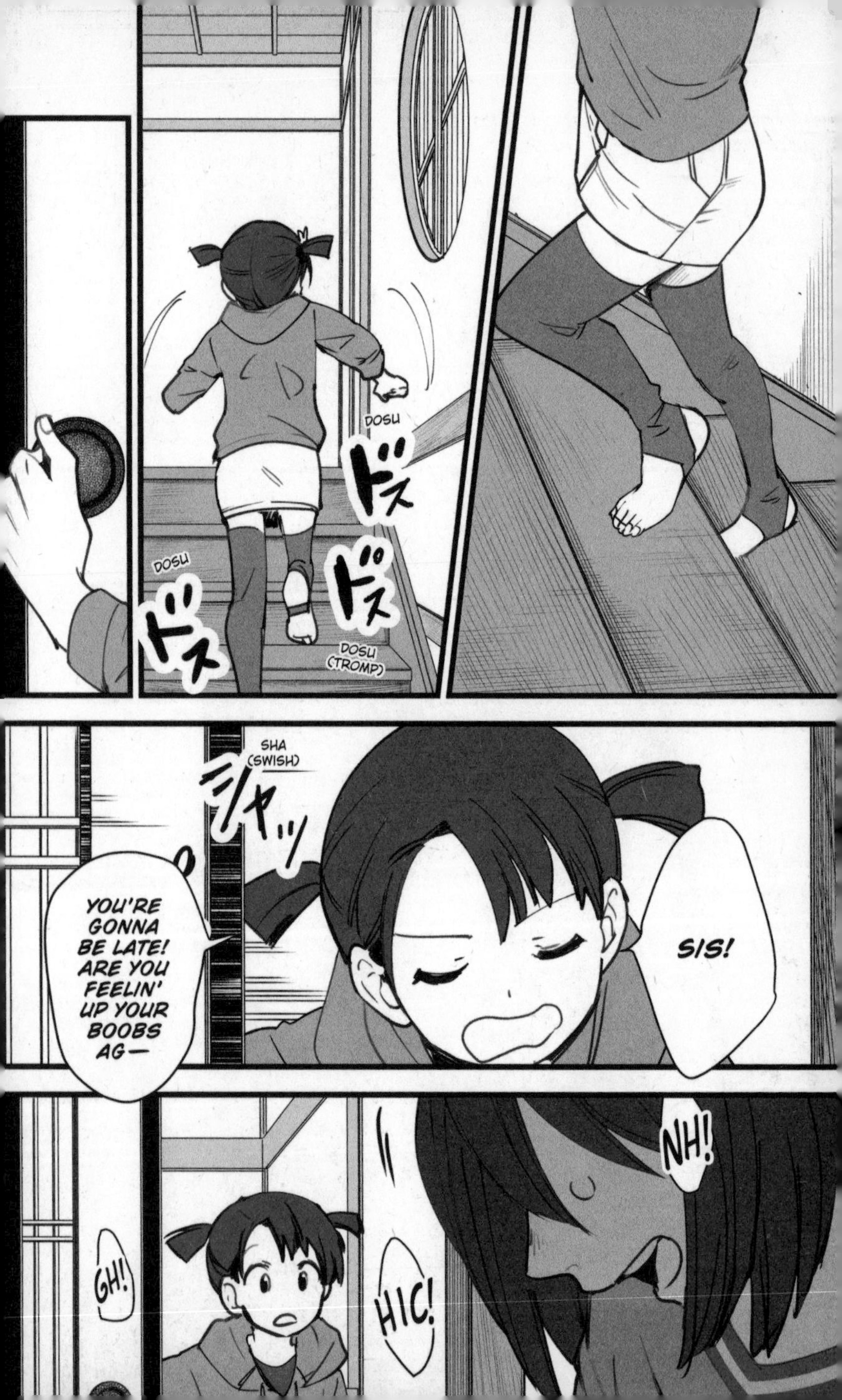
DOSU
ドス
ドス
DOSU (TROMP)
DOSU
ドス
SHA (SWISH)
シャッ
SIS!
YOU'RE GONNA BE LATE! ARE YOU FEELIN' UP YOUR BOOBS AG—
NH!
HIC!
GH!

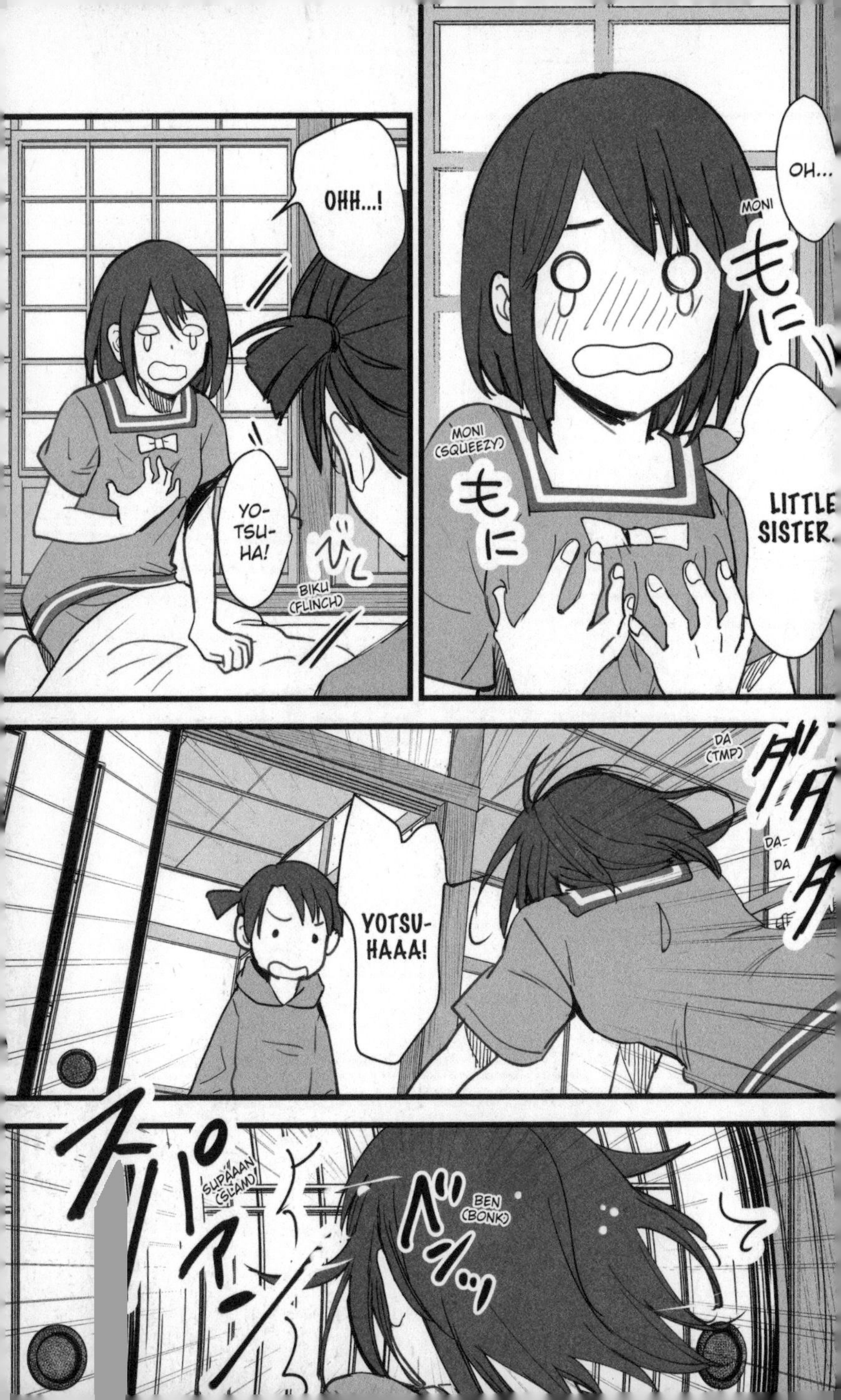

OH...
MONI
もに
MONI (SQUEEZY)
もに
LITTLE SISTER.
OHH...!
YO-TSU-HA!
びく
BIKU (FLINCH)
DA (TMP)
DA-DA
ダタタ
YOTSU-HAAA!
BEN (BONK)
SUPAAAN (SLAM)

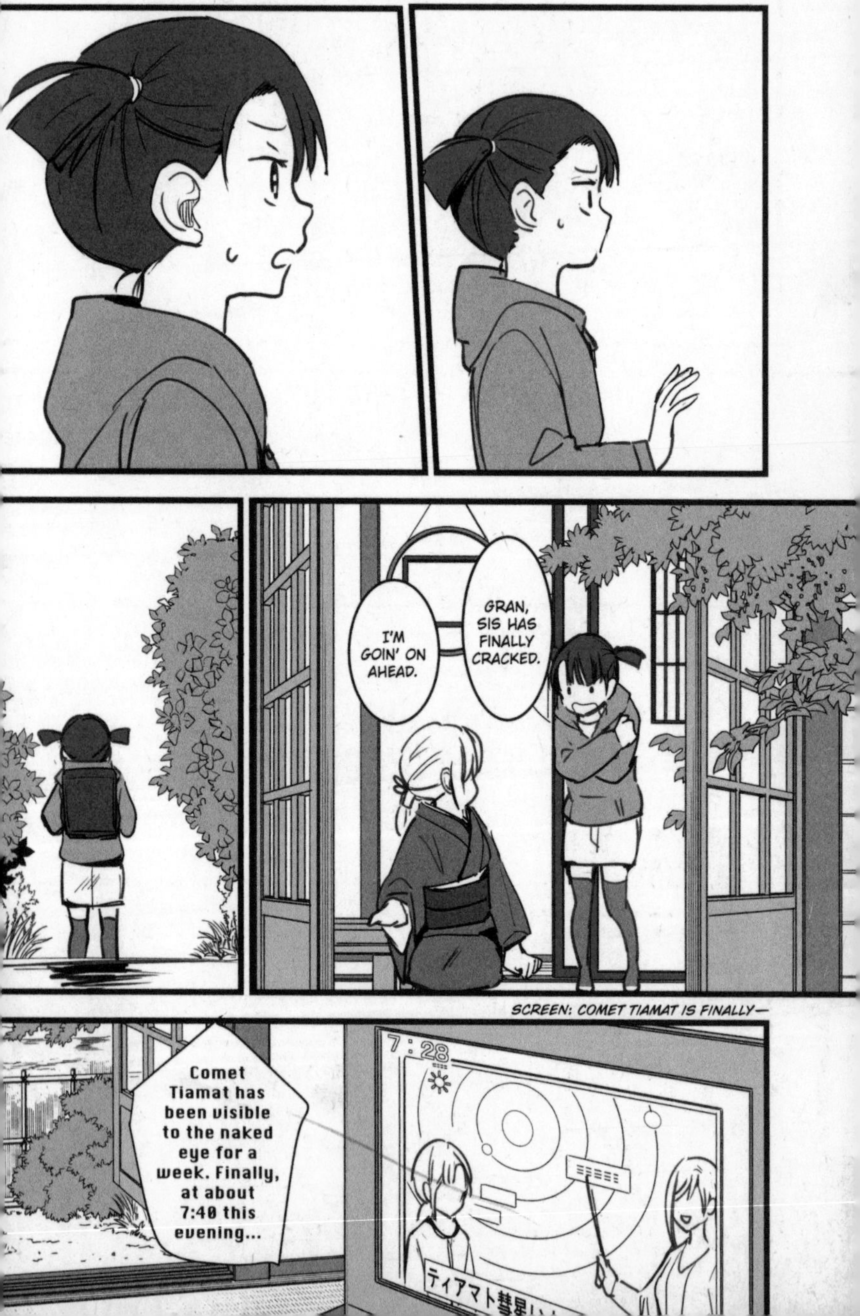
GRAN, SIS HAS FINALLY CRACKED.
I'M GOIN' ON AHEAD.
SCREEN: COMET TIAMAT IS FINALLY—
ティアマト彗星
Comet Tiamat has been visible to the naked eye for a week. Finally, at about 7:40 this evening...

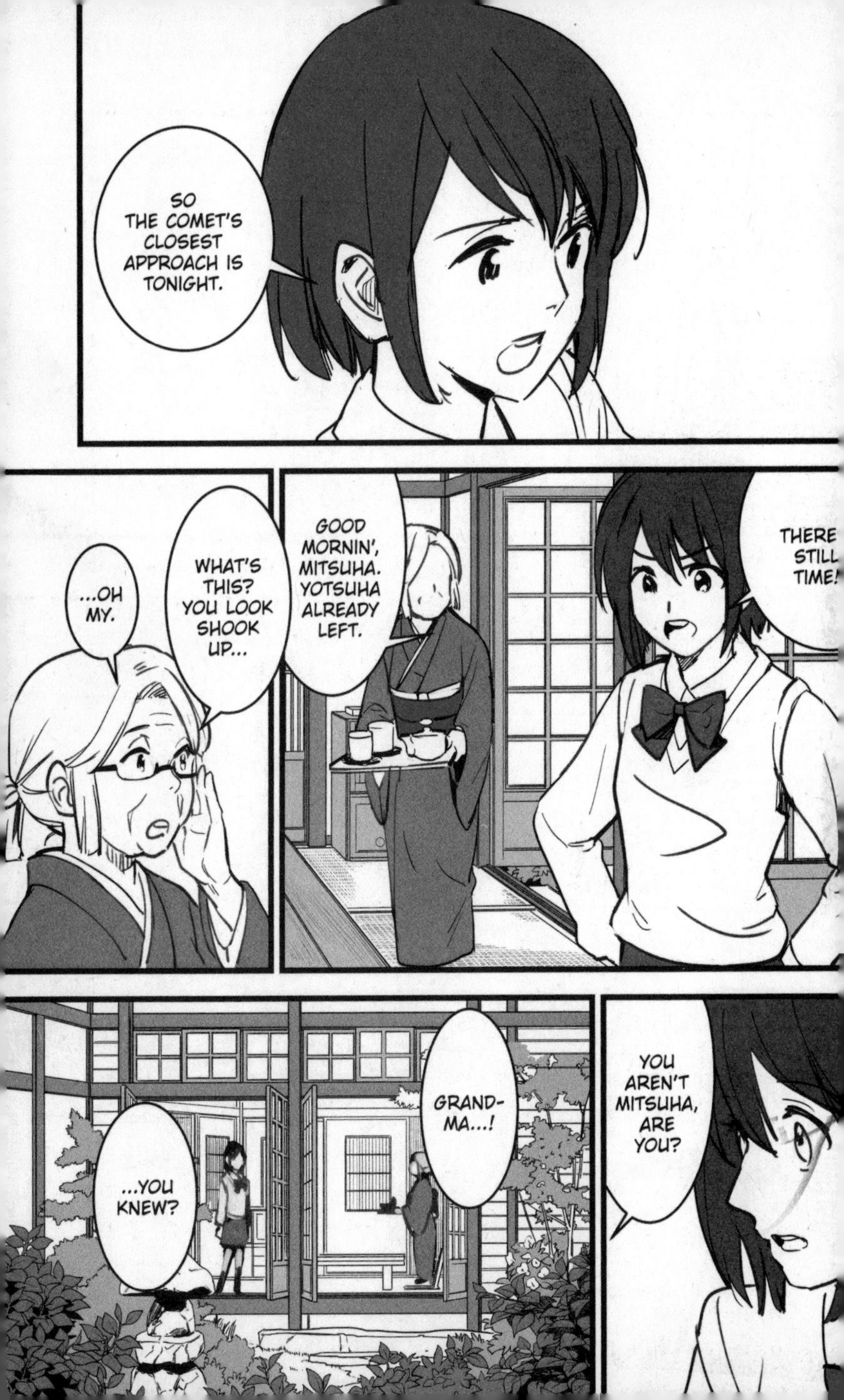
SO THE COMET'S CLOSEST APPROACH IS TONIGHT.
THERE STILL TIME!
GOOD MORNIN', MITSUHA. YOTSUHA ALREADY LEFT.
WHAT'S THIS? YOU LOOK SHOOK UP...
...OH MY.
YOU AREN'T MITSUHA, ARE YOU?
GRAND-MA...!
...YOU KNEW?

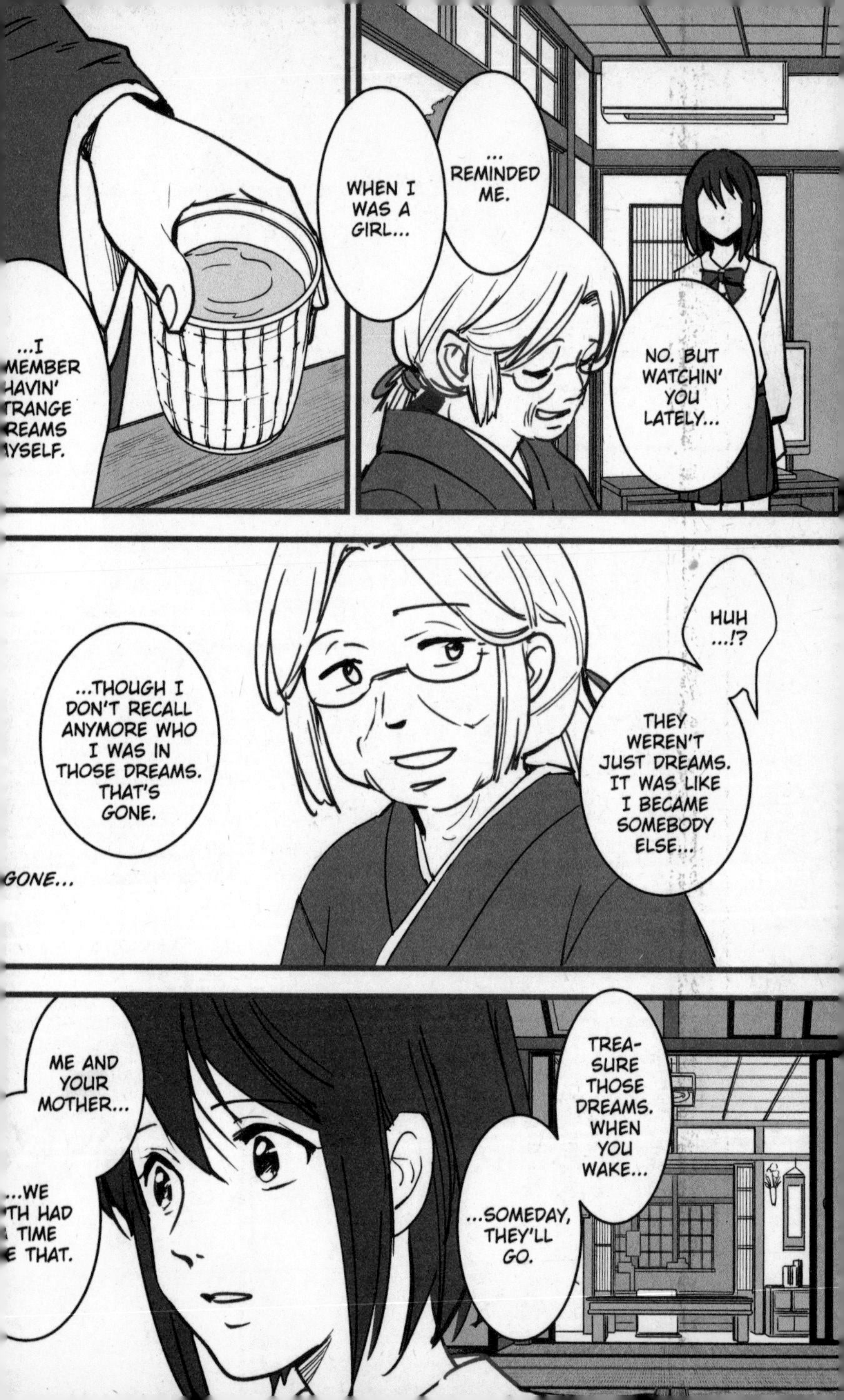

NO. BUT WATCHIN' YOU LATELY...
...REMINDED ME.
WHEN I WAS A GIRL...
...I MEMBER HAVIN' TRANGE REAMS YSELF.
HUH ...!?
THEY WEREN'T JUST DREAMS. IT WAS LIKE I BECAME SOMEBODY ELSE...
...THOUGH I DON'T RECALL ANYMORE WHO I WAS IN THOSE DREAMS. THAT'S GONE.
GONE...
TREA-SURE THOSE DREAMS. WHEN YOU WAKE...
...SOMEDAY, THEY'LL GO.
ME AND YOUR MOTHER...
...WE TH HAD TIME E THAT.

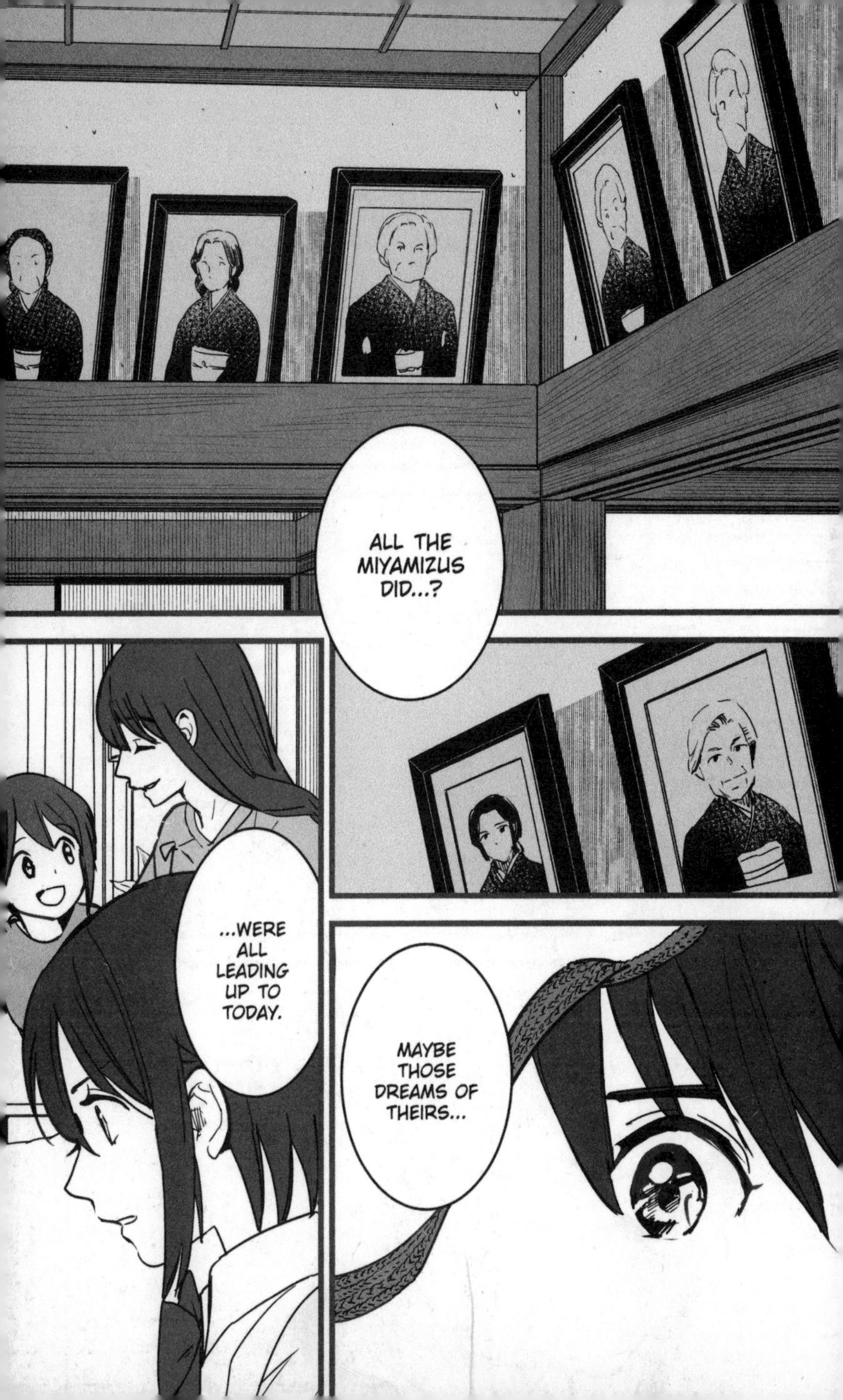
ALL THE MIYAMIZUS DID...?
MAYBE THOSE DREAMS OF THEIRS...
...WERE ALL LEADING UP TO TODAY.

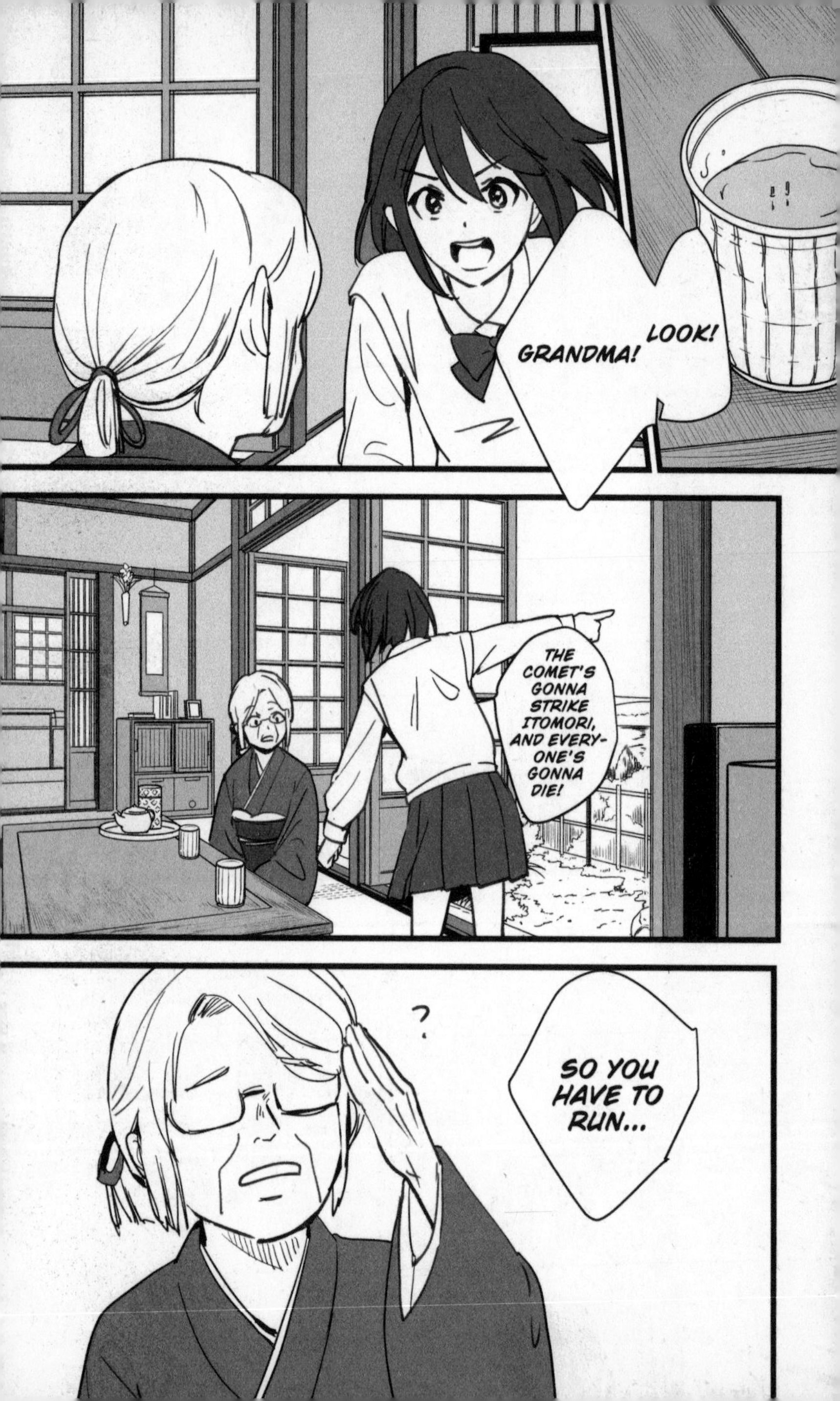
LOOK! GRANDMA!
THE COMET'S GONNA STRIKE ITOMORI, AND EVERY-ONE'S GONNA DIE!
?
SO YOU HAVE TO RUN...

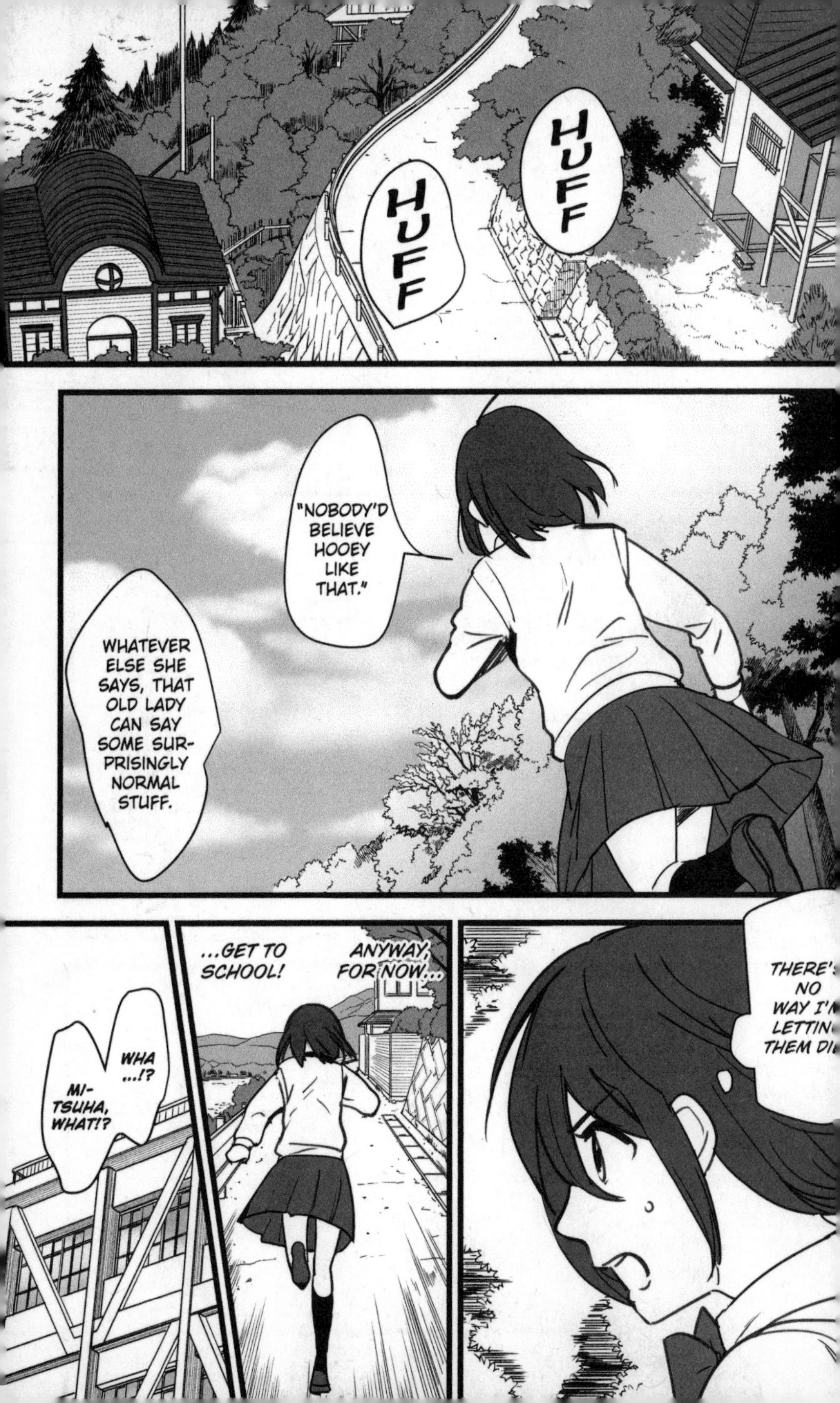
HUFF
HUFF
"NOBODY'D BELIEVE HOOEY LIKE THAT."
WHATEVER ELSE SHE SAYS, THAT OLD LADY CAN SAY SOME SUR-PRISINGLY NORMAL STUFF.
THERE'S NO WAY I'M LETTIN THEM DI
ANYWAY, FOR NOW...
...GET TO SCHOOL!
WHA ...!?
MI-TSUHA, WHAT!?

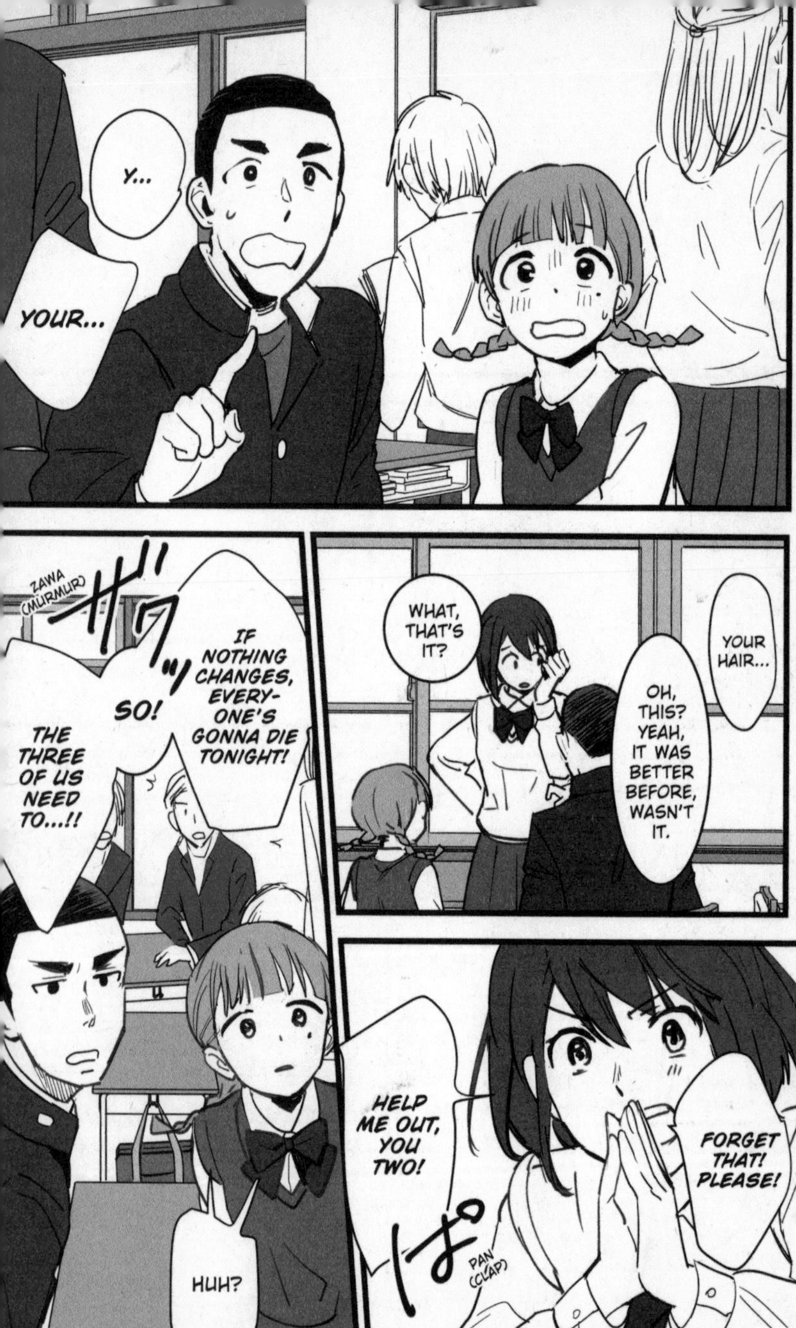
Y...
YOUR...
YOUR HAIR...
WHAT, THAT'S IT?
OH, THIS? YEAH, IT WAS BETTER BEFORE, WASN'T IT.
FORGET THAT! PLEASE!
HELP ME OUT, YOU TWO!
PAN (CLAP)
IF NOTHING CHANGES, EVERY-ONE'S GONNA DIE TONIGHT!
SO!
ZAWA (MURMUR)
THE THREE OF US NEED TO...!!
HUH?

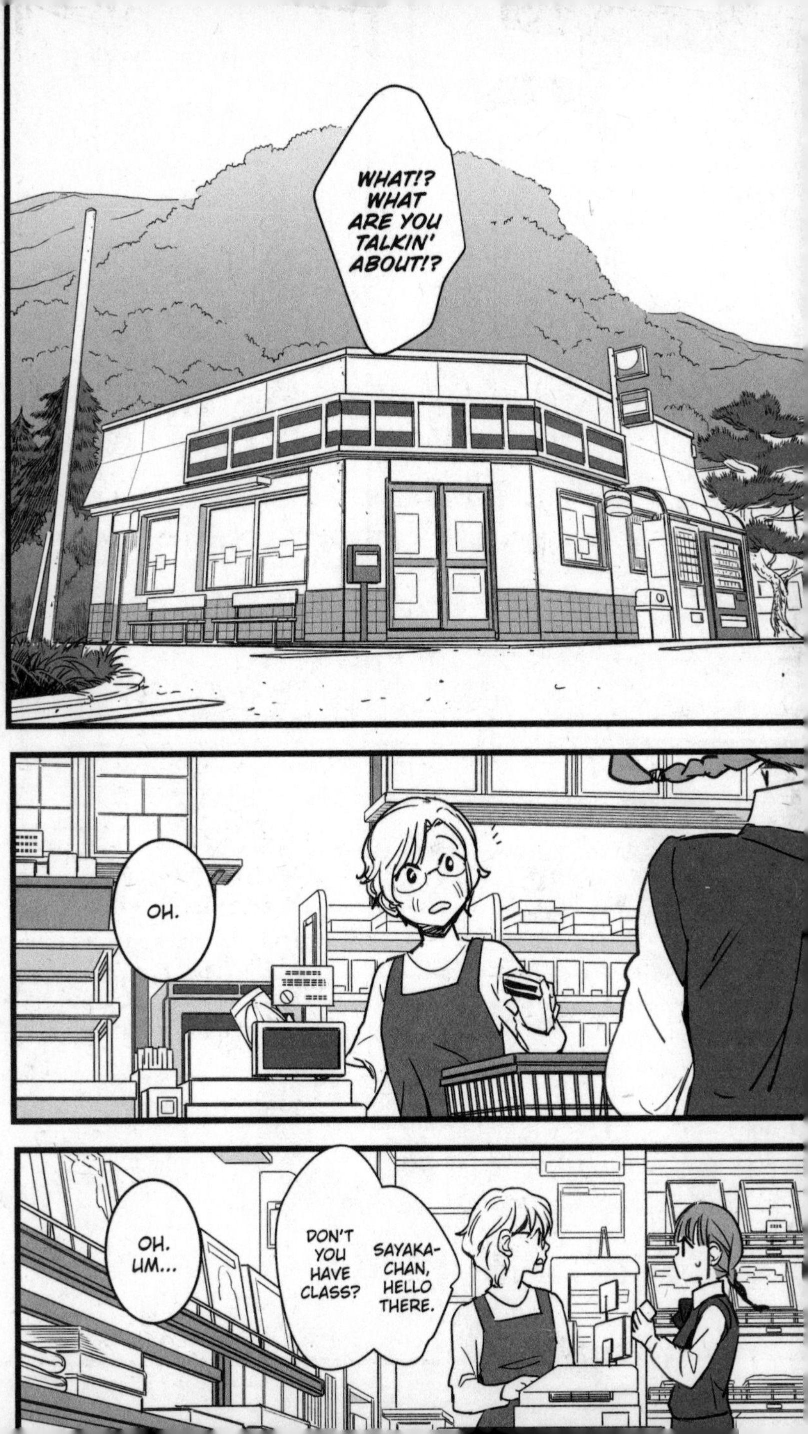
WHAT!? WHAT ARE YOU TALKIN' ABOUT!?
OH.
SAYAKA-CHAN, HELLO THERE.
DON'T YOU HAVE CLASS?
OH. UM...

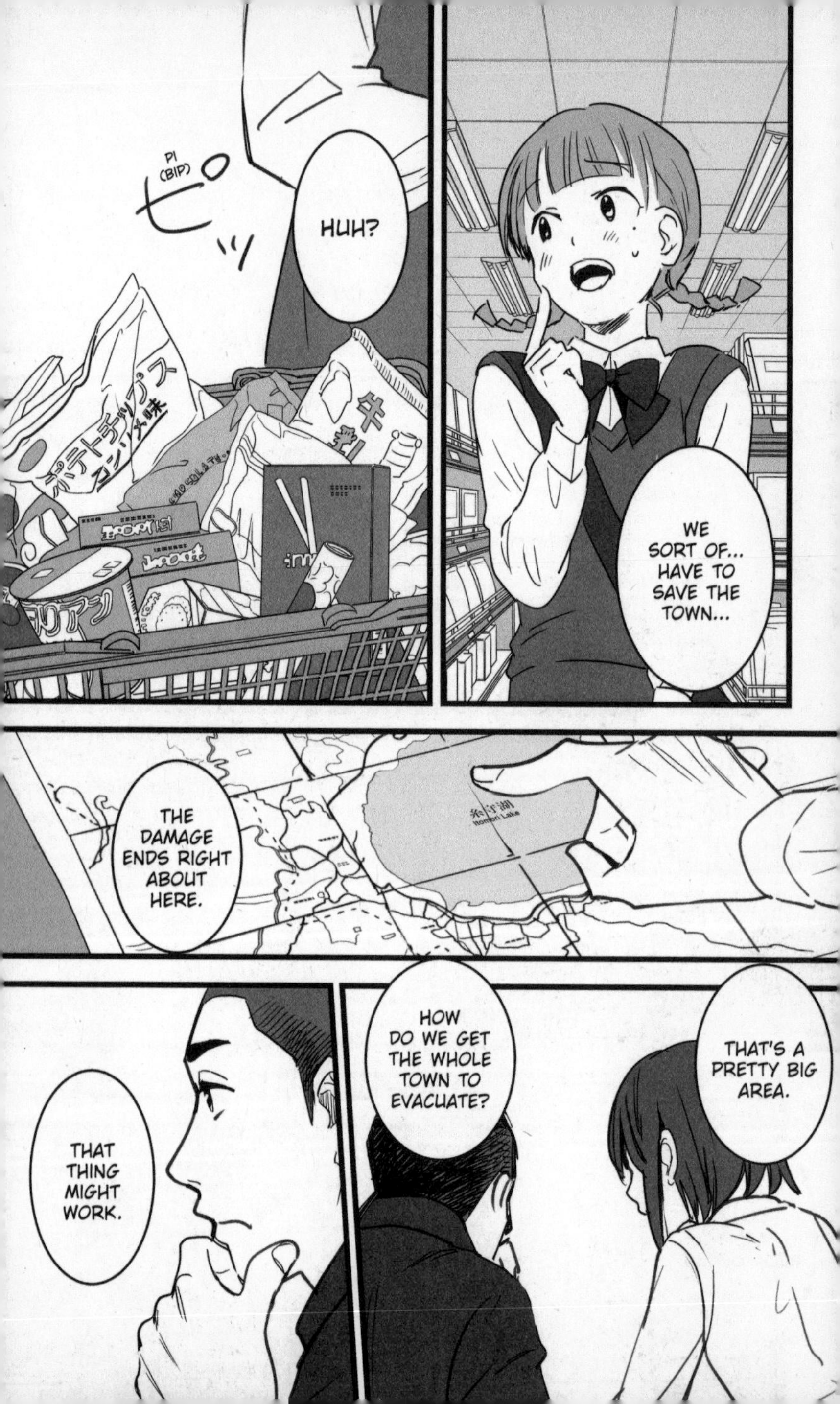
WE SORT OF... HAVE TO SAVE THE TOWN...
HUH?
ピッ
PI (BIP)
ポテトチップス
コンソメ味
THE DAMAGE ENDS RIGHT ABOUT HERE.
糸守湖
Itomori Lake
THAT'S A PRETTY BIG AREA.
HOW DO WE GET THE WHOLE TOWN TO EVACUATE?
THAT THING MIGHT WORK.

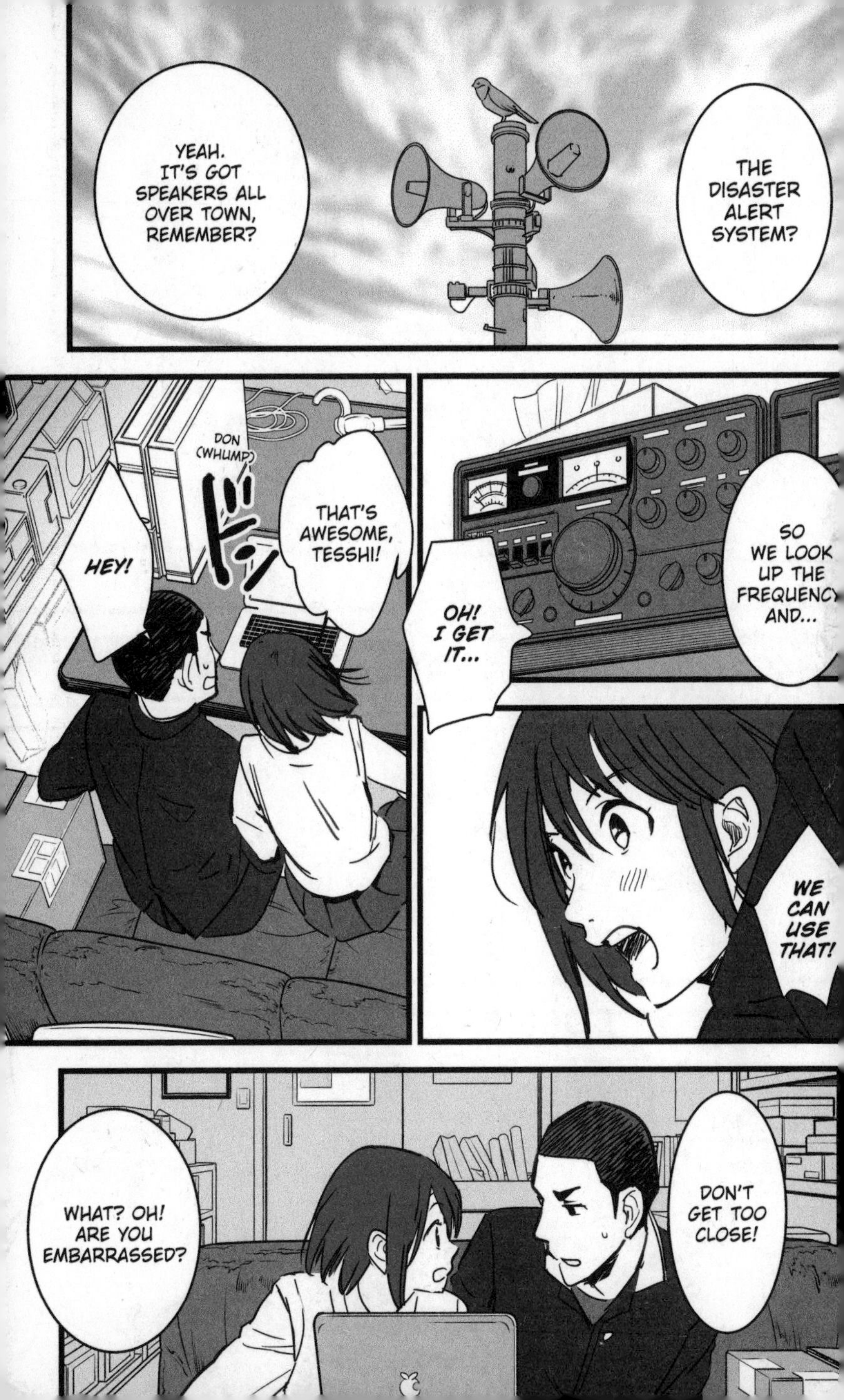
THE DISASTER ALERT SYSTEM?
YEAH. IT'S GOT SPEAKERS ALL OVER TOWN, REMEMBER?
SO WE LOOK UP THE FREQUENCY AND...
OH! I GET IT...
WE CAN USE THAT!
THAT'S AWESOME, TESSHI!
DON (WHUMP)
ドン
HEY!
DON'T GET TOO CLOSE!
WHAT? OH! ARE YOU EMBARRASSED?

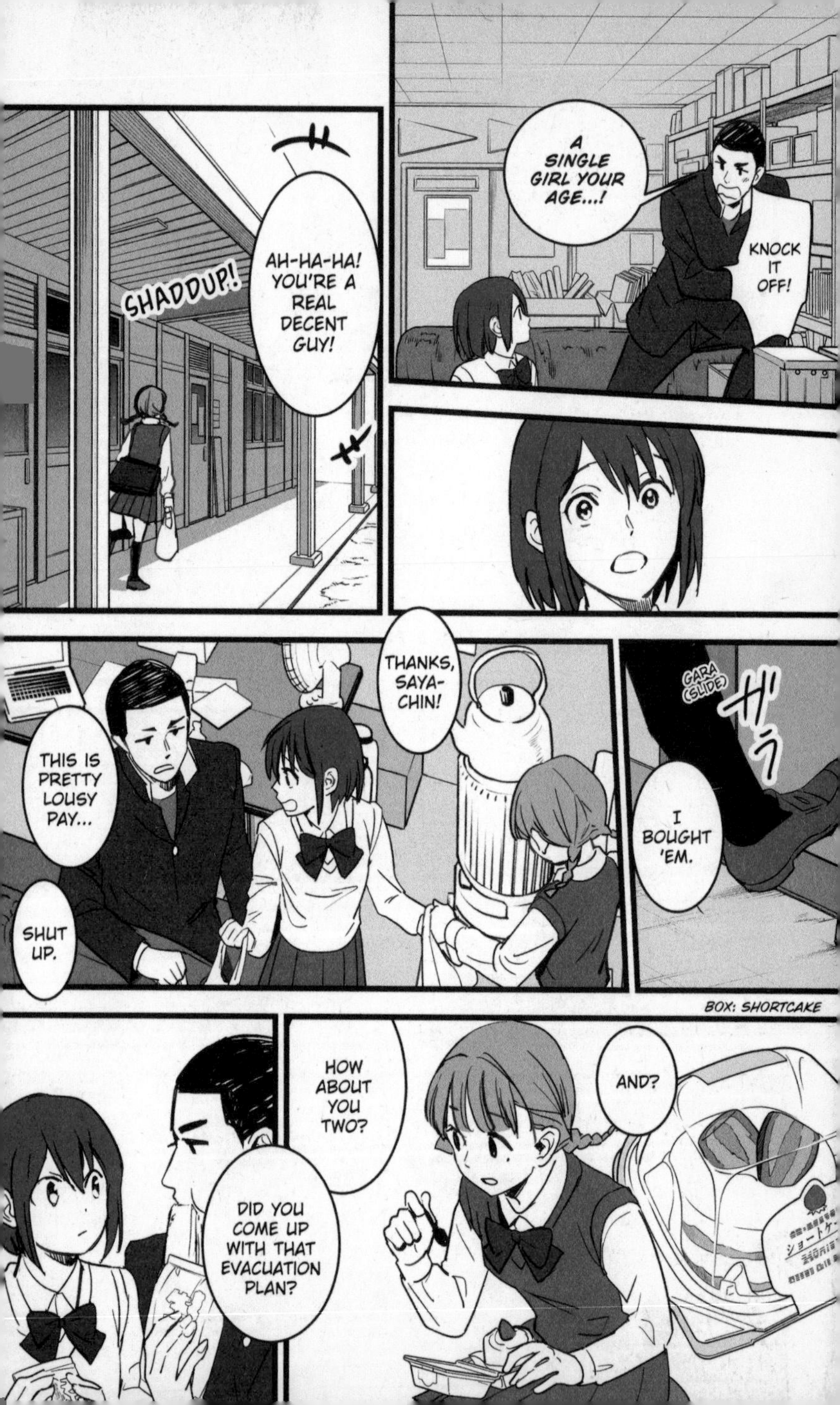
A SINGLE GIRL YOUR AGE...!
KNOCK IT OFF!
AH-HA-HA! YOU'RE A REAL DECENT GUY!
SHADDUP!
GARA (SLIDE)
I BOUGHT 'EM.
THANKS, SAYA-CHIN!
THIS IS PRETTY LOUSY PAY...
SHUT UP.
AND?
HOW ABOUT YOU TWO?
DID YOU COME UP WITH THAT EVACUATION PLAN?
BOX: SHORTCAKE

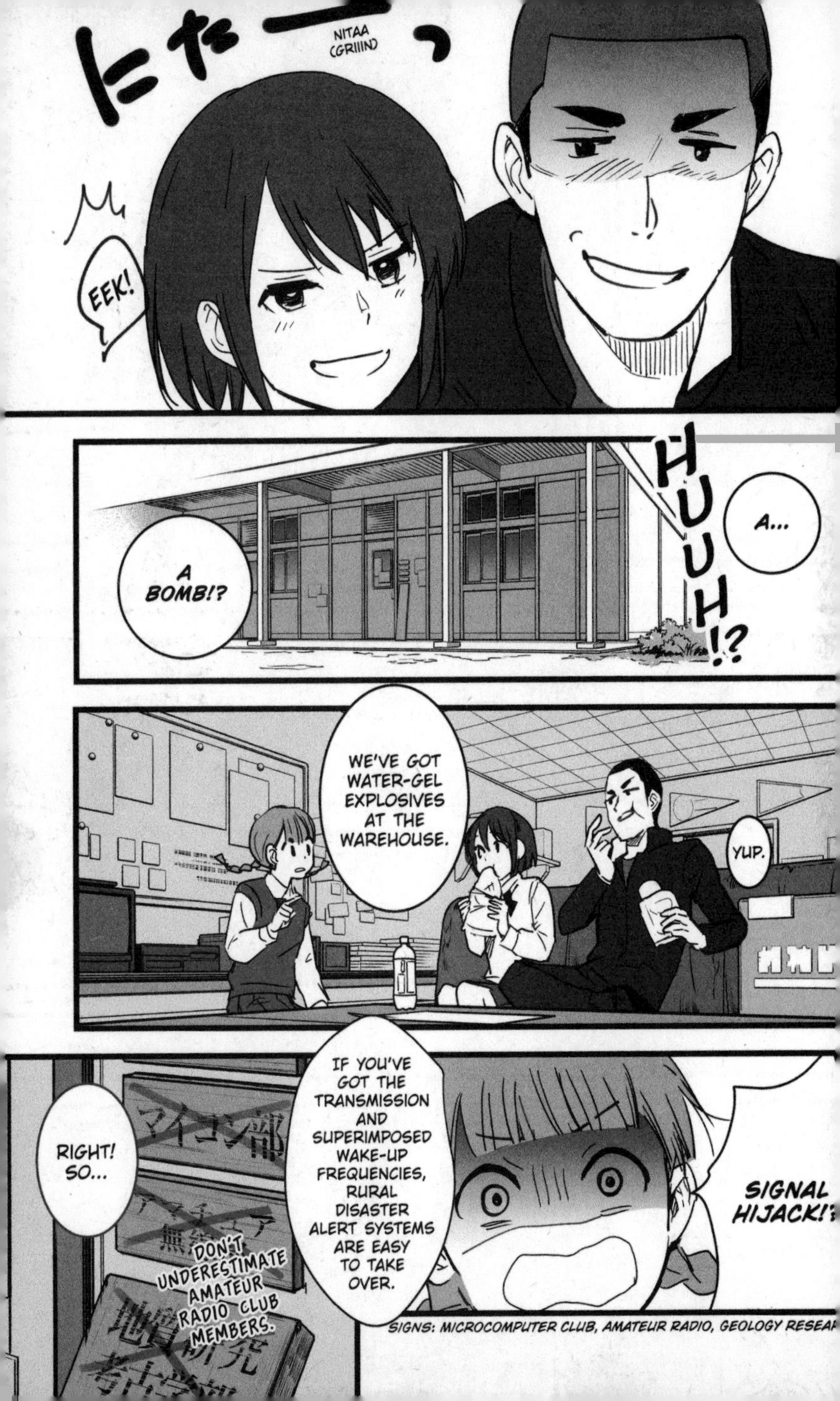
にたーっ
NITAA (GRIIIN)
EEK!
A...
HUUH!?
A BOMB!?
YUP.
WE'VE GOT WATER-GEL EXPLOSIVES AT THE WAREHOUSE.
SIGNAL HIJACK!?
IF YOU'VE GOT THE TRANSMISSION AND SUPERIMPOSED WAKE-UP FREQUENCIES, RURAL DISASTER ALERT SYSTEMS ARE EASY TO TAKE OVER.
RIGHT! SO...
DON'T UNDERESTIMATE AMATEUR RADIO CLUB MEMBERS.
SIGNS: MICROCOMPUTER CLUB, AMATEUR RADIO, GEOLOGY RESEAR

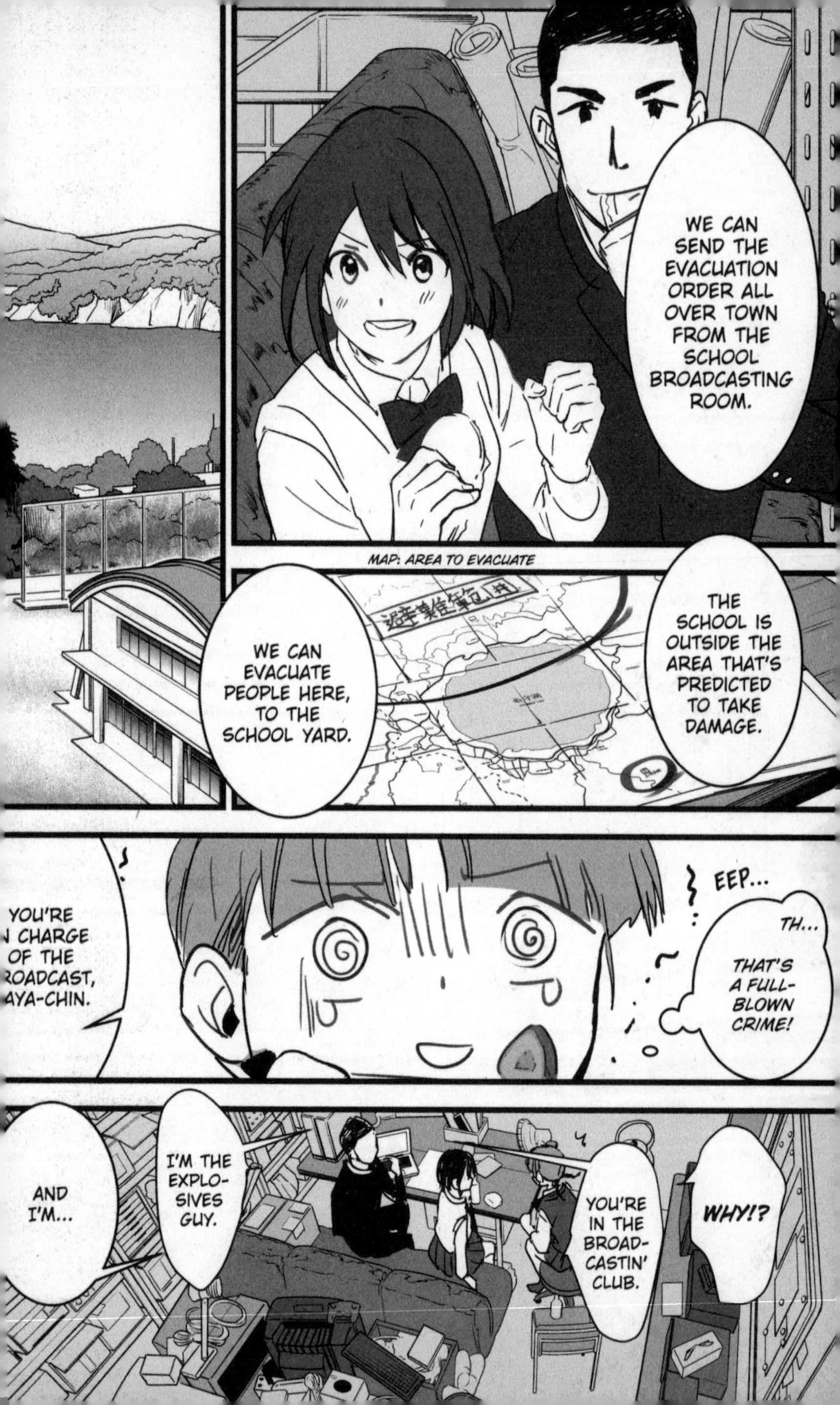
WE CAN SEND THE EVACUATION ORDER ALL OVER TOWN FROM THE SCHOOL BROADCASTING ROOM.
MAP: AREA TO EVACUATE
THE SCHOOL IS OUTSIDE THE AREA THAT'S PREDICTED TO TAKE DAMAGE.
WE CAN EVACUATE PEOPLE HERE, TO THE SCHOOL YARD.
EEP...
TH... THAT'S A FULL-BLOWN CRIME!
YOU'RE N CHARGE OF THE ROADCAST, AYA-CHIN.
WHY!?
YOU'RE IN THE BROAD-CASTIN' CLUB.
I'M THE EXPLO-SIVES GUY.
AND I'M...

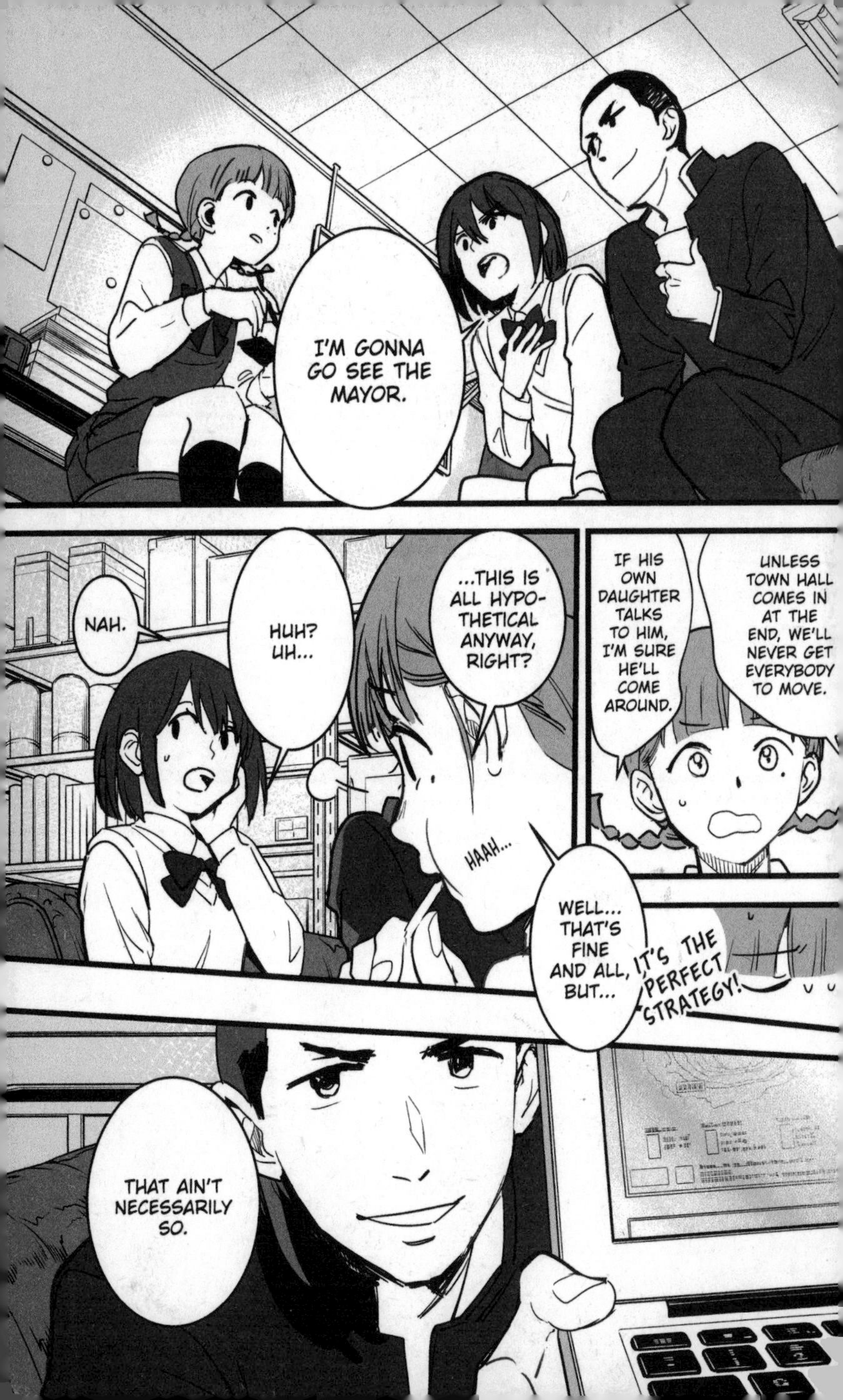
I'M GONNA GO SEE THE MAYOR.
UNLESS TOWN HALL COMES IN AT THE END, WE'LL NEVER GET EVERYBODY TO MOVE.
IF HIS OWN DAUGHTER TALKS TO HIM, I'M SURE HE'LL COME AROUND.
IT'S THE PERFECT STRATEGY!
...THIS IS ALL HYPO-THETICAL ANYWAY, RIGHT?
HUH? UH...
NAH.
HAAH...
WELL... THAT'S FINE AND ALL, BUT...
THAT AIN'T NECESSARILY SO.

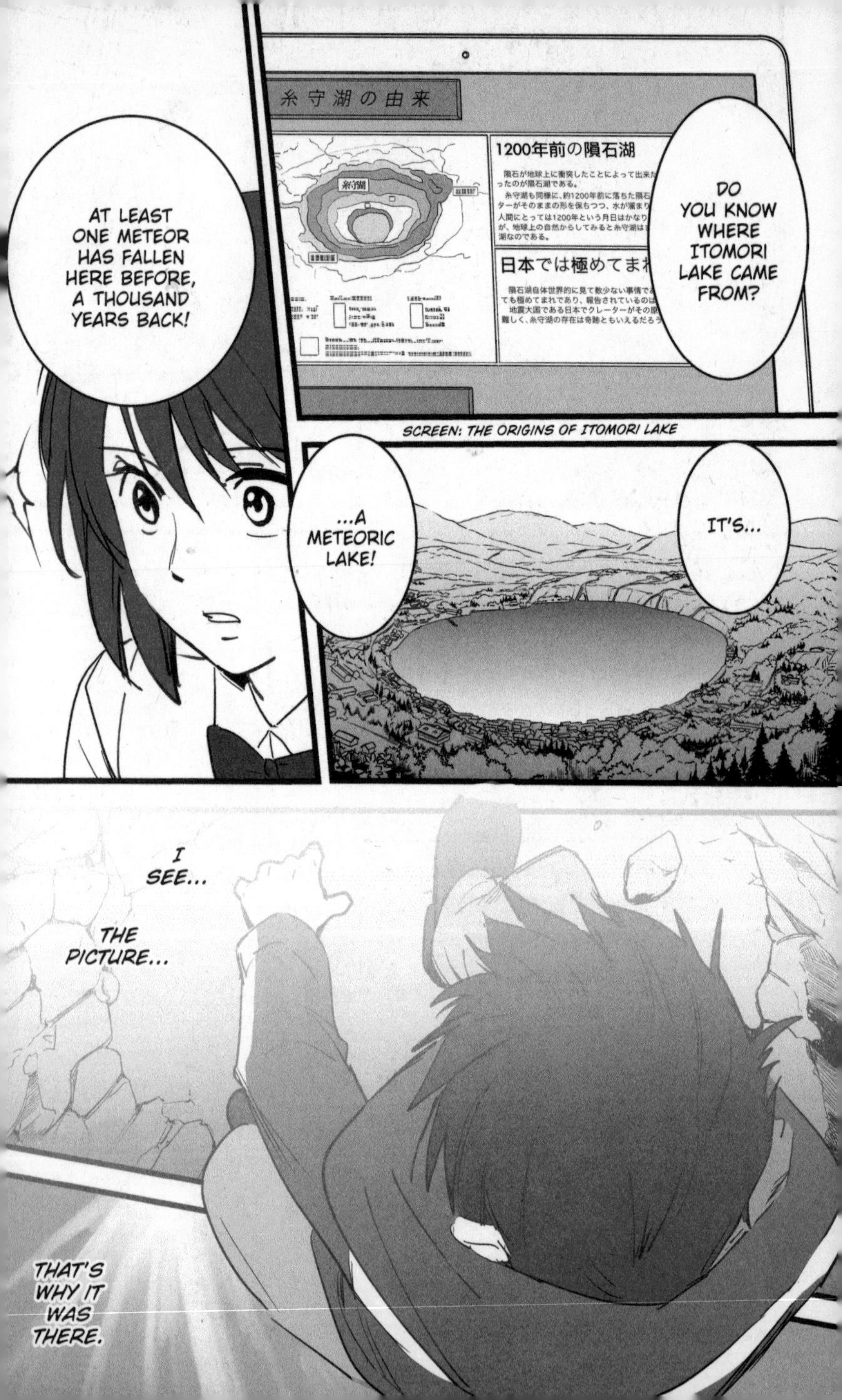

DO YOU KNOW WHERE ITOMORI LAKE CAME FROM?
糸守湖の由来
1200年前の隕石湖
SCREEN: THE ORIGINS OF ITOMORI LAKE
IT'S...
...A METEORIC LAKE!
AT LEAST ONE METEOR HAS FALLEN HERE BEFORE, A THOUSAND YEARS BACK!
I SEE...
THE PICTURE...
THAT'S WHY IT WAS THERE.

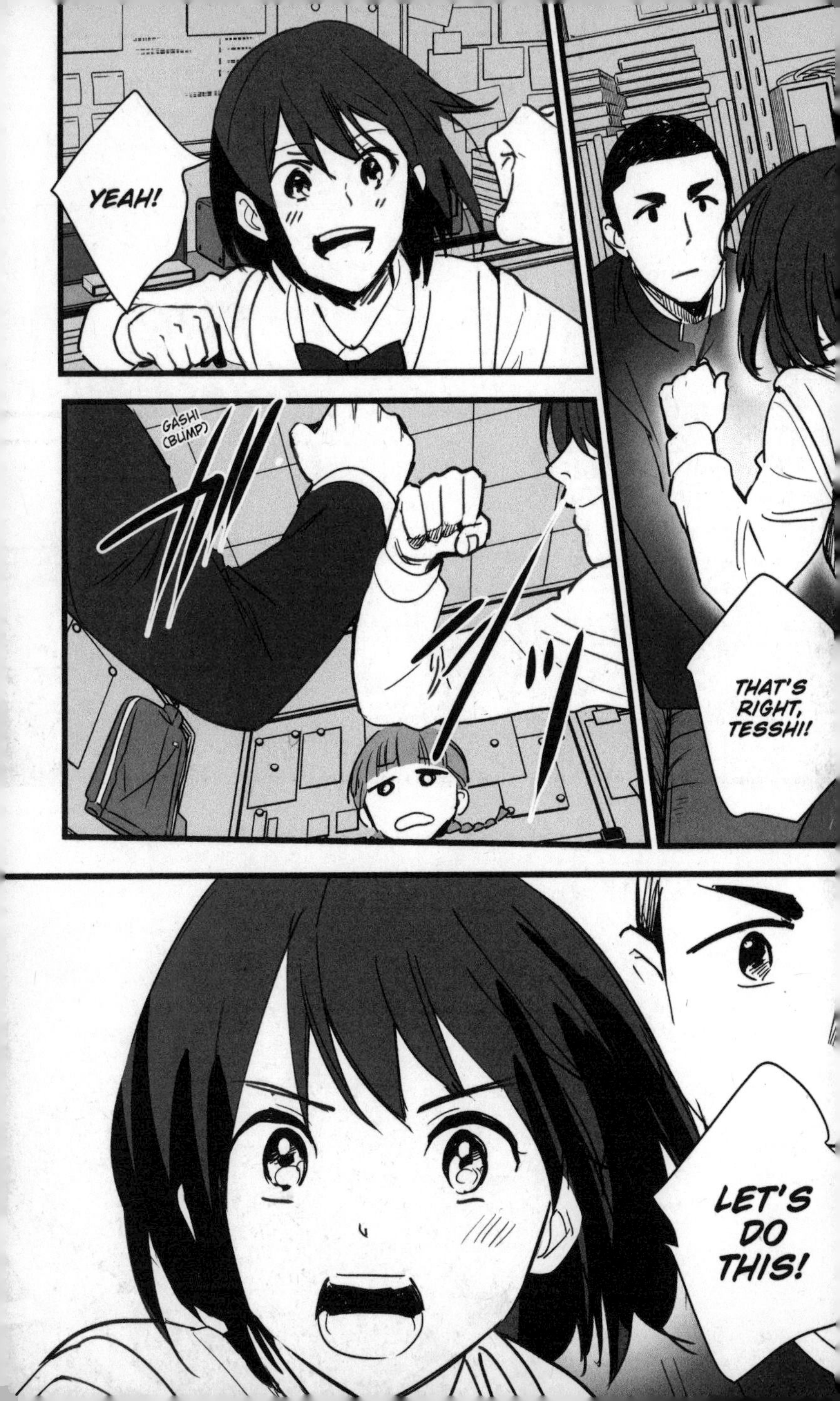
THAT'S RIGHT, TESSHI!
YEAH!
GASHI (BUMP)
LET'S DO THIS!

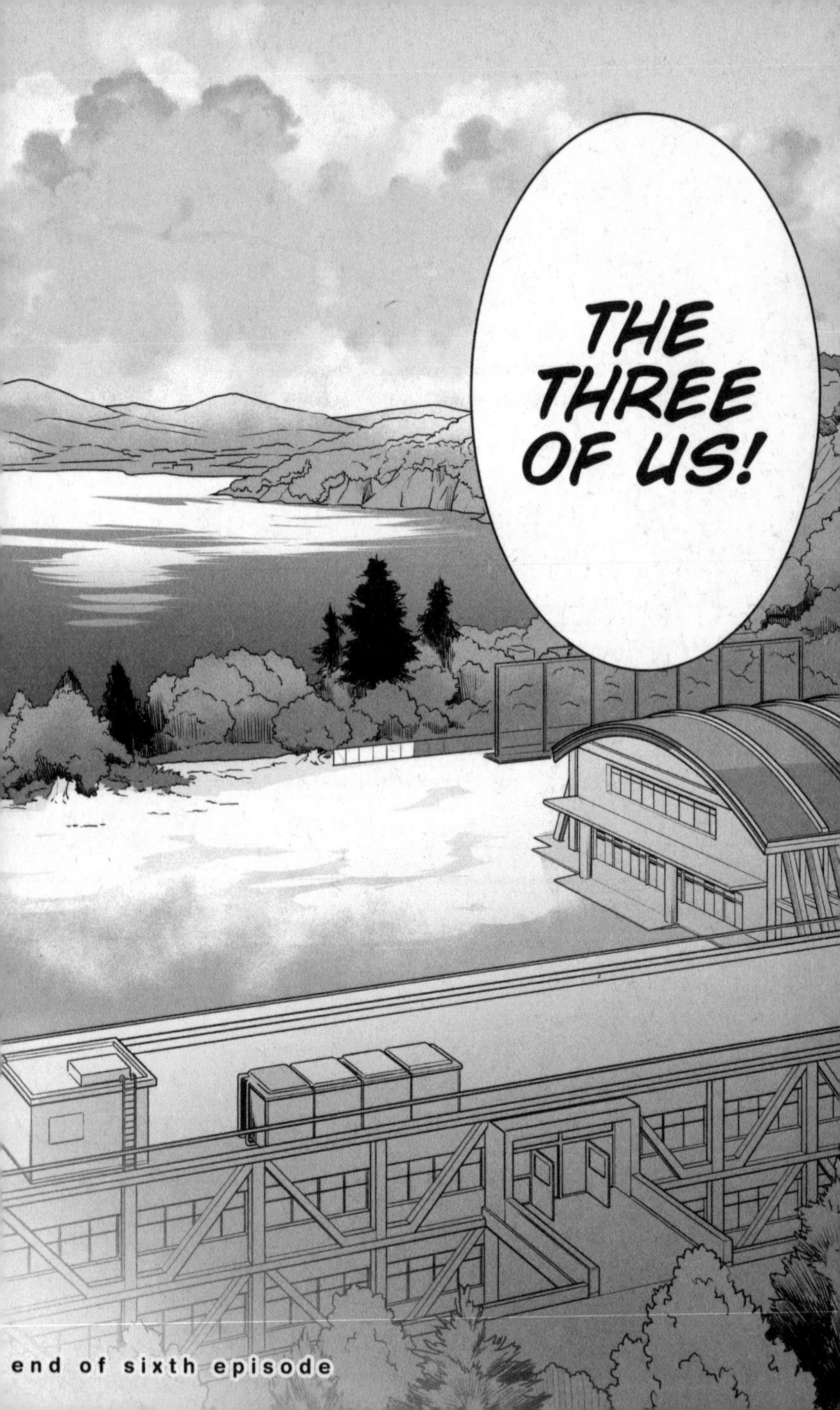
THE THREE OF US!

end of sixth episode

your name

02

end
continued in Vol. 03

your name.

Translation: Taylor Engel
Lettering: Abigail Blackman

YOUR NAME. Vol. 2
©Ranmaru Kotone 2016
©2016 TOHO CO., LTD. / CoMix Wave Films Inc. / KADOKAWA CORPORATION / East Japan Marketing & Communications, Inc. / AMUSE INC. / voque ting co., ltd. / Lawson HMV Entertainment, Inc.
First published in Japan in 2016 by KADOKAWA CORPORATION, Tokyo. English translation rights arranged with KADOKAWA CORPORATION, Tokyo through TUTTLE-MORI AGENCY, INC., Tokyo.

English translation © 2017 by Yen Press, LLC

Yen Press
1290 Avenue of the Americas
New York, NY 10104

Visit us at yenpress.com
facebook.com/yenpress
twitter.com/yenpress
yenpress.tumblr.com
instagram.com/yenpress

First Yen Press Edition: November 2017

Yen Press is an imprint of Yen Press, LLC.
The Yen Press name and logo are trademarks of Yen Press, LLC.

The publisher is not responsible for websites (or their content) that are not owned by the publisher.

Library of Congress Control Number: 2017934009

ISBNs: 978-0-316-41288-9 (paperback)
       978-0-316-52112-3 (ebook)

10 9 8 7 6 5 4 3 2 1

BVG

Printed in the United States of America